**Oryx Sourcebook Series
in Business and Management**

Retirement
Benefit Plans
An Information
Sourcebook

Oryx Sourcebook Series in Business and Management
Paul Wasserman, Series Editor

**Oryx Sourcebook Series
in Business and Management**

Retirement Benefit Plans
An Information Sourcebook

by Herbert A. Miller, Jr.
Librarian, The Wyatt Company

Phoenix • New York
ORYX PRESS
1988

The rare Arabian Oryx is believed to have inspired the myth of the unicorn. This desert antelope became virtually extinct in the early 1960s. At that time several groups of international conservationists arranged to have 9 animals sent to the Phoenix Zoo to be the nucleus of a captive breeding herd. Today the Oryx population is over 400, and herds have been returned to reserves in Israel, Jordan, and Oman.

Library of Congress Cataloging-in-Publication Data

Miller, Herbert A.
   Retirement benefit plans : an information sourcebook / by Herbert A. Miller, Jr.
   p. cm. — (Oryx sourcebook series in business and management; no. 8)
   Includes indexes.
   ISBN 0-89774-282-6
   1. Old age pensions—United States—Bibliography.   2. Pension trusts—United States—Bibliography.   I. Title.   II. Series.
Z7164.P4M54   1988
[HD7105.35.U6]
016.33125′2′0973—dc19   87-22500

Meinen Eltern

Contents

Acknowledgements

For my wife, Judy, and for my children, Caroline and Joseph, the time spent doing this work has been mostly time that should have been spent with them. I am grateful for their forbearance, and I hope to make it up to them in the future. I owe other debts of gratitude. Nevin W. Raber, Librarian Emeritus and my superior in the former Business Library at Indiana University, taught me much of what I know and mentioned me to Professor Wasserman when the latter was looking for authors. Sylvester Schieber, my current boss, afforded me some of the resources that I needed and patiently did without some of the overtime that I certainly owe him. I bounced a number of questions and problems off Lori Travers, a helpful colleague in the library profession who works for a competitor. Erica Feibes, June Lynn, and Millicent Watkins, who work with me in the Wyatt Company Library, were each of help. Whenever I could make the interests of the company coincide with getting this book done, I did so. I wish I could have done that more often. Nancy Ann Pecar and Judy Welch prepared the manuscript and did an admirable job. When this book proves useful to someone, it may very well be because of the input of the above persons.

Introduction

Retirement plans have as their aim the providing of retirement income for their participants. As complex and pervasive creatures, they really only date from World War II. It follows that practitioners in the area have not been born into it. Very few people have been able to follow a parent into retirement plan work, and there is no single distinguishable profession in the field. The eight-year-old who has forsaken firefighting or jet piloting to announce a career in pension work has probably not been born.

Instead, the practitioners come from a number of different professions, each with its distinctive and abstruse jargon. There are lawyers, actuaries, economists, data processors, and accountants just down the hall from my library. As people with differing backgrounds enter the field, they assume various roles with regard to the different types of plans. They can be plan administrators, consultants, communicators, or government regulators, just to name a few.

Further adding to this complexity is the fact that the plans differ considerably one from another. In putting down the boundaries within which this book would be done, I chose to ignore the late 1985 introduction of a bill which would divide qualified plans into two categories: retirement plans and nonretirement or capital accumulation plans. I did so because there are a number of prominent examples of organizations which obviously expect their employees to use their capital accumulation plans as retirement vehicles because no other type of plan is provided.

And so we have the prospect of a recognizably distinct segment of our economy in which an actuary serving as a consultant to defined benefit plans has almost no vocabulary in common with a lawyer who designs leveraged ESOPs (Employee Stock Ownership Plans) even though they are both engaged in providing income to future retirees. It is probable that neither one of them is upset by this, but the employee benefits manager who did an undergraduate degree in personnel has to have some smattering of understanding of both of them. Pity even more the communicator whose background in Milton and Pope is supposed to provide the ability to describe a retirement plan to the person for whom all this complexity exists. This latter, the plan participant, comes from any walk of life, and most participants are ignorant of at least some aspects of their own retirement packages.

None of this lack of coherence would matter much if this were not an important field. It is important, however, from the personal milieu through the macroeconomic level. Each individual retirement plan participant should know as much as possible about the retirement plan in which that participant is enrolled and about the universe of such plans. Career decisions, for example, should definitely not be made in ignorance of their retirement implications. Each organization must set and monitor its retirement plan policy, having as much knowledge of its environment as is feasible. Finally, federal policies must be set and monitored in the knowledge that pension funds own 16.7 percent of the total financial assets of the U.S. That figure is vintage 1984, and it is up from 3 percent in 1950.

The situation is analogous to that hackneyed but useful Hindu allegory of the blind men and how they feel about the elephant. If you, as a practitioner in the retirement plan area, are perfectly satisfied with your knowledge of the elephant based on those portions of pachydermal anatomy that have come your way, you are not in need of this book. If you think you might be better off with a little more knowledge of the beast, you are invited to use this book to try to find that knowledge.

No cures for blindness are guaranteed, of course. To a very considerable extent, any bibliography is at second remove from real information. What has been attempted in this book is a listing according to format of the various sources that exist, sometimes with indications of their importance or relevance. The indexes may help the user to sharpen a search for a hazily remembered publication, or they may lead to information that is new to that user. Of course, it is certainly possible that there is no better information than that already had, that the information sought exists but is not published, or that it has escaped my nets. In any event, it is a good thing to cover all the bases when one is dealing with the golden years of a lot of people.

Retirement Benefit Plans

Surveys

The following is a list of surveys having at least some coverage of retirement plans. Some of them are voluminous treatments of complex topics. Others are primarily compensation surveys that might have one paragraph or a footnote on retirement plans in a particular industry. Some are very expensive. Others are free. Some, whether expensive or not, are proprietary and tightly controlled. This gives rise to considerable problems in bibliographic description. I have had to resort to descriptions from telephone interviews in some cases. The user will notice that the beginning date of a serial survey and its frequency are often a matter of uncertainty. The expenditure of time and telephone charges to pin down better information was considered excessive. It is true, moreover, that the expenditure would very often be to no avail. Many of the best surveys in this area are produced in organizations wherein the continuity of personnel is minimal. The failure of these organizations to keep publication records or even a backfile of the survey is common. In my own company, there exists a rather important survey which, from internal evidence, has gone through seventeen editions. If a backfile exists prior to 1979, I am not aware of it. Of course, considering the attitude of business folk toward their libraries, it might be a prudent thing to keep such material elsewhere. In any event, most of the benefits industry has little use for yesterday's information.

1. *ABA's Incentive Compensation Practices Survey; Summary Report.* Prepared by Towers, Perrin, Forster & Crosby, Inc. Washington, DC: American Bankers Association, 1982. 102 p.
   Includes profit sharing and thrift coverage.

2. *ACME Survey of Key Operating Statistics on Management Consulting.* New York: The Association of Management Consulting Firms, 1984–. (Annual)
   There is one table which gives cost of pension, profit sharing, or other retirement benefits as a percentage of revenue for consulting firms by size of firms.

3. *AMS New Benefits Survey.* Willow Grove, PA: Administrative Management Society, 1986. 6 p.
   There is one graph showing prevalence of 401(k) plans in flexible benefits arrangements.

4. *AMS Office Benefits Survey for the United States and Canada.* Willow Grove, PA: Administrative Management Society, n.d. (Annual)
> This touches only upon the question of whether employees share in the cost of the pension plan.

5. *Analysis of Possibilities for ORP/TDA Tax Sheltered Savings.* Austin, TX: Texas Association of College Teachers, n.d. (Annual)
> Because of an interesting and unique retirement situation obtaining for Texas college teachers, TACT devotes its August issue of *TACT Bulletin* to a treatment of investment options available to its membership. This issue should be of consuming interest to all other 403(b)-eligible parties. In effect, what TACT is doing is causing major insurance companies to put their best foot forward in going after 403(b) retirement money. Not-for-profit organizations all over the country can see the picture in Texas for the price of a single issue of *TACT Bulletin* and can negotiate their own deals from an informed position.

6. *ASAE Association Executive Compensation Survey.* Washington, DC: American Society of Association Executives, 1980–. (Irregular)
> The section on retirement benefits, though brief, constitutes a better picture than we have for most professions or industry segments.

7. *A. S. Hansen, Inc. Fall Planning Conference; Instant Survey National Results.* Deerfield, IL: A. S. Hansen, Inc., 1982?–. (Annual)
> This is the survey of participants in a particular conference held annually. There is some plan prevalence information given.

8. *ASPA-BNA Survey; Personnel Activities, Budgets, and Staffs.* Washington, DC: Bureau of National Affairs, Inc., 1969?–. (Annual)
> The importance of this survey is that it gives some inkling of how retirement plans are administered in the private sector.

9. *ASPA-Saratoga Institute Human Resource Effectiveness Survey.* Saratoga, CA: Saratoga Institute, 1986. Various pagings.
> The benefits section of this survey does not deal explicitly with retirement plan costs as a percentage of revenues or expenses, but it *does* deal with total benefits costs in that way. The survey is sponsored by the American Society of Personnel Administrators.

10. *Bankers Trust Study of Employee Savings and Thrift Plans.* New York: Bankers Trust Co., 1961–1977. (Irregular)
> The five editions of this study were each, at their publishing dates, unique and very important surveys. Although it was expected that another edition would be published in 1983, the publisher evidently abandoned the idea. After a lengthy discussion of plan provisions, each study outlines numerous specific plans. Unlike the *Corporate Pension Plan Study*, each company was named. It is probable that this title is now only of historical interest.

11. *Banking Industry Management Perquisite Survey.* Boston: Olney Associates, Inc., n.d. (Annual?)
> This is a survey of ninety-five Northeast banking institutions. It covers prevalence, by size of bank, for deferred compensation, pension plans, supplemental pension plans, profit sharing plans, and thrift plans.

12. *The BEA Pension Survey.* New York: BEA Associates, Inc., 1976–. (Annual)
> This survey covers only forty major firms, but it gives analyses you do not see anywhere else. The survey tracks pension expenses, pension liabilities, and the ability of the company to pay the pensions if the trusts do not suffice. The forty companies are all household names.

13. Beller, Daniel J. *Estimates of Participant and Financial Characteristics of Private Pension Plans.* Washington, DC: U.S. Government Printing Office, 1983. 36 p.

14. Beller, Daniel J. *Patterns of Worker Coverage by Private Pension Plans; A Survey.* . . . Washington, DC: U.S. Department of Labor, 1980. 23 p.

15. Brown, James K. *Retirement Pay and Deferred Compensation for Outside Directors.* Corporate Directorship Practices. Conference Board Research Bulletin, 115. New York: Conference Board, 1982. 7 p.

16. *Buck's 1984 Report on the Funded Status of Corporate Pension Plans in the United States.* New York: Buck Consultants, Inc. 1985. 18 p.
　　Here, the title suggests that this survey is serial.

17. *Company Practices in Voluntary (Nonqualified) Deferred Compensation; Survey Highlights.* Lincolnshire, IL: Hewitt Associates, 1986. 17 p.

18. *Compensation and Benefits for Outside Directors in the Fortune 100 Industrials.* Lincolnshire, IL: Hewitt Associates, n.d. (Annual)
　　There is given for *named* companies' eligibility, amount, and duration of payment information.

19. *Compensation Survey Report of Management Positions in Not-for-Profit Organizations.* Washington, DC: Towers, Perrin, Forster & Crosby, Inc., 1982–. (Annual?)
　　This contains prevalence information for different types of retirement plans in associations.

20. *A Confidential Survey of Benefit Managers by Segal Associates.* New York: Martin E. Segal Co., 1978–. (Biennial)
　　This survey covers salary, responsibilities, problems, personal data, employment data, and professional organizational affiliations of *Fortune* 1,000 benefit managers.

21. Cooper, Robert D. *Pension Fund Operating Expenses; The Summary Report.* Brookfield, WI: International Foundation of Employee Benefit Plans, 1980. 30 p.

22. Cooper, Robert D. *Pension Fund Operating Expenses; The Summary Report and Fact Book.* Brookfield, WI: International Foundation of Employee Benefit Plans, 1984. 53 p.

23. Cooper, Robert D.; Crabb, Connie Ann; and Carlsen, Melody A. *Pension Fund Operations and Expenses; The Technical Report.* Brookfield, WI: International Foundation of Employee Benefit Plans, 1984. 102 p.

24. *Corporate Director's Compensation.* Conference Board Report, 877. New York: The Conference Board, Inc., 1986. 20 p.
　　One segment of this report covers incidence of retirement benefit plans for outside directors.

25. *Corporate Pension Plan Study.* New York: Bankers Trust Co., 1943–1980. (Irregular)
　　The eleven editions of this survey, which Bankers Trust has decided to abandon, were widely cited and heavily used. A complete run would be cardinal to a study of the history of pensions in the U.S. After a lengthy analysis of various provisions of retirement plans, the last edition describes nearly 300 plans including a special section for small companies. For each plan it covers the eligibility, vesting, early retirement,

disability, death benefits, benefit formulae, and replacement ratios. No company names were ever used.

26. *Credit Union Management Compensation Manual.* Prepared by Allan McNabb et al. Conducted by Maritz Market Research, Inc. Madison, WI: The Credit Union Executives Society, 1976–. (Irregular)
There is coverage of retirement programs in this survey.

27. Davis, Harry E. *Early Retirement Provisions of Pension Plans, 1971.* Report, 429. Washington, DC: U.S. Department of Labor, Bureau of Labor Statistics, 1974. 8 p.

28. Dennis, William J. *Small Business Employee Benefits, December 1985.* Washington, DC: National Federation of Independent Business. Research & Education Foundation, 1986?. 47 p.
There is not much information in the small business area. This is therefore very useful.

29. *Digest of Pension Plans; 1976–1978 Edition.* Washington, DC: U.S. Bureau of Labor Statistics, 1977. 363 p.
This volume was updated at least twice. The second update came out about May 1979.

30. *Digest of Profit-Sharing, Savings, and Stock Purchase Plans, Winter, 1961–62. (20 Selected Plans).* Bulletin, 1325. Washington, DC: U.S. Department of Labor, 1962. 31 p.

31. *Disclosures of Pension Information.* Financial Report Survey, 22. New York: American Institute of Certified Public Accountants, 1982.

32. *Edison Electric Institute Benefits Survey.* Conducted by Organization Resources Counselors, Inc. Washington, DC: Edison Electric Institute, 1977–. (Annual)
This surveys electrical utilities only. There is no summary of the various plan provisions. Instead, table after table lays forth each provision plan by plan. The names of the companies are divulged but the provisions are coded so that it is not possible to find a picture of the plans for a particular company.

33. *Employee Benefits.* Washington, DC: U.S. Chamber of Commerce, Survey Research Section, 1949?–. (Annual)
This important survey is primarily concerned with benefits as a whole, but several of its tables break out pension plan payments and profit sharing and thrift plan payments. One can thus learn percentage of payroll, cents per hour, and dollars per year per employee figures which are interesting to many. A shortcoming of the survey is that it treats only employees who are not exempt from the provisions of the Fair Labor Standards Act. Except in banking, professional employees are not covered. Another shortcoming is that the data is over a year old when first published. This is nevertheless the best known and most used benefits survey.

34. *Employee Benefits; An RIA Survey.* New York: Research Institute of America, Inc., 1986.
This survey makes a useful distinction between union and nonunion plans.

35. *Employee Benefits Historical Data; 1951–1979.* Washington DC: U.S. Chamber of Commerce, Survey Research Center, 1981. 40 p.
This was a Chamber of Commerce attempt to show changes in the benefit picture over much of the period in which they had been keeping statistics. It was well done, but it has not been redone. Streams of data can often be updated since 1979 through the use of the annual *Employee Benefits*.

36. *Employee Benefits in Medium and Large Firms.* Washington, DC: U.S. Department of Labor, Bureau of Labor Statistics, n.d. (Annual)
Three-eighths of the 1985 survey, published in July 1986, has to do with retirement plans. This is an excellent survey if your approach is from the macro level. Government policymakers no doubt find it extremely useful. But, if you are in charge of benefits for a 400-employee, $30 million revenue, consumer goods manufacturer in Oklahoma, you should not expect it to tell you what companies in your situation are affording their employees.

37. *Employee Retirement and Insurance Benefits Cost Survey.* New York: Teachers Insurance Annuity Association/College Retirement Equity Fund, 1977–. (Biennial)
This is a survey that imparts percentage of payroll and dollars per year per employee for retirement and insurance benefits in higher education.

38. *Employer Attitudes toward Employee Benefits and Tax Change; A Mercer-Meidinger Survey, September 1984.* New York: Wm. M. Mercer-Meidinger, 1984. 26 p.

39. *ERISA Related Changes in Corporate Pension Plans.* New York: Bankers Trust Co., 1976. 8 p.

40. *ESOP Survey.* Washington, DC: The ESOP Association, n.d. (Annual)
A survey of firms having employee stock ownership plans and belonging to the publishing association.

41. *Estimates of Participant and Financial Characteristics of Private Pension Plans.* Washington, DC: U.S. Department of Labor, 1983. 36 p.
The data in this study were taken from 1978 filings.

42. *Executive Compensation and Benefits in the Food-Service Industry.* Compiled and analyzed by Laventhol & Horwath. Philadelphia, PA: National Restaurant Association, n.d. (Quadrennial?)
The 1985 survey was the third. The data were gathered in late 1984 and include prevalence of pensions, profit sharing plans, and savings plans by type of restaurant. The profit sharing contributions are given for nineteen positions from chief executive through head bartender.

43. *Executive Compensation; Annual Report.* Princeton, NJ: Sibson & Co., Inc., 1966–. (Annual)
This has its roots in the *Annual Management Compensation Study.* Current editions of this survey reportedly contain some information on retirement plans and supplemental retirement plans for executives. Sibson & Co. is now owned by Johnson & Higgins. Mr. Sibson himself is still publishing under the former title, but an examination of his twenty-first edition does not disclose retirement plan coverage.

44. *Executive Engineering Compensation Survey.* Phoenixville, PA: D. Dietrich Associates, Inc., 1977–. (Annual)
A page or two of this survey refers to retirement plans for executives in engineering and architectural firms.

45. *Executive Perquisites.* Franklin Park, NJ: Compensation Resources, 1984. 113 p.
One page in this survey covers prevalence of early retirement provisions for corporate executives.

46. *Executive Report on Large Corporate Pension Plans.* New York: Johnson & Higgins, 1978–. (Annual)
    This is a study of corporate pension expense and funding. The introduction treats current issues in the area. The figures for expense as a percentage of corporate profit and the funding ratios to be found here are useful.

47. Eymonerie, Maryse. *The Availability of Fringe Benefits in Colleges and Universities.* Washington, DC: American Association of University Professors, 1980. 44 p.
    This was the fruit of a project funded by the Ford Foundation.

48. *Facts and Issues.* Princeton, NJ: Sibson & Co., Inc., n.d. (Annual)
    This publication summarizes the preceding year's happenings in the entire compensation area. It also speculates as to the coming year's trends.

49. *Findings from the Survey of Private Pension Benefit Amounts.* Washington, DC: U. S. Department of Labor, 1985. 77 p.
    All findings are vintage 1978.

50. *Flexible Benefit Programs; A Comprehensive Look at Flexible Spending Accounts and Broad-Based Plans, A TPF&C Survey Report, May 1985.* New York: Towers, Perrin, Forster & Crosby, Inc., 1985. 12 p.

51. *Flexible Compensation, 1985; A National Survey of Cafeteria and 401(k) Plans.* Washington, DC: Employers Council on Flexible Compensation, 1985. 13 p.

52. Foote, George H., and McLaughlin, David J. *Corporate Retirement Programs; A Survey of Benefit Levels, Cost Allocations, and Retirement Plan Features among 490 Large Companies in 33 Industries.* New York: McKinsey & Co., Inc., 1965. 113 p.

53. *401(k) Plans; Survey of the State of the Art, February 1984.* New York: Buck Research Corp., 1984. 47 p.

54. *401(k) Survey Report.* Springfield, MA: Massachusetts Mutual Life Insurance Co., 1984–. (Annual)

55. *401(k)s and Tax Reform Proposals; Telephone Survey.* New York: Buck Research Corp., 1985. 8 p.

56. *Fringe Benefits for Teachers in Public Schools.* ERS Report. Part 3 of *National Survey of Fringe Benefits in Public Schools.* Arlington, VA: Educational Research Service, Inc., 1976–. (Biennial)
    There is very little retirement plan coverage in this survey.

57. Greene, Mark R., et al. *Early Retirement; A Survey of Company Policies and Retirees' Experiences.* Eugene, OR: University of Oregon, Graduate School of Management and Business, 1969. 89 p.

58. *Hansen Survey of Defined Benefit Plans and Retirement Practices.* Deerfield, IL: A. S. Hansen, Inc., n.d.
    This is available to participants only, and I have never seen anything except "executive highlights."

59. *The Hay/Huggins Benefits Comparison.* Philadelphia, PA?: Hay/Huggins Co., Inc., n.d. (Annual)
Formerly entitled the *Noncash Compensation Comparison,* this is reputedly an excellent survey which includes a good deal of information on numerous plan provisions. Although about a thousand organizations are surveyed, no company names are mentioned and the industry breakdown is rudimentary. The survey is tightly controlled. I believe that a copy may be obtained only by participants.

60. *Health and Insurance Benefits and Pension Plans for Salaried Employees, Spring 1963.* Washington, DC: U.S. Department of Labor, Bureau of Labor Statistics, 1964. 13 p.

61. Herzog, Austin L. *Pension Plan Provisions of State and Federal Public Employee Retirement Systems.* New York: Ebasco Risk Management Consultants, Inc., 1980. 120 p.

62. *Hewitt Associates SpecBook.* Lincolnshire, IL: Hewitt Associates, 1979?–. (Annual)
Reputed recently to have grown to three volumes from two, this survey has extensive coverage of retirement plans. The specifications of the plans are not summarized as in most surveys. Instead, such information as benefit formula, integration provisions, eligibility requirements, and type of plan are listed for 700 to 800 *named* companies. This survey is strictly controlled and, I believe, available to participants only. Summaries are sold to all comers under the title *Salaried Employee Benefits.* . . . See entries 120 and 121.

63. *HMCS; Hospital Management Compensation Survey.* Compiled by the Compensation Institute, a Mercer-Meidinger Co. Louisville, KY: Compensation Institute, 1980–. (Annual)
This contains information on incidence of supplemental retirement programs among hospital executives.

64. *Hospitality Industry Compensation Survey.* By the American Hotel & Motel Association with the assistance of Peat, Marwick, Mitchell & Co. New York: American Hotel & Motel Association, 1974?–. (Annual?)
There is only one table on pensions. It shows the relative prevalence of defined benefit and defined contribution plans.

65. *Hot Topics in Retirement Plans.* Lincolnshire, IL: Hewitt Associates, 1983?. 39 p.

66. *How Major Industrial Companies View Employee Benefit Programs; A Survey by Fortune Market Research.* New York: Time, Inc., 1975. Various pagings.

67. *Inc. Executive Compensation Study.* Compiled and analyzed by *Inc.* and Peat, Marwick, Mitchell & Co. Boston: Inc. Publishing Co., n.d. (Annual)
This survey is important because it restricts its sample to small business. Three pages give prevalence of the various kinds of plans by size of company, by industry, and by region. Because there are nondiscrimination rules, the figures have considerable relevance for rank and file in these companies, and this is not just an executive compensation survey.

68. *Industrial Flight Survey.* Minneapolis, MN: General Mills, Inc., n.d. (Annual)
This title contains some information about retirement benefits afforded pilots by companies employing them.

69. *Initial Results of a Survey on Employee Stock Ownership Plans and Information on Related Economic Trends.* Washington, DC: U.S. General Accounting Office, 1985. 46 p.

70. *Interest Rate Assumptions Used for Pension Disclosure in . . . Corporate Annual Reports; Industrials.* New York: Buck Consultants, Inc., n.d. (Annual)
> The subtitle suggests that Buck publishes these by industry segment. I have never seen anything except the industrials.

71. *International Benefit Guidelines.* London: Wm. M. Mercer International, 1976?–. (Annual)
> Although the international scene is not within the compass of this bibliography, the above publication affords a rare opportunity to view the U.S. retirement picture in an international context. Coverage of retirement issues in each of fifty-eight countries amounts to a couple of paragraphs apiece.

72. *Inventory of Construction Industry Multiemployer Pension Plans.* Washington, DC: Associated General Contractors of America, n.d. (Annual?)
> For more than a thousand multiemployer plans, this survey gives information on contributions, participants, assets, liabilities, and interest rate assumptions. There is also a funding ratio given. Because it is compiled from Department of Labor Form 5500 filings, the information is wanting in currency, but it is nevertheless useful.

73. *IRAs; The People's Choice.* Washington, DC: Investment Company Institute, 1985. 60 p.
> This report presents results of a household survey done in late 1984.

74. *IRS Curtailment of Flexible Benefit Plans; A Survey of Employer Reactions.* New York: Buck Research Corp., 1984. 39 p.

75. Knowlton, P. A. *Profit Sharing Patterns; A Comparative Analysis of the Formulas and Results of the Plans of 300 Companies with 730,000 Employees.* Evanston, IL: Profit Sharing Research Foundation, 1954. 144 p.

76. *Large Corporate Pensions; Report to Participants.* Greenwich, CT: Greenwich Associates, 1973–. (Annual)
> This has coverage of things not surveyed elsewhere. Mainly, it has to do with the investment practices of pension funds, but there is treatment of gross contributions and distributions; actuarial assumptions; participants' age, service, and vesting; postretirement increases; and use of 401(k)s. The 1973 edition has a statistical history of pensions.

77. *Listening Exercise; Results of the Corporate Communication Practices Survey.* Johnson & Higgins Communications, n.d. 24 p.
> This is post-ERISA, but there is nothing to indicate the date of publication more precisely.

78. *Living with ERISA; A Survey of Current Corporate Practices.* New York: Peat Marwick, Mitchell & Co., 1977. 15 p.

79. Livingston, David T. *Investment Practices of Jointly Trusteed Pension Plans.* Research Survey Report, 2. Brookfield, WI: International Foundation of Employee Benefit Plans, 1974?. 29 p.

80. Louis Harris & Associates, Inc. *Retirement and Income; A National Research Report of Behavior and Opinion Concerning Retirement, Pensions and Social Security.* New York: Garland Publishing, Inc., 1984. 121 p.
> This covers inflation and attitudes toward the pension system and Social Security.

81. *Lump Sum Distribution Options in Pension Plans Covering Salaried Employees; Survey Results.* Lincolnshire, IL: Hewitt Associates, 1980. 17 p.

82. *Management Compensation Survey of the Banking Industry.* Princeton, NJ: Sibson & Co., Inc., n.d. (Annual?)
This publication contains at least some information on the retirement picture in the banking industry.

83. *Management Compensation Survey of the Insurance Industry.* Princeton, NJ: Sibson & Co., Inc., n.d. (Annual?)
This survey is known to be divided into two parts. One of these pertains to property and casualty companies. The other is devoted to life companies. A minor amount of each survey has to do with pension plans, profit sharing plans, and thrift plans in each industry.

84. *Martin E. Segal Company Survey of the Funded Position of Multiemployer Plans.* New York: Martin E. Segal Co., 1983–. (Annual)
This is a survey that monitors the health by one measure of Taft-Hartley-type plans. The plans are all clients of Segal which allows them access to current information. Only relatively aged information would be available to the public through Department of Labor filings.

85. Metzger, Bert L. *Profit Sharing in 38 Large Companies; Piece of the Action for 1,000,000 Participants.* Evanston, IL: Profit Sharing Research Foundation, 1975. 249 p.
This is volume one of a two-volume study. The content is pre-ERISA.

86. Metzger, Bert L. *Profit Sharing in 38 Large Companies; Piece of the Action for 1,000,000 Participants.* Evanston, IL: Profit Sharing Research Foundation, 1978. 460 p.
This is the second volume of a two-volume study. The first was published before ERISA made its effects felt. This is the post-ERISA survey.

87. Mruk, Edwin S., and Giardina, James A. *Organization & Compensation of Boards of Directors.* Sponsored by the Financial Executives Institute. New York: Arthur Young, n.d. (Annual?)
There is prevalence information for retirement plans and deferred compensation arrangements. The prevalence is broken down by size and a useful number of industrial divisions. There is also some information on actual provisions of the plans. Coverage is getting better inasmuch as the 1983 edition has scant material relative to the 1985 edition.

88. *The National Executive Compensation Survey.* Coordinated by MIMA, the Management Association. Chicago: MIMA, 1976–. (Annual)
This survey focuses upon manufacturing management and includes prevalence of several kinds of deferred arrangements, including profit sharing. It does not touch upon other kinds of retirement plans however.

89. *National Survey of Corporate Law Departments Compensation and Organization Practices.* Volume I. Compensation Study. New York: The Association of the Bar of the City of New York/Arthur Young, 1978–. (Annual)
This has a small amount of information on retirement plan prevalence.

90. *National Survey of Employee Benefits for Full-Time Personnel of U.S. Municipalities.* Washington, DC: Edward H. Friend & Co., ?–1982. (Biannual?)
I learned by telephone conversation in 1985 that this probably would not be published again. The 1982 edition was the fifth. It was cosponsored by the Labor-Management Relations Service of the United States Conference of Mayors and the International City Management Association.

91. *National Survey of the Compensation of Hospital Managers and Executives.* Chicago: The Sullivan Group, Inc., 1978–. (Annual)
Through 1985, there was some coverage of the retirement picture among hospital executives. It included information on the IRC 403(b) annuities widespread among not-for-profit hospitals. The 1986 survey does not include this coverage.

92. *1985 Survey of 401(k) Plans; Summary of Responses.* New York: Towers, Perrin, Forster & Crosby, Inc., 1985. 16 p.

93. *1978 Survey of Changes in Normal Retirement Benefits.* New York: Bankers Trust Co., 1978. 14 p.
This is a survey to investigate the changes in retirement plans caused by ERISA.

94. *Non-Cash Benefits' Survey.* Phoenixville, PA: D. Dietrich Associates, Inc., 1974–. (Annual)
About one-ninth of each survey is concerned with profit sharing, savings, and pension plans of the kinds of firms that Mr. Dietrich's organization surveys. These are engineering and architectural firms.

95. *NRMA Pension Survey.* New York: National Retail Merchants Association, 197?–.

96. *Nursing Home Salary and Benefits Report.* Hawthorne, NJ: John R. Zabka Associates, Inc., 1979–. (Annual)
There is a minor amount of coverage of pension and profit sharing plans. The coverage is only prevalence and source of contributions with a regional breakdown of each.

97. *The 100 Largest Retirement Plans, 1960–1966.* Washington, DC: U.S. Department of Labor, Labor-Management Services Administration, 1968. 24 p.

98. *PAYSOP Survey of Fortune Directory Companies.* Lincolnshire, IL: Hewitt Associates, 1984. 21 p.

99. *Pension Plans & The Impact of ERISA.* PPF Survey, 119. Washington, DC: Bureau of National Affairs, Inc., 1977. 47 p.

100. *Pensions & Other Retirement Benefit Plans.* PPF Survey, 134. Washington, DC: Bureau of National Affairs, Inc., 1982. 58 p.
This is a survey of 246 personnel executives regarding type of plan, retirement policies, and investment practices.

101. *Pensions & Other Retirement Benefits.* PPF Survey, 103. Washington, DC: Bureau of National Affairs, Inc., 1973. 22 p.

102. *Plan Design and Experience in Early Retirement Windows and in Other Voluntary Separation Plans.* Lincolnshire, IL: Hewitt Associates, 1986. 11 p.

103. President's Commission on Pension Policy. *Preliminary Findings of a Nationwide Survey on Retirement Income Issues.* Washington, DC, 1980. 21 p.

104. *Professional Engineer Income and Salary Survey.* Prepared by Abbott Langer & Associates. Alexandria, VA: National Society of Professional Engineers, 1952–. (Annual)
> The 1984 edition contained brief but useful pension coverage. This was not carried in the 1985 edition.

105. *Profile of Employee Benefits.* Conference Board Report, 645. New York: The Conference Board, Inc., 1974. 103 p.
> Used in conjunction with the 1981 edition of the same title, one might see effects of ERISA on the retirement field.

106. *Profile of Employee Benefits.* 1981 Edition. Conference Board Report, 813. New York: The Conference Board, Inc., 1981. 58 p.
> This is a survey of 3,083 companies. About one-sixth of the publication is concerned with retirement income and capital accumulation plans.

107. *Profit Sharing Manual; Containing a Digest and Analysis of Eighty-Four Representative Profit Sharing Plans.* Columbus, OH: Council of Profit Sharing Industries, 1948. 647 p.

108. *Profit Sharing Survey.* Conducted by Hewitt Associates in cooperation with the Profit Sharing Council of America. Chicago: Profit Sharing Council of America, 1958–. (Annual)
> This item surveys contributions as a percentage of pay, investment choices, asset mix, rates of return, and a number of other provisions of profit sharing plans.

109. *Public Pension Funds; Report to Participants.* Greenwich, CT: Greenwich Associates, 1977?–. (Annual)
> This publication does for public plans what the same publisher does for the private sector in its *Large Corporate Pensions.* Although it primarily covers investment practices, it also touches on actuarial assumptions, workforce characteristics, benefit levels and formulae, vesting, brokerage, and participation.

110. *Public Pension Investment Targeting; A Survey of Practices.* Prepared by . . . Municipal Finance Officers Association. n.p.: Alliance Capital Management Corp., 1983. 52 p.

111. *Public Retirement Systems; Summaries of Public Retirement Plans Covering Colleges and Universities.* New York: Teachers Insurance Annuity Association, 1976–. (Annual?)

112. *Recording Industry; Survey of Compensation and Benefits.* Conducted by M&M Resources Corp. New York: Recording Industry Association of America, n.d. (No information on frequency)
> This survey purportedly goes into considerable detail on defined benefit plans in the industry and includes data on prevalence of defined contribution plans.

113. *Report on State Pension Commissions.* New York: Johnson & Higgins, 1978–. (Annual)
> This report is actually done by the Pension Commission Clearinghouse. The latter was a service of Edward H. Friend & Co. which was purchased by Johnson & Higgins at some point in the early 80s. After a summary and overview of the retirement picture for state employees, there is a state-by-state summary of important events in the year past and the prognosis for the year to come.

114. *Residential Builders Compensation Survey.* San Diego, CA: Stephens & Associates, n.d. (Annual)
One very tiny portion of this executive compensation survey has to do with prevalence of pensions, profit sharing plans, and savings or thrift plans.

115. *Retirement Equity Act of 1984; A Survey of Employers' Reaction.* New York?: Buck Research Corp., 1986. 19 p.

116. *Retirement Savings; Attitudes & Practices; A Survey.* Conducted for Employers Council on Flexible Compensation by Opinion Research Corp. Washington, DC: ECFC, 1986. 21 p.

117. *Retirement System Provision Survey.* Washington, DC: National Education Association, 19?–. (Frequency unknown)
I have seen only a 1979 edition that gave the provisions of sixty-eight plans. There were earlier editions, but I have no knowledge of more recent ones.

118. *A Review and Comparison of Employee Savings Plans.* New York: Bankers Trust Co., 1979. 77 p.
This is an analytical summary of the *Bankers Trust Study of Employee Savings and Thrift Plans* which is described in entry 10.

119. *Revised Profit Sharing Manual; Containing a Digest and Analysis of Ninety-One Representative Profit Sharing Plans.* Akron, OH: Council of Profit Sharing Industries, 1953. 316 p.

120. *Salaried Employee Benefits Provided by Major U.S. Employers.* Lincolnshire, IL: Hewitt Associates, n.d. (Annual)
About a quarter of each survey has to do with stipulations of retirement and capital accumulation plans.

121. *Salaried Employee Benefits Provided by Major U.S. Employers; A Comparison Study.* Lincolnshire, IL: Hewitt Associates, 1980?– (Annual)
This survey shows changes in benefits over time, year by year, since 1979.

122. *Salary Budget and Benefit Trends.* Deerfield, IL: A. S. Hansen, Inc., n.d. (Annual)
There is a little prevalence information given.

123. *Salary Reduction Plans; Design Features and Plan Experience, A TPF&C Survey Report.* New York: Towers, Perrin, Forster & Crosby, Inc., 1983. 12 p.

124. *Salary Reduction Plans; Maximizing Employee Participation, A TPF&C Survey Report.* New York: Towers, Perrin, Forster & Crosby, Inc., 1984. 16 p.

125. *Stock Ownership Plans for Employees.* New York: New York Stock Exchange, 1956. 207 p.

126. *Study of Public Employee Retirement Systems.* New York: Bankers Trust Co., 1984. 254 p.
After a lengthy discussion of structure, administrative practices, investment management, and plan provisions, the survey discusses individual plan summaries by plan group. Groups include state, local, teacher, higher education, fire, law enforcement, forestry, judicial, transport, utility, and elected official plans.

127. *A Study of State Government Employee Benefits.* Developed and compiled by AGE National Office. Washington, DC: Assembly of Governmental Employees, n.d. (Annual)
> This title contains a pretty complete and compact synopsis of the retirement plans for all fifty states.

128. *A Study on Employee Benefits in Major U.S. Corporations from the Perspective of Benefit Plan Directors and Managers.* Princeton, NJ: Opinion Research Corp., 1985. 2 vols.

129. *Survey of Actuarial Assumptions and Funding; Pension Plans with 1,000 or More Active Participants.* Washington, DC: The Wyatt Co., 1969?–. (Annual)
> The title varied slightly in earlier editions. The 1985 edition says it is the seventeenth in a series. This publication covers, for 948 plans, interest rate and salary growth assumptions, the social security and retirement age assumptions, security ratios, and value of assets and disclosure interest rates.

130. *Survey of Pension Plans; 1978.* Chicago: Coopers & Lybrand, 1978. 12 p.
> This appears to have been a one-shot survey of midwestern plans. It covers participation and vesting, benefit formulae, age at retirement, and other provisions of plans.

131. *Survey of Retirement and Savings/Capital Accumulation Benefit Plans Covering Salaried Employees of U.S. Employers.* Washington, DC: The Wyatt Co., 1987–. (Biennial)
> At this writing, the first edition of this has yet to see the light of day. Judging from the survey instrument, it is to be an all-encompassing survey of prevalence of plan provisions in minute detail. How much of the detail will be published and whether the survey will be available to nonparticipants are yet moot points.

132. *Survey of the Compensation of Employee Physicians and High-Level Professional Jobs in U.S. Hospitals.* Chicago: The Sullivan Group, Inc., 1984?–. (Irregular)
> There is included some small amount of coverage of the retirement picture including 403(b) annuities.

133. *Technical Support in the Development of Modifications to the Civil Service Retirement System: Task I; Review of Non-Federal Retirement Practices and Costs.* Washington, DC: U. S. Office of Personnel Management, 1984. Paged in sections.
> This study, carried out by consultants Towers, Perrin, Forster & Crosby and ICF Incorporated, gives a picture of retirement plan coverage, provisions, benefits, and costs in the nonfederal portion of the U.S economy in 1984.

134. Tennant, W. Jack; Gates, Jack; and Trumble, Steve. *Benefits Survey: Public Employee Retirement Systems; A Study of Benefits and Related Provisions in Selected Large PERS.* Washington, DC: The Wyatt Co., 1981. 152 p.

135. *Thrift Industry Management Perquisite & Employee Benefit Survey.* Boston: Olney Associates, Inc., 1984?–.
> The group surveyed is New England thrift institutions. Pension plans and thrift plans are covered as to prevalence and some provisions.

136. *TIAA-CREF College and University Retirement Plan Provisions.* New York: Teachers Insurance and Annuity Association/College Retirement Equity Fund, Educational Research, n.d. (Biennial?)
> Institution by institution for nearly 1,500 colleges and universities, the particulars of eligibility, contributions, and age are covered. This book is a godsend for the academic job hopper.

137. *Top 50; A Survey of Retirement, Thrift and Profit-Sharing Plans Covering Salaried Employees of 50 Large U.S. Industrial Companies.* Washington, DC: The Wyatt Co., 1968–. (Annual)
> This is the only survey I know of that attempts to project the retirement benefits that will be received by employees covered by certain plans. Admittedly employees of the firms surveyed here are hardly typical of the labor force as a whole. There are hundreds of thousands of them, however. Furthermore, the plan provisions are given, and hundreds of other companies are thus able to assess roughly the adequacy of their own retirement plans.

138. *Top 100 Executive Benefits Study.* New York: Towers, Perrin, Forster & Crosby, Inc., 1982. 28 p.
> For a hundred named companies, this item surveyed Supplemental Executive Retirement Plans, (SERPs) and excess plans, if any, from proxy statements. In November 1985, Towers, Perrin, Forster & Crosby, Inc., had no intention of updating this survey.

139. *Top 100 Industrial Executive Compensation Study.* New York: Towers, Perrin, Forster & Crosby, Inc., n.d. (Annual)
> There is a section of this survey that gives prevalence of excess plans, Supplemental Executive Retirement Plans (SERPs), and supplemental executive savings plans.

140. *Top 100 U.S. Industrial Companies; Analysis of Retirement Arrangements for Outside Directors as Disclosed in Proxy Statements.* New York: Towers, Perrin, Forster & Crosby, Inc., 1985. 5 p.
> For thirty-one named companies, eligibility, benefit amount, duration, and some miscellaneous conditions are disclosed.

141. *Valuation Interest Rate and Salary Scale Assumptions Used in Funding Corporate Pension Plans.* New York?: Buck Consultants, Inc., 1983–. (Annual?)

142. *Wages and Benefits in U.S. Construction Contracts, 1985.* Washington, DC: Construction Data Services, Inc., 1985. 509 p.
> By region, state, and city, this is a book that shows negotiated pension costs for each of the construction trades.

143. *What Makes 401(k) Plans Appealing? A Survey of Design Features and Plan Experience, A TPF&C Survey Report.* New York: Towers, Perrin, Forster & Crosby, Inc., 1986. 16 p.

144. *The Wyatt Communications Survey Report; An Executive Summary.* Chicago: The Wyatt Co., 1986. 32 p.
> Although this is a general survey of communications professionals on current issues, the nature of the publisher dictates content relevant to retirement.

Promotional Literature

Some of the most current and choice literature in the area of retirement plans is not indexed or even tracked bibliographically. Its very authors frequently do not keep backfiles of it, and they rarely know when their periodical was begun.

The primary purpose of the literature is promotional. The content is sometimes very substantial, but always the idea is to convey to a client or prospect that the publisher has services or facilities for hire. The publishers are usually banks, insurance companies, or consultants. The latter include the consulting subsidiaries of insurance brokers and accountancies as well as firms that do nothing but consult.

This chapter lists most of the promotional literature of the various consulting firms. Also included are publications from some insurance companies and from a few banks. Undoubtedly banks and insurance companies publish a great deal of material of which I am not aware, but I am confident that I have the greater part of the consulting firms' publications listed if they have retirement plan content.

Although there is generally no charge for these publications, they are not necessarily freely available. The organizations that go to great expense to put them out can only recoup the expense if they drum up business as a result. Requesting a title from a regional firm when they have no office in your vicinity will often be a waste of time. Further, although it would be untrue to say that these materials all say the same thing at the same time, someone blessed with all of this literature would find it highly repetitive. Finally, getting and keeping track of this material would be a trial. It is ephemeral to a great degree. The industry has a high employee turnover and the editorial philosophies, titles, frequencies, and formats change at least as often as the people.

Because of competitive conditions in the industry and lack of editorial continuity, I had more than the usual amount of trouble with bibliographic description in this chapter. Some of the material was garnered by telephone interview, and at least one call was made to each publisher from whom information was needed. I am fairly certain that I have not included house organs or other material meant for internal distribution.

145. *Act Now.* New York: Johnson & Higgins, 1980–1983?.
No longer in publication, past issues may have had some retirement plan content.

146. *The Advanced Underwriter.* Hartford, CT: Connecticut Mutual Life, 1946?–.
(Monthly)
Only occasional retirement plan coverage, but the pieces that appear are substantial.

147. *The Agenda.* Briarcliff Manor, NY: Frank B. Hall Consulting Co., 1984–.
(Published as required by events and not frequent)
Four- to six-page newsletter covering all benefits.

148. *Annual Reporting & Disclosure Calendar for Benefit Plans.* New York: Segal
Associates, n.d. (Annual)

149. *At Issue; Summaries of Issues and Legislation Currently under Public Debate.*
Hartford, CT: Aetna Life Insurance Co., Employee Benefit Division, 1985–.
(Monthly?)
Four-page newsletter with some retirement plan coverage.

150. *Benefit Benchmarks; Court Cases on Employee Benefits.* Briarcliff Manor,
NY: Frank B. Hall Consulting Co., 1984–. (Published as required by events)

151. *Benefit Briefs; A Monthly Newsletter about Current Developments in the Field
of Employee Benefit Plans.* Atlanta, GA: Tillinghast, Nelson & Warren,
1978?–1986. (Monthly)

152. *Benefit Bulletin; An Executive Guide to Current Developments.* New York:
Johnson & Higgins, 1980–. (Irregular)
A two- to four-page newsletter that covers all benefits.

153. *Benefit Input.* Atlanta, GA: Hazlehurst & Associates, Inc., 1971–.
(Bimonthly)
Formerly published under another title, this newsletter covers all benefits.

154. *Benefit Newsbeat.* New York: Johnson & Higgins, 1977–1983?. (Published as
required by events)
This covered all benefits. Publication might resume.

155. *Benefit Spotlight on. . . .* New York: Johnson & Higgins, 1980–1986.
(Irregular)
This is a four- to six-page newsletter which was usually not confined to one benefit
topic. It has ceased with the advent of *BeneNet Spotlight.*

156. *Benefit Update.* Briarcliff Manor, NY: Frank B. Hall Consulting Co., 1982–.
(Irregular)
This two- to six-page newsletter is almost weekly in frequency and covers regulation
and legislation of all benefits. It replaces *Technical Release.*

157. *Benefits Alert.* St. Louis, MO: Powers, Carpenter, Hall, Inc., 1978–.
(Published as warranted by events)
This newsletter covers all benefits.

158. *BenefitsLetter.* New York: Peat, Marwick, Mitchell & Co., n.d. (Irregular)
This newsletter has been superseded by another title (see entry 204). In 1981 it was a
four-page newsletter of some relevance to our topic.

159. *BeneNet Spotlight.* New York: Johnson & Higgins, 1986–. (Published as warranted by events)
This covers legislation and regulation for all types of benefits. Frequency may be nearly monthly.

160. *BeneNet Washington Letter.* New York: Johnson & Higgins, 1986?–. (Irregular)

161. *BookeMarks.* Winston-Salem, NC: Booke & Co., 1969–. (Monthly)
This six-page newsletter covers mainly legislative and regulatory issues.

162. *The Browser.* Chicago: William M. Mercer-Meidinger, 1976?–. (Monthly)
This is a listing by subject of articles appearing in the business press on benefit subjects. Each article is briefly abstracted. This is very like *Nutshell* (see entry 370). The same criticism applies.

163. *Buck Consultants for Your Benefit.* . . . New York: Buck Consultants, Inc., 1972?–. (Prepared at intervals)
This item appears when Buck has something definitive to say. Each issue is five to fifteen pages devoted to a single topic. Some of the coverage may not be retirement plan related, but much is.

164. *Bulletin.* New York: Martin F. Segal Co., 1983–. (Irregular?)
Because I have seen this in two different formats with a great interval between dates of publication, I can only say that each issue deals with one particular topic.

165. *C&M Communications & Management.* New York: Towers, Perrin, Forster & Crosby, n.d. (Bimonthly)
My last issue of this is four years old as I write, but it would appear to have usefulness for communicators in the retirement arena.

166. *Capitol Ideas; A Regulatory/Legislative Update on Employee Benefits.* Briarcliff Manor, NY: Frank B. Hall Consulting Co., 1983–1987. (Published as developments warrant)

167. *CG Perspective; A Report on Current Insurance Issues.* Hartford, CT: Connecticut General Life Insurance Co., 1977–1982. (Monthly)
This had some retirement plan content.

168. *The Compensation and Benefits File.* Washington, DC: The Wyatt Co., 1985–. (Monthly)
This is a newsletter almost become a magazine. It covers all benefits and salary issues as well. There is, therefore, only a fair percentage of coverage which is topical to this book. At this writing, there have been two special issues that have both been entitled *Compensation and Benefits Alert.*

169. *Coopers & Lybrand Actuarial, Benefits & Compensation Information Release.* New York?: Coopers & Lybrand (U.S.A.), n.d. (Irregular)
This is more frequent than monthly and varies from three to sixteen pages depending on what there is to cover and how exhaustively it is covered.

170. *Coopers & Lybrand Benefits Briefing.* Detroit, MI: Coopers & Lybrand, 1986–. (Irregular)
The very first issue, which is all that has been published at this writing, has four of thirteen pages relevant to retirement plans.

171. *Corroon & Black Benefits Quarterly.* New York?: Corroon & Black Corp., n.d. (Quarterly)
This covered mostly legislative and regulatory events for all benefits. Its publication has ceased.

172. *EHF Quarterly Newsletter.* Washington, DC: Edward H. Friend & Co., 1976–. (Quarterly)
This has ceased. My last holding is a 1979 issue. It had a good deal of coverage of public retirement plans as that was a specialty of the firm.

173. *Emphasis.* Atlanta, GA: Tillinghast, Nelson & Warren, 1979?–. (Bimonthly)
There is a certain amount of coverage of retirement topics in this magazine which has grown out of the newsletter format. Whether that will continue in light of the recent Tillinghast merger, I cannot speculate. Beginning in 1987, it will be published quarterly. During 1985 and 1986, it was bimonthly.

174. *The Employee Benefits File.* Washington, DC: The Wyatt Co., 1984. (Irregular?)
This newsletter was superseded by *Compensation and Benefits File,* see entry 168.

175. *Executive Letter.* Washington, DC: Martin E. Segal Co., 1977–. (Quarterly)
This is a two-page newsletter that usually treats a particular retirement plan issue. It is now quarterly, but it has been bimonthly in the past.

176. *Flex News.* Washington, DC: The Wyatt Co., 1983–. (Bimonthly)
This should be of interest to retirement plan practitioners who work in the context of "cafeteria" benefits.

177. *Flex3.* New York?: Towers, Perrin, Forster & Crosby, Inc., n.d. (Irregular?)
Reports and provides commentary on flexible benefits.

178. *Focus; On Government Activity Affecting Group Pension Business.* Hartford, CT: Connecticut General Life Insurance Co., 1979–. (Bimonthly)

179. *For Your Information.* New York: Buck Consultants, Inc., 1972–. (Published as events warrant)
Treatments are more brief than those in its companion, *Buck Consultants for Your Benefit.*

180. *Guide to ERISA Reporting and Disclosure Requirements.* New York?: Coopers & Lybrand, n.d. (Annual)

181. *Hansen Reviews: . . .* Deerfield, IL: A. S. Hansen, Inc., n.d. (Irregular)
Each issue is on one particular topic, and that issue is the subtitle that follows the colon in the title proper.

182. *Hansen Viewpoint: . . .* Deerfield, IL: A. S. Hansen, Inc., n.d. (Irregular)
This publication covers all benefits.

183. *Hay/Huggins Bulletin; Recent Developments in Employee Benefits & Actuarial Services.* Philadelphia, PA: Hay/Huggins, n.d. (Monthly?)

184. *Hewitt Associates on Flexible Compensation.* Lincolnshire, IL: Hewitt Associates, 1983–. (Monthly?)
Trends and developments in flexible compensation are the subject of this four-page publication.

185. *HRM Alert.* Newburyport, MA: Alexander & Alexander, Inc., n.d. (Biweekly)
This two-page publication seems always to include something on qualified plans.

186. *HRM Update.* Newburyport, MA: Alexander & Alexander, Inc., 1981–.
(Irregular)
This item is less frequent than monthly and varies from two to four pages. Each issue
covers only one topic.

187. *Impact on Group Pension & Financial Services.* Washington, DC: Aetna Life
& Casualty, Employee Benefits Division, n.d. (Monthly or nearly so)

188. *Kwasha Lipton Bulletin.* Englewood Cliffs, NJ: Kwasha Lipton, 1970–.
I have not inspected either this or the following *Newsletter*, but when a firm publishes
titles in tandem, they usually devote one to more or less exhaustive treatments and the
other to newsy brief items.

189. *Kwasha Lipton Newsletter.* Englewood Cliffs, NJ: Kwasha Lipton, 1960?–.
(Approximately bimonthly?)
See entry 188.

190. *Kwasha Lipton Reprint.* Fort Lee, NJ?: Kwasha Lipton, 1973–. (Irregular)
These are reprints of articles authored by Kwasha personnel and appearing first in the
general business and benefits presses.

191. *Management Update on Employee Benefit Plans.* Washington, DC: American
Security Bank, Investor Services Group, n.d. (Quarterly)

192. *The Mercer-Meidinger Bulletin.* New York: William M. Mercer-Meidinger,
1975?–. (Monthly)
This four-page newsletter is not be confused with *The Mercer Bulletin* (itself formerly
the *Mercer Actuarial Bulletin*), a Canadian publication. This publication seems to have
had the title *The Mercer Bulletin* before the 1984 merger with Meidinger. No doubt
this led to confusion in Detroit and Windsor. Content seems about evenly divided
between retirement and welfare issues.

193. *Mercer-Meidinger Information Release.* Louisville, KY: William M. Mercer-
Meidinger, 1985?–. (Irregular)
This one- to four-page newsletter may be the safety valve to get information out when
the various other newsletters published by this firm do not offer good timing. Most
issues have relevance for retirement practitioners.

194. *The Mercer-Meidinger Public Sector Report.* Washington, DC: William M.
Mercer-Meidinger, 1981–. (Quarterly)
This is a two-page quarterly that covers public plans. Retirement issues get their share
of coverage.

195. *Monthly Update. . . .* Atlanta, GA: Hazlehurst & Associates, Inc., 198?–.
(Monthly)
This is a two- to four-page newsletter that covers all benefits. Publication is coordi-
nated with *Benefit Input* (see entry 153) by the same firm.

196. *NewsLetter.* New York?: Martin E. Segal Co., 1957–. (Quarterly)
This is a four- to six-page newsletter that sometimes covers a retirement issue but is
more often devoted to coverage of other benefits. It may be the grand old man of
newsletters covering retirement plans. A thirty-year period of editorial consistency is
certainly remarkable.

197. *Perspective; Review of Emerging Executive Compensation Issues.* Philadelphia, PA: Hay/Huggins, 1983–. (Infrequent)
Apparently this will concern itself only with those retirement plan issues that bear on executive compensation.

198. *Private Opinion; Insurance and Benefit Ideas for Management.* New York?: Johnson & Higgins, 1978?–. (Quarterly)
I think this is mostly devoted to other benefits, but there is likely to be retirement plan content.

199. *Reporting Calendar; Multiemployer Pension and Welfare Plans under ERISA.* Washington, DC: The Wyatt Co., 1982?–. (Annual)

200. *Reporting Calendar; Single Employer Pension, Profit-sharing and Welfare Plans under ERISA.* Washington, DC: The Wyatt Co., n.d. (Annual)

201. *Social Security News.* Louisville, KY: William M. Mercer-Meidinger, n.d. (Quarterly)

202. *Speaking Out.* New York?: William M. Mercer-Meidinger, n.d. (Irregular)
This would appear to be the text of significant speeches delivered by Mercer consultants. I am aware of only three issues having been published in 1986.

203. *A Special Report to Clients.* Lincolnshire, IL: Hewitt Associates, n.d. (Irregular)
These would appear to be substantial treatments of very important topics.

204. *Spectrum.* Washington, DC: Peat Marwick, Mitchell & Co., 1982–. (Irregular)
From inspection of one issue, I would say that this newsletter has at least occasional relevance to our topic. Before 1982 it was entitled *Benefits-Letter* (see entry 157). It is published six to ten times each year.

205. *TPF&C Letter.* New York: Towers, Perrin, Forster & Crosby, Inc., n.d. (Monthly)
Occasional retirement plan coverage in a two-page newsletter.

206. *TPF&C Update.* New York: Towers, Perrin, Forster & Crosby, Inc., n.d. (Irregular?)
I have only two issues of this from 1984, but it seems that each issue is a substantial treatment of a particular topic.

207. *U.S. Broker; Employee Benefits Edition.* Boston: John Hancock Mutual Life Insurance Co., 1982–. (Monthly)
There is some retirement plan coverage, but most coverage is relevant to other benefit issues.

208. *U.S. Broker; Pension Consultant Edition.* Boston: John Hancock Mutual Life Insurance Co., 1985–. (Monthly)
Published for retirement fund and institutional investment brokers and consultants.

209. *Update: Pension Investment Strategy & Performance Review.* Washington, DC: Aetna Life Insurance Co., Employee Benefits Division, 1982?–. (Quarterly)

210. *The Wyatt Communicator.* Chicago: The Wyatt Co., 1983–. (Quarterly, but occasionally triannual)
A fair proportion of the material published is of interest to those charged with the communication of retirement benefits.

211. *The Wyatt Company Special Memorandum.* n.p.: The Wyatt Co., n.d. (Irregular)
Several offices of this company will publish one of these whenever a need is seen. They are unnumbered and sometimes undated. There is no central backfile, and they are generally mailed only to clients and prospects.

212. *Wyatt Public Plans Bulletin.* Washington, DC: The Wyatt Co., 1980–1985. (Irregular)
There was considerable coverage of public retirement plans in this publication, which was folded into the *Compensation and Benefits File* (see entry 168).

213. *Wyatt Washington Commentary.* Washington, DC: The Wyatt Co., 1981–1983. (Irregular)
This four- to ten-page publication was not a newsletter so much as technical treatises arising from government actions. It was, to some extent, superseded by other Wyatt publications.

Periodicals

This chapter on periodical literature includes annuals, irregulars, and updated services. Surveys and free newsletters are not covered here but have separate chapters of their own. The most frequent reference questions asked about retirement plans have to do with prevalence of various practices. The best sources to answer these questions are surveys, so a separate chapter on them was warranted. As to newsletters, they make up the bulk of the chapter on promotional literature.

A bigger problem was what to include in a bibliography of periodicals on retirement plans. In 1979 or 1980, *Playboy* gave space to an article that was a pretty fair treatment of the differences between defined benefit and defined contribution plans. You will not find *Playboy* in this chapter, however. The only magazine with a centerfold is *Pension World*, which publishes, in its January issue, a compliance calendar for employee benefit practitioners. It is not very racy.

Any periodical publication that deals wholly with retirement plans or with the entire field of employee benefits is fair game for this chapter. Also included are those titles that have regular pertinent content even though the bulk of their coverage is irrelevant. Thus, publications in the areas of human resource management and accounting, for example, are included. Finally, general business titles, whether scholarly or not, whether aimed at the executive suite or the mass market, are included. The employee benefits manager must not only do a modicum of professional reading; in addition, that manager must know what superiors and plan participants are likely to have read. For this reason, magazines such as *Harvard Business Review, Across the Board*, and *Business Week* are included.

Although it is true that following current periodicals is the single best way to keep up with changes in the world of retirement plans, the most current of periodicals, the newspaper, is not very important in the literature. The man on the street would rather read buggy whip advertisements than articles on pensions. In addition, even those papers that can afford to pay journalists who have some sophistication in business matters have the problem that the retirement area is a very abstruse and minor subset of the business world. There is, therefore, only one newspaper listed in this chapter.

Included in this chapter are a number of titles the authors of which thought they were producing monographs. When librarians see a piece in a ring binder, not only do they think of scarred shelves and books falling off them, but also of updates that may arrive at some future time. When forced to choose a main entry, a cataloger will opt for title, because compilers, editors, and authors frequently change in the course of several years publication while titles remain relatively constant. It is also true that publishers have tested the market with what was intended to be a loose-leaf service. The market having proved cold, the publisher forbears to update, and the publication becomes effectively a monograph. And so, what may be considered monographs by some are included among the periodicals and vice versa. One does the best one can and hopes the indexing will render the material available in the case of mistakes.

Finally, it is a good idea to make a statement regarding the reasons for including a chapter on periodicals in a subject bibliography. Such a chapter is useful to a practitioner in making decisions about which publications should be monitored for current awareness. It can be useful to the librarian in determining the strengths of a collection. But it is only minimally useful in seeking specific information. It is a failure of business pedagogy that there still exist many otherwise competent people who think that the way to find literature on a particular topic is to find periodicals likely to cover that topic. Then, having located runs of the periodicals in question, they pray for an annual index, and failing that, they will go from issue to issue examining tables of contents. It is true that many publications are not indexed, but if you recognize yourself in the above description, please hie yourself to a competent business reference librarian and ask for an introduction to the likes of ABI-INFORM or BUSINESS PERIODICALS INDEX.

214. *ACA News.* Scottsdale, AZ: American Compensation Association, 1958–. (Monthly)
ACA, as an organization, is slanted toward nonretirement compensation, but retirement plans are not ignored by any means. In addition to articles, this newsletter contains book reviews and announcements of pamphlet publications.

215. *Academy Alert; Pensions & Employee Benefits.* Washington, DC: American Academy of Actuaries, 1987–. (Irregular)
At this writing none have seen the light of day, but the purpose is to inform actuaries on current issues that concern them professionally.

216. *Accounting and Auditing for Employee Benefit Plans.* Boston: Warren, Gorham & Lamont, Inc., 1978–. (Annual)
The original 1978 volume was authored by Geoffrey M. Gilbert, Gregory J. Lachowicz, and James F. Zid. Annual cumulative supplements are prepared by a team headed by Paul Rosenfeld.

217. *Across the Board.* New York: The Conference Board, Inc., 1939–. (Monthly)
The occasional retirement plan coverage of this magazine is highly influential.

218. *The Actuarial Digest.* Atlanta, GA: Triple E Publications, 1982–. (Bimonthly)
This newsletter is not affiliated with any of the actuarial bodies as far as I can see. It is refreshing in that it has cartoons and a crossword which is more accurately described as a crossnumber.

219. *Actuarial Notes.* n.p., Railroad Retirement Board, 1972?–. (Irregular)

220. *Actuarial Notes.* n.p., Social Security Administration, 1963–. (Irregular)

221. *Actuarial Studies.* n.p., Social Security Administration, 1934?–. (Irregular)

222. *The Actuarial Update.* Washington, DC: American Academy of Actuaries, 1971–. (Monthly)

223. *The Actuary; The Newsletter of the Society of Actuaries.* Itasca, IL: Society of Actuaries, 1967–. (Monthly)

224. *Administering Pension Plans; Course Manual.* By Bernard Forseter and Daniel Sussman. Washington, DC: Federal Publications, 1980?–. (Annual)

225. *Advanced Law of Pensions and Deferred Compensation; ALI-ABA Course of Study Materials.* Philadelphia, PA: American Law Institute-American Bar Association. Committee on Continuing Professional Education, 198?–. (Annual?)

226. *ALI-ABA Course Materials Journal.* Philadelphia, PA: American Law Institute-American Bar Association, 1976–. (Bimonthly)
There is occasional, excellent material on various legal aspects of retirement plans.

227. *American Academy of Actuaries Yearbook.* Washington, DC: American Academy of Actuaries, 1966?–. (Annual)
This is more than a listing of members. The 1982 edition, for example, contains thirty pages of pension plan recommendations and interpretations and fifty pages of financial reporting recommendations and interpretations. There is also a good deal of material on professional conduct. The academy is the umbrella organization for the four other actuarial bodies in the U.S.

228. *American Demographics.* Ithaca, NY: American Demographics, Inc., 1979–. (Monthly)
There is occasional, useful coverage of material interesting to retirement plan practitioners.

229. *American Institute of Actuaries Yearbook.* Chicago: American Institute of Actuaries, 1909?–1948. (Annual)
This is mostly a listing of members of one of the precursors to the Society of Actuaries.

230. *Annual Conference on Employee Benefits. Proceedings.* New York: Trusts and Estates; Pension & Welfare News, 1967–. (Annual)

231. *Annual Report.* Washington, DC: Pension Benefit Guaranty Corp., 1975–. (Annual)

232. *Basic Law of Pensions and Deferred Compensation; ALI-ABA Course of Study Materials.* Philadelphia, PA: American Law Institute-American Bar Association. Committee on Continuing Professional Education, 198?–. (Annual?)
This is cosponsored by various law schools.

233. *Benefits News Analysis.* New Haven, CT: Benefits News Analysis, Inc., 1979–. (10/yr.)
Most of the articles have to do with how a particular company is handling a particular benefit or problem. Because interest in how others do the job is nothing short of avid, this is a very useful periodical.

234. *Benefits Quarterly.* Brookfield, WI: International Society of Certified Employee Benefits Specialists, 1985–. (Quarterly)
This is a scholarly, referred journal. In addition to articles, there are book reviews, abstracts of articles appearing in other publications, and a legal/legislative update. The latter is analytic rather than newsy.

235. *Benefits Today.* Washington, DC: Bureau of National Affairs, Inc., 1984–. (Fortnightly)
This newsletter covers Congress, regulation, the courts, policy and practice prevalence, and news in all benefit areas.

236. *Best's Insurance Reports; Life-Health.* Oldwick, NJ: A. M. Best Co., 1906–. (Annual)
This is not just a directory of insurance companies, many of which provide services to pension funds, it is a rating of their financial condition. If a fund hires an insurance company for any of several purposes, it is prudent to have checked their Best's rating.

237. *Best's Retirement Income Guide.* Oldwick, NJ: A. M. Best Co., 1979–. (Biannual)
This lists insurance companies that offer certain kinds of annuity and gives the provisions of each.

238. *Best's Review.* Life/Health Insurance Edition. Oldwick, NJ: A. M. Best Co., Inc., 1899–. (Monthly)

239. *The Blue Book of Pension Funds; The Standard Reference for Major United States Pension Funds.* Washington, DC: ERISA Benefit Funds, Inc., 1980–1986. (Annual)
The 1985–86 edition may have been the last. The rights were sold to Dun & Bradstreet which may, or may not publish. The 85–86 edition arrived at six volumes, and the cost was considerable, but this was an invaluable marketing tool for companies in pension services. Persons wanting to purchase back copies or to check on future issues are advised to call Dun's Marketing Services at (800) 524-2859.

240. *BNA Pension Reporter.* Washington, DC: Bureau of National Affairs, Inc., 1974–. (Weekly)
This extremely important publication covers legislation, the courts and regulations by the various federal agencies. It is indexed frequently, but the indexing is not cumulative beyond the quarterly, and the index is always at least two weeks behind the issues. This shortcoming can be overcome by accessing the expensive BNA online packages discussed in another chapter. Included are lists of upcoming educational seminars.

241. *Books on Benefits.* Brookfield, WI: International Foundation of Employee Benefit Plans, n.d. (Irregular)
This advertises IFEBP publications.

242. *Bulletin to Management.* Washington, DC: Bureau of National Affairs, Inc., 1950–. (Weekly)
This newsletter successfully targets a select group, and its retirement coverage, although not comprehensive, is important.

243. *Business Insurance.* Chicago: Crain Communications, Inc., 1967–. (Weekly)
This publication is extremely important to the retirement plan practitioner. Although it targets all benefits as well as risk management and the insurance industry, there is considerable coverage of retirement plan news. Special issues include a May (or thereabout) directory of employee benefit plan computer systems and a late December issue listing employee benefit consultants. A July or August issue announces employee benefit communications awards. Through sponsoring such awards, this magazine may

have done more to make benefits comprehensible to employees than have all government regulations yet printed.

244. *Business Insurance Directory of Corporate Buyers of Insurance, Benefit Plans and Risk Management Services.* Chicago: Crain Communications, Inc., 1983?–. (Annual)
Listings of chief financial officers, risk managers, employee benefit managers, personnel managers, and pension/retirement plan managers in more than 2,000 major United States companies.

245. *Business Week.* New York: McGraw-Hill, Inc., 1929–. (Weekly)
There is not a great deal of retirement plan coverage in this publication, but so many business people read it that any coverage has high impact. In the late 70s and early 80s, *Business Week* convulsed pension professionals by emphasizing the relatively low funding levels of many plans. Economic factors resulting in better funding levels have put an end to that slant, at least temporarily.

246. *Census of Certified Employee Benefit Specialists; Results.* Brookfield, WI: International Society of Certified Employee Benefit Specialists, n.d. (Quarterly)
This is a sampling of opinion on various matters among employee benefit practitioners.

247. *Claims Processing for Benefit Plans.* Brookfield, WI: International Foundation of Employee Benefit Plans, 197?–. (Annual)
Text of speeches given at an annual conference. At first glance, this would not seem relevent to pensions, as one outside the area tends to think of claims in a welfare benefits context, but the 1985 issue is more than half taken up with retirement plan considerations.

248. *Code of Federal Regulations.* Washington, DC: Office of the Federal Register, National Archives and Records Administration, n.d. (Annual)
This is the codification of regulations first printed in the *Federal Register* (see entry 306). It has many titles, and most titles have more than one volume.

249. *Collective Bargaining Negotiations and Contracts.* Washington, DC: Bureau of National Affairs, Inc., 1945–. (Biweekly)
This two-volume loose-leaf service contains some information on collectively bargained retirement arrangements. The coverage is nowhere near what one would wish. The service is accompanied by an irregular, but more frequent than monthly, newsletter entitled *What's New in Collective Bargaining Negotiations & Contracts.*

250. *Communicating Employee Benefits.* Brookfield, WI: International Foundation of Employee Benefit Plans, 197?–. (Annual)
This collection of speeches was once entitled *Communications Institute Proceedings.*

251. *Communicating Employee Benefits; Ideas and Strategies.* Greenvale, NY: Institute for Management, 1986–. (Annual)
A collection of speeches or essays on diverse topics, some touching on retirement plans.

252. *Compensation & Benefits Management.* Greenvale, NY: Panel Publishers, Inc., 1984–. (Quarterly)
Substantive articles with a relatively low fog index.

253. *Compensation & Benefits Manager's Report.* Englewood Cliffs, NJ: Prentice-Hall, Inc., 1987–. (Fortnightly)
According to its prepublication advertisement, this newsletter is to cover all compensation, including that with which this book is concerned.

254. *Compensation and Benefits Review.* Saranac Lake, NY: American Management Association, 1969–. (Bimonthly)

Formerly entitled *Compensation Review*, this publication retains an orientation toward cash compensation, but the retirement plan articles that appear are out of the top drawer. In addition to articles, there are reprints selected from other periodicals, book reviews, and a news section entitled "In Brief."

255. *CompFlash: New Developments in Compensation and Benefits.* Saranac Lake, NY: American Management Association, 1977–. (Monthly)

This is a newsletter with a heavy bent toward cash compensation, but it does have some relevance for retirement plan professionals.

256. *Compliance Guide for Plan Administrators.* Chicago: Commerce Clearing House, Inc., 1976–. (Fortnightly)

This two-volume loose-leaf title is accompanied by a fortnightly newsletter intended for routing and subsequent filing with the service. It covers welfare benefits as well as retirement plans. By type of plan, it covers the various reporting requirements mandated by federal law. Because plans must report, either regularly or on a significant event basis, to the Department of Labor, the Internal Revenue Service, the Pension Benefit Guaranty Corporation, and participants, there is a definite market for this among administrators of benefit plans.

257. *Computer Applications for Employee Benefit Plans.* Brookfield, WI: International Foundation of Employee Benefit Plans, 198?–. (Annual?)

Texts of speeches given at a conference. A former title was *EDP; Applications for Employee Benefit Plans.*

258. *The CPA Journal.* New York: New York State Society of Certified Public Accountants, 1931–. (Monthly)

In addition to occasional in-depth coverage from the accounting perspective, employee benefit plans have a section to themselves in most issues.

259. *Daily Labor Report.* Washington, DC: Bureau of National Affairs, Inc., 1941–. (Daily)

260. *Daily Report for Executives.* Washington, DC: Bureau of National Affairs, Inc., 1942–. (Daily)

261. *Daily Tax Report.* Washington, DC: Bureau of National Affairs, Inc., 1954–. (Daily)

A typical issue has about 25 percent of its pages relevent to retirement plan topics. Because of its daily currency, this title is of great usefulness to those who must be on top of government legislation, regulation, and court decisions as events happen. The majority of practitioners should be able to do without it, however. The indexing is frequent and good but always less up to date than one wishes.

262. *Digest.* Brookfield, WI: International Foundation of Employee Benefit Plans, 1964–. (Monthly)

This newsletter consists of announcements, abstracts of readings newly released, and full-blown articles on benefits in general.

263. *Directory of Registered Investment Advisors . . . with the Securities and Exchange Commission.* Charlottesville, VA: Money Market Directories, Inc., 1987–. (Annual)

264. *Dun's Business Month.* New York: Dun & Bradstreet Publications Corp., 1893–. (Monthly)

Retirement plan coverage is infrequent, but the readership is influential.

265. *EBPR Research Reports.* Chicago: Charles D. Spencer & Associates, Inc. 1954–. (Weekly updates)

Less than half of this seven-volume loose-leaf service is concerned with the retirement area, but that is enough to render it indispensable. It is published in tandem with *Employee Benefit Plan Review* (see entry 272). It is accompanied by *Weekly News Digest,* a newsletter that is intended to be routed and then filed with the service. The emphasis is on surveying the world of benefits and explaining it to someone at the level of a personnel practitioner. Prevalence of various practices, samples of particular plans, and synopses of exemplary studies are the main content. Considerable pieces of regulation lifted from the *Federal Register* and other background documents are placed in context. The weakness of this service is in its arrangement. The use of decimals in the page numbers is no hindrance to the seasoned user. It constitutes a formidable barrier to the new or occasional user. The index could be much better. More thought should be given to the range of vocabulary with which users approach the index.

266. *EBRI Issue Brief.* Washington, DC: Employee Benefit Research Institute, n.d. (Irregular)

Each *Issue Brief* is a thorough treatment of a particular topic, and many of the topics are retirement plan related.

267. *EBRI News.* Washington, DC: Employee Benefit Research Institute, n.d. (Irregular)

These news releases are published whenever EBRI has something to say and cannot wait for the normal release of *Employee Benefit Notes.*

268. *ECFC Bulletin.* Washington, DC: Employers Council on Flexible Compensation, n.d. (Irregular)

Sometimes this resembles a news release, but it is just as often a substantive treatment of a legislative or regulatory topic. The publication is, in a word, flexible.

269. *ECFC Newsletter.* Washington, DC: Employers Council on Flexible Compensation, n.d. (Monthly?)

Flexible compensation or "cafeteria plans" usually allow contributions to a plan that can be used for retirement. Therefore this newsletter, which largely covers legislation and regulation, is relevant to the topic of this volume.

270. *Effective Collection of Employer Contributions.* Brookfield, WI: International Foundation of Employee Benefit Plans, 19?–. (Biennial?)

This is the text of speeches given at a conference. It has been variously titled in the past. Most of the titles contain the phrase *Institute on Employer Contributions.*

271. *Employee Benefit Notes.* Washington, DC: Employee Benefit Research Institute, 1980–. (Monthly)

This newsletter has more substantial treatment of retirement plan issues than is usual in a newsletter.

272. *Employee Benefit Plan Review.* Chicago: Charles D. Spencer & Associates, Inc., 1946–. (Monthly)

This is aimed at the benefits manager rather than at the actuary or attorney, but it is useful to the latter as well. The articles are brief and newsy. Each issue contains an internal section entitled "Multinational Benefits Review" which is a good way to keep up with foreign trends. There is also a good listing of upcoming educational seminars.

273. *Employee Benefit Plans under ERISA; Federal Regulations.* Englewood Cliffs, NJ: Prentice-Hall, Inc., 197?–. (Annual)

274. *Employee Benefits Annual, 1985; Proceedings of the Annual Employee Benefits Conference.* Brookfield, WI: International Foundation of Employee Benefit Plans, 1956?–. (Annual)
This compendium of speeches given at a major conference of the IFEBP has had several titles. Cites to it tend to puzzle even experienced business reference librarians. It has been called *Annual Educational Conference Proceedings* (with various subtitles); *Textbook for Employee Benefit Plan Trustees, Administrators and Advisors;* and *Textbook for Welfare and Pension Trustees and Administrators.* Because the audience to whom the speeches are made varies greatly in level of expertise, the material varies from sophomoric to abstruse. On balance it can be quite useful, and I know of nothing that gives a better picture of what employee benefit administrators really do.

275. *Employee Benefits Cases.* Washington, DC: Bureau of National Affairs, Inc., 1981–. (Weekly)
This loose-leaf service includes bound volumes that provide text and indexed coverage of opinions of federal and state courts and selected decisions of the National Labor Relations Board and arbitrators on employee benefits issues from September 1974 to the point at which the loose leaf takes over. All of this is available in various sources in a good law library, but to have it in one-half shelf is a great advantage to an employee benefits attorney.

276. *Employee Benefits Cases: Cumulative Digest and Index, Table of Cases, Covering Volumes 1–.* Washington, DC: Bureau of National Affairs, Inc., 1985–.
Frequent retrospective use of EBC, as it is commonly cited, renders the purchase of this advisable.

277. *Employee Benefits Compliance Coordinator.* New York: Research Institute of America, Inc., 1986?–. 4 vols.

278. *Employee Benefits for Nonprofits: A Monthly Newsletter for Nonprofit Organizations.* Washington, DC: NP Publishing, Inc., 1985?–. (Monthly)
This newsletter covers federal legislation and regulation from the point of view of nonprofit organizations. Because of tax code implications, associations, foundations, governments, universities, private schools, and other not-for-profit organizations can have very different retirement arrangements from private sector employers.

279. *Employee Benefits; Information Sources.* Compiled by Dee Birschel. Brookfield, WI: International Foundation of Employee Benefit Plans, 1972?–. (Annual)
This is a subject listing of source materials published by the foundation. The title may therefore be a little presumptuous because most readers would not infer from the title that this is a publisher's catalog. But the foundation is an excellent source of information on most benefits topics. Furthermore, the subject scheme according to which the items are arranged could be of use to those who keep files of information on benefits topics.

280. *Employee Benefits Journal.* Brookfield, WI: International Foundation of Employee Benefit Plans, 1975–. (Quarterly)
This publication specializes in substantive but readable articles that cover the entire gamut of employee benefits.

281. *Employee Benefits Report.* Boston: Warren, Gorham & Lamont, Inc., 1974–. (Monthly)
Formerly *Executive Compensation and Employee Benefits Report,* and before that, *Executive Compensation Report,* this periodical now has some retirement plan coverage. It covers trends in benefits and does a lot of commentary on federal regulations.

282. *Employee Benefits Symposium; Proceedings.* Brookfield, WI: International Society of Certified Employee Benefit Specialists, 1982–. (Annual)
   Speeches given at an annual conference.

283. *Employee Ownership.* Arlington, VA: National Center for Employee Ownership, 1981–. (Bimonthly)
   This is a newsletter covering Employee Stock Ownership Plans.

284. *Employee Relations Report.* Washington, DC: Chamber of Commerce of the United States, n.d. (Irregular)
   Until sometime in 1984, the chamber published two newsletters entitled *Employee Benefits Report* and *Human Resources Report.* Two telephone calls to the chamber have left me with the impression that these two publications were merged into the above title. At this writing, there is only one issue to go by, but it appears that retirement plan coverage will certainly be less.

285. *Employee Retirement Income Security Act;. . .Report to Congress.* Washington, DC: U.S. Department of Labor, 1975?–. (Annual)

286. *Enrolled Actuaries Listed Geographically.* Washington, DC: American Academy of Actuaries, n.d. (Biennial)

287. *Enrolled Actuaries Report.* Washington, DC: American Academy of Actuaries, 1976?–. (Bimonthly)

288. *ERIC Legislative Directory.* Washington, DC: The ERISA Industry Committee, 197?–. (Annual?)
   This is a directory of who's on first in Congress, especially with regard to employee benefits.

289. *ERIC; The Executive Report.* Washington, DC: The ERISA Industry Committee, n.d. (Fortnightly)
   This newsletter is generally not available to nonmembers. Its subject matter is coverage of legislative and regulatory issues in employee benefits.

290. *ERISA Citator.* Washington, DC: Washington Service Bureau, Inc., 1985–.
   This one-volume loose-leaf service is updated monthly. It ties together the Employee Retirement Income Security Act of 1974 with related statutes, regulations, case law, and administrative rulings.

291. *ERISA Compliance Guide.* n.p., Alexander & Alexander, Inc., 1979–. (Loose leaf)

292. *ERISA Opinion Letter(s).* Washington, DC: U.S. Department of Labor, 1975?–. (Irregular)
   These are available from the Department of Labor which sends them out in clumps whenever a clump can be said to have accumulated. Many of the more meaningful ones are available in loose-leaf services, and all are available on LEXIS. Commerce Clearing House's *Pension Plan Guide* refers to them as *Pension and Welfare Benefits Administration Opinion Letters.*

293. *ERISA Source Manual.* Compiled and edited by Leo Brown. New York: Law Journal Seminars Press, 1982–.

294. *ERISA; The Law and the Code, as Amended. . . .* Washington, DC: Bureau of National Affairs, Inc., 198?–. (Irregular)

295. *ERISA Update.* Washington, DC: Washington Service Bureau, Inc., n.d. (Monthly)
> This service indexes and updates Pension Benefit Guaranty Corporation opinion letters, ERISA opinion letters from the Department of Labor, and prohibited transactions.

296. *ESOP in the News.* Washington, DC: The Employee Stock Ownership Association of America, n.d. (Annual)
> A pamphlet of press clippings.

297. *ESOP Report.* Washington, DC: The Employee Stock Ownership Association of America, n.d. (Monthly)
> This newsletter reports on government happenings that are likely to affect ESOPs.

298. *Estate Planning.* Boston: Warren, Gorham & Lamont, Inc., 1973–. (Bimonthly)
> The occasional retirement plan coverage tends here to be targeted at pensions for the self-employed. Because there is not a lot of material written on this facet, this periodical arrives at a degree of importance in the literature that one might not expect. Practitioners dealing with partnerships and sole proprietorships as well as professional corporations and subchapter S corporations may find this a useful magazine.

299. *Estate Planning Review.* Chicago: Commerce Clearing House, Inc., 1974–. (Monthly)
> Published as a part of CCH's financial and estate planning service, this newsletter has good retirement plan coverage. This is especially so in the area of small business where there is not a lot of published material.

300. *Executive Compensation.* Englewood Cliffs, NJ: Prentice-Hall, Inc., n.d. (Monthly)
> This three-volume loose-leaf service is updated monthly with a newsletter that indicates that it is authored by Arthur H. Kroll. There is retirement plan coverage, but one should not purchase this title in the belief that it must cover supplemental executive retirement plans (SERPs) or ERISA excess plans.

301. *Executive Compensation & Taxation Coordinator.* New York: The Research Institute of America, Inc., 1978–. (Fortnightly)
> This loose-leaf three-volume set is accompanied by the fortnightly *Employee Benefits Alert.* Retirement plan coverage is restricted as implied by its former title *Executive Compensation Alert.*

302. *Executive Compensation Reports: An Executive Service Covering Corporate Compensation Programs.* Alexandria, VA: DP Publications Co., 1981–. (Fortnightly)
> This publication, which is compiled from SEC filings, contains some retirement plan information for "high five" people at a few major corporations.

303. *FE; The Magazine for Financial Executives.* Morristown, NJ: Financial Executives Institute, 1932–. (Monthly)
> This magazine targets the corporate CFO who usually has some responsibility for the investment of retirement plan assets. Its occasional retirement plan coverage is, therefore, important.

304. *Federal Employees Almanac.* Falls Church, VA: Federal Employees' News Digest, Inc., 1954–. (Annual)
> This has a concise and up-to-date treatment of the Civil Service Retirement System from the viewpoint of the participant.

305. *Federal Pension Law Service.* Washington, DC: Matthew Bender, 1974–. (Loose leaf)

306. *Federal Register.* Washington, DC: Office of the Federal Register, National Archives and Records Administration, n.d. (Daily)
Regulations promulgated by the Department of Labor, the Internal Revenue Service, the Pension Benefit Guaranty Corp., and other agencies first see the light of day in this publication. An employee benefits attorney will need access to this.

307. *Federal Reserve Bulletin.* Washington, DC: U.S. Federal Reserve System, Board of Governors, 1915–. (Monthly)
This is a good source of interest rate and foreign exchange information for those interested in retirement fund investment.

308. *Federal Securities Law Reporter.* Chicago: Commerce Clearing House, Inc., n.d. (Weekly)
This seven-volume loose-leaf publication is germane to retirement plan literature partly because employer securities are extensively used in funding retirement plans. Securities laws and regulations are therefore important to many employee benefit practitioners.

309. *Federal Tax Forms.* Chicago: Commerce Clearing House, Inc., n.d. (Monthly)
This three-volume loose-leaf service contains the most current edition of at least fifteen forms of interest to the retirement plan practitioner. Instructions for completing the forms are also found here. It is true that all of this material is available free from the government. It is also true that the delays and other frustrations of dealing with the government enable CCH to sell this service.

310. *Federal Taxes: Private Letter Rulings.* Englewood Cliffs, NJ: Prentice-Hall, Inc., 1977?–. (Weekly)
Commerce Clearing House (CCH) and Prentice-Hall (P-H) have differing philosophies on how to provide this service. P-H chooses to publish annual volumes of summaries of private letter rulings (PLRs) supplemented by a loose leaf which contains summaries of those rulings most recently issued. This has the disadvantage that the reader will nearly always have to resort to a database or to express mail for the full text of a given ruling. (cf. the CCH treatment in entry 343, *IRS Letter Rulings.*)

311. *Fiduciary Responsibilities under the New Pension Reform Act.* By George E. Ray and Harvey V. Lamon. Ann Arbor, MI: Institute of Continuing Legal Education, 1975–.

312. *Filing Requirements for Employee Benefit Plans.* Publication 1048. Washington, DC: Internal Revenue Service, 19?–. (Annual?)

313. *Financial Analysts Journal.* New York: Financial Analysts Federation, 1945–. (Bimonthly)
There is heavy retirement plan content from the viewpoint of fund investment.

314. *Financial Directory of Pension Funds.* Parsippany, NJ: Dun's Marketing Services, 1977–. (Annual)
This is now in 104 volumes covering geographic segments of the U.S. It was formerly published out of Washington, DC by ERISA Benefit Funds, Inc. A.k.a. *The Red Book.*

315. *Financial Planning.* Atlanta, GA: International Association for Financial Planning, Inc., 1971–. (Monthly)
There is regular coverage of retirement plans and retirement planning/counseling. This is particularly relevant to smaller companies and to executives at companies where retirement counseling is provided as a benefit.

316. *Financial World.* New York: Financial World Partners, 1902–. (Fortnightly)
There is occasional material relevant to retirement plans from the perspective of fund investment.

317. *Forbes.* New York: Forbes, Inc., 1917–. (Fortnightly)
There is only occasional coverage of issues relevant to retirement plans, but there is a wide and influential readership.

318. *Forms and Workbook for Pension and Profit Sharing Plans.* By Irving Schreiber and Carmine V. Scudere. Rev. ed. Greenvale, NJ: Panel Publishers, Inc., 1979–. (Loose leaf)

319. *Fortune.* New York: Time, Inc., 1930–. (Biweekly)
The occasional retirement plan coverage is widely read. Moreover, the "*Fortune* 500" is the survey list of choice among benefits surveys.

320. *The 401(k) Reporter; The Newsletter for Sponsors of Qualified Cash or Deferred Arrangements under Section 401(k) I.R.C.* Cleveland, OH: Protean Financial Corp., 1985–. (Monthly)
This covers legislation, regulation, and current conditions in the markets and the world of employee benefits.

321. *Fund Advisors Institute; Proceedings.* Brookfield, WI: International Foundation of Employee Benefit Plans, 197?–. (Annual)
A collection of speeches given at an annual conference.

322. *Handbook for Benefit Plan Professionals.* Brookfield, WI: International Foundation of Employee Benefit Plans, 198?–. (Biennial?)

323. *Harvard Business Review.* Boston: Harvard University, Graduate School of Business Administration, 1922–. (Bimonthly)
The occasional retirement plan coverage in this scholarly publication is widely read and is considered authoritative.

324. *How to Set Up and Run a Qualified Pension or Profit Sharing Plan for a Small or Medium Business.* By Irving Schreiber and Carmine V. Scudere. Rev. ed. Greenvale, NY: Panel Publishers, Inc., 1980–.

325. *HR/PC; Personal Computing for Human Resource Professionals.* Pacific Palisades, CA: DGM Associates, 1985–. (Irregular)
This newsletter has, at this writing, not done anything specifically confined to retirement plan operations, but it is yet very new. Computer applications in the field are legion, and most corporate retirement practitioners fall under the rubric of human resources.

326. *IMPACT; Prentice-Hall Information for Managers on Personnel and Current Trends in Human Resources.* Englewood Cliffs, NJ: Prentice-Hall, Inc., 1983–. (Fortnightly)
The occasional retirement plan coverage by this newsletter is not impressive. It could be used by nonbenefits managers to keep up on benefits happenings and by benefits managers to maintain an awareness of the larger context of personnel management.

327. *Individual Retirement Plans (IRAs).* Publication 590. Washington, DC: Internal Revenue Service, 19?–. (Annual)

328. *Institutional Investor.* New York: Institutional Investor, Inc., 1967–. (Monthly)
Considerable and regular coverage of retirement fund investment. For more than a decade, the January issue has contained a directory of large funds.

329. *Insurance; Abstracts and Reviews.* Rotterdam, The Netherlands: Nationale-Nederlanden, 1984–. (Quarterly)
Although the subject coverage is mostly irrelevant to this book, this has indexing of *Transactions of the Society of Actuaries,* and it does include pension literature among the subjects indexed.

330. *Insurance and Employee Benefits Literature.* n.p., Special Libraries Association, Insurance and Employee Benefits Division, 1933–. (Bimonthly)
This is a bibliography of recently appearing publications. Retirement plan coverage is not extensive, but it is useful.

331. *Insurance Contract Profiles; Defined Benefit Edition.* Westport, CT: Evaluation Associates, Inc., ?–1986. (Monthly)
See annotation on the defined contribution edition, entry 332.

332. *Insurance Contract Profiles; Defined Contribution Edition.* Westport, CT: Evaluation Associates, Inc., ?–1986. (Monthly)
Although this publication has ceased, it may remain in occasional demand from time to time. It gives interest rates and provisions of GICs (Guaranteed Insurance Contracts) offered to managers of defined contribution plans. It is a monthly snapshot of the GIC market and might yet be handy for performance evaluation or litigation.

333. *Insurance Guide.* Englewood Cliffs, NJ: Prentice-Hall, Inc., n.d. (Monthly)
Aimed at insurance agents, this one-volume loose-leaf service affords them with the ammunition they need in selling all kinds of benefit plans to their prospects. The retirement sections are therefore very much oriented to the small employer. There is a monthly updating newsletter.

334. *Insurance; Mathematics and Economics.* Amsterdam, The Netherlands: Elsevier Science Publishers. 1982–. (Quarterly)
Occasional, very technical items relevant to retirement plans are included in this journal.

335. *Insurance Sales.* Indianapolis, IN: Rough Notes Co., Inc., 1878–. (Monthly)
This magazine targets insurance agents who have a definite niche in the retirement plan business. It is full of advice on how to sell and news with implications for agents.

336. *Internal Revenue Bulletin.* Washington, DC: Internal Revenue Service, 1919–. (Weekly)
In this publication, IRS publishes revenue rulings, revenue procedures, IRS announcements, IRS notices and a number of other types of pronouncements. Regulations generally are introduced here, and those dealing with benefits are then reprinted in a number of other sources. This, however, is the first and most reliable source of them.

337. *International Benefits.* Brookfield, WI: International Foundation of Employee Benefit Plans, 198?–. (Annual?)
This is the text of speeches given at a conference.

338. *International Tax Journal.* Greenvale, NY: Panel Publishers, Inc., 1974–. (Quarterly)
There is a regular feature on international benefits planning, which, more often than not, deals with retirement plan issues in multinational companies.

339. *Investment Manager Profiles.* Westport, CT: Evaluation Associates, Inc., 1976?–.
Fiduciaries have an obligation not to sit on retirement funds but rather to invest them. Should they choose to hire a professional investment manager rather than using in-house expertise, they have the problem of finding such "money runners" and weighing them against one another. This two-volume loose-leaf service consists largely of profiles of more than a hundred such investment management firms. In each case, a profile indicates something about the style and track record of the firm. Also included are some truly yummy tables of market statistics and performance statistics of money managers in general for use as gauges against which individual managers may be measured. This service is also accompanied by a monthly newsletter entitled *Report Letter* and by *Flash Reports*.

340. *Investments Institute; Proceedings.* Brookfield, WI: International Foundation of Employee Benefit Plans, 197?–. (Annual)
A collection of speeches given at an annual conference.

341. *IRA Compliance Manual.* Englewood Cliffs, NJ: Prentice-Hall, Inc., n.d. (Monthly)
Updated monthly, this one-volume loose-leaf publication covers individual retirement arrangements, Keogh plans and simplified employee pension plans.

342. *IRAs, SEPs and Self-Employed Plans Compliance Guide.* By Carmine V. Scudere. Albany, NY: Matthew Bender, 1986–. 2 vols. (Bimonthly)
A flier for this service promises bimonthly updates and a monthly newsletter.

343. *IRS Letter Rulings.* Chicago: Commerce Clearing House, Inc., 1977–. (Weekly)
There is a base volume and sheaf after sheaf of the rulings themselves. Commerce Clearing House (CCH) and Prentice-Hall (P-H) have differing philosophies on how to provide this service. CCH provides full text of each letter ruling from the beginning of the subscription or thereabouts. I have rarely known an employee benefits attorney to be satisfied with less than instantaneous full text. On the other hand, the CCH approach eats shelf space. (cf. the P-H treatment at *Federal Taxes; Private Letter Rulings*, entry 310.)

344. *IRS Publications.* Chicago: Commerce Clearing House, Inc., n.d.
Again, it is true that everything in this three-volume loose-leaf service is available free from the government. There are a number of IRS publications that are of use to practitioners in the retirement plan arena.

345. *Issues Digest.* Washington, DC: American Academy of Actuaries, 1982–. (Annual)
A compilation and summary of major issues facing the actuarial profession.

346. *J. K. Lasser's All You Should Know about IRA, Keogh, and Other Retirement Plans.* New York: Simon & Schuster, 198?–. (Annual)

347. *Journal of Accountancy.* New York: American Institute of Certified Public Accountants, 1905–. (Monthly)
There is little retirement plan coverage, but the coverage is important.

348. *Journal of Compensation and Benefits.* Boston: Warren, Gorham & Lamont, Inc., 1985–. (Bimonthly)
Much of the material published here is relevant to retirement plans. This publication is very important to practitioners.

349. *Journal of Insurance Regulation.* Kansas City, MO: National Association of Insurance Commissioners, 1982–. (Quarterly)
Although there is little, if any, explicit coverage of retirement plans in this publication, it is a long way from being irrelevant to the topic.

350. *Journal of Pension Planning & Compliance.* Greenvale, NY: Panel Publishers, Inc., 1974–. (Quarterly)
This journal is indispensable to the retirement plan practitioner.

351. *Journal of Portfolio Management.* New York: Institutional Investor, Inc., 1975–. (Quarterly)
Material of considerable interest to those charged with the investment of plan assets is published here. The fog index is as low as the subject matter will allow.

352. *Journal of Risk and Insurance.* Athens, GA: American Risk and Insurance Association, Inc., 1933–. (Quarterly)
This scholarly journal publishes articles relevant to retirement plans with considerable frequency. The articles tend to be highly technical, and their subject matter has a greater time horizon than does most benefits literature. For the benefits manager who is trying to divine what has happened in the last few months, this publication will not be particularly useful. There is a use for it among those who can afford the luxury of a longer term viewpoint.

353. *Journal of Taxation.* Boston: Warren, Gorham & Lamont, Inc., 1954–. (Monthly)
Practitioners interested in the legal and regulatory environment have pronounced this to be an indispensable publication. It is generally not easy reading.

354. *Labor & Investments.* Washington, DC: Industrial Union Department, AFL-CIO, 1981–. (10/yr.)
This newsletter may be unique in giving the union viewpoint on pension and benefit funds. Considerable attention is given to control of the funds by participants.

355. *LAN: Life Association News.* Washington, DC: National Association of Life Underwriters, n.d. (Monthly)
The relatively small amount of retirement plan coverage is mostly oriented toward how to sell the plans. The target audience is the insurance agent.

356. *Legal Legislative Reporter.* Brookfield, WI: International Foundation of Employee Benefit Plans, 1966–. (Monthly)
This is a legislative and regulation newsletter covering all benefits.

357. *Legislative & Regulatory Report.* Washington, DC: Association of Private Pension and Welfare Plans, n.d. (Monthly)
The title is a good description of this newsletter.

358. *Life Insurance Fact Book.* Washington, DC: American Council of Life Insurance, 1946–. (Annual)
There are a few pages on private pension plans with life insurance companies.

359. *Managing Corporate Benefit Plans.* Brookfield, WI: International Foundation of Employee Benefit Plans, 198?–. (Annual)
Former title: *Corporate Benefit Management Conferences; Proceedings.* This is the text of conference speeches.

360. *Managing Employee Benefits.* By Linda Bennett and Christine Watt Finnerty. Paramus, NJ: Prentice-Hall Information Services, 1987–. (Quarterly)
This one-volume loose-leaf service covers all benefits and therefore has relatively minor coverage of retirement and deferred compensation. Having looked at the section on that topic, I must say that it would make a very good introductory two hours' reading for someone new to the field.

361. *Managing Employee Benefits Guidelines.* Paramus, NJ: Prentice-Hall Information Services, 1987–. (Monthly)
Newsletter to accompany the service in entry 360.

362. *The Money Market Directory of Pension Funds and Their Investment Managers.* Charlottesville, VA: Money Market Directories, Inc., 1970–. (Annual)
This is very useful for the funds looking for money runners and vice versa. It also has rankings of funds and advisors and other material of use in fund investment. These rankings have been published separately as pamphlets and a midyear update pamphlet has appeared.

363. *Monthly Benefit Statistics.* Washington, DC: U.S. Social Security Administration, n.d. (Monthly)
This is a source of numbers of retirees under Social Security. Because there are not reliable statistics of retirees under other plans, these numbers are of some interest.

364. *Monthly Labor Review.* Washington, DC: U.S. Bureau of Labor Statistics, 1878–. (Monthly)
The occasional retirement plan coverage is widely read and influential. Its audience is more among those interested in government policy than among other kinds of practitioners.

365. *National Conference of State Retirement Administrators; Proceedings.* n.p., n.d. (Annual)
Speeches presented at a conference.

366. *National Council on Teacher Retirement; Proceedings.* n.p., n.d. (Annual)

367. *NBER Digest.* Cambridge, MA: National Bureau of Economic Research, n.d. (Monthly)
This newsletter summarizes selected NBER working papers. The latter, some of which are listed in the chapter on monographs, are informal treatises in economics. Because retirement plans have come to have socioeconomic and financial importance, a good percentage of these working papers treat of various facets of such plans.

368. *NBER Reporter.* Cambridge, MA: National Bureau of Economic Research, n.d. (Quarterly)
There is occasional coverage of NBER's project on pensions and synopses of technical and working papers that are of some interest to the benefits practitioner. NBER writings have considerable importance, but they are not intended to address the day to day needs of benefits managers.

369. *NCTR Newsletter.* Austin, TX: National Council on Teacher Retirement, 1982?–. (Monthly)
This newsletter is normally provided only to members of NCTR. From the two issues I have seen, it would be interesting to anyone in the area of public plans.

370. *Nutshell: A Monthly Digest of Employee Benefits Publications.* Aspen, CO: The Country Press, Inc., n.d. (Monthly)
Nutshell can be extremely useful in keeping its subscriber informed. It is especially useful to those who have no access to a good benefits library. Because there are few such libraries, its potential audience is wide. It consists of abstracts of articles

appearing in a broad array of publications, most of them listed in this book. The weakness of the publication is that it is inevitably slow. A May issue, consisting of abstracts written on items mostly dated in May, was received in my library on 1 July. Thus the average item in the issue hits the street about six weeks before *Nutshell* can represent it to its reader. That said, one must admit that *Nutshell* is useful even in a good benefits library. It can be used to make certain that important acquisitions were made, and its article supply service is modestly priced.

371. *Pay Planning.* Englewood Cliffs, NJ: Institute for Benefit Planning, 1979–1983?

This was a loose-leaf service that had some useful information on executive retirement vehicles.

372. *PBGC Opinion Letters.* Springfield, VA: National Technical Information Service, 1974–. (Quarterly?)

These are written at the Pension Benefit Guaranty Corporation. While they are being reported upon by the press and handed from contact to contact, they are also accumulating until someone feels that librarians have been goaded enough. Then a quarterly collection may, or may not, be issued by NTIS to those on standing order. This method of distribution ensures that most libraries will not have the letters most requested and that "old boy" networks will continue to have social utility.

373. *The Pension Actuary.* Washington, DC: American Society of Pension Actuaries, 1975?–. (Monthly)

This newsletter is generally available only to members of ASPA.

374. *Pension Administrator's Form Book.* Greenvale, NY: Panel Publishers, Inc., 1986–.

375. *Pension and Annuity Income.* Publication 575. Washington, DC: Internal Revenue Service, 19?–. (Annual)

376. *Pension and Employee Benefits; Code, ERISA, Regulations.* Chicago: Commerce Clearing House, Inc., n.d. (Irregular)

Editions of this irregular serial have appeared as of 4/15/78, 5/8/81, 8/19/83, and 4/5/85. A 1987 edition is said to be forthcoming.

377. *Pension and Profit Sharing.* Englewood Cliffs, NJ: Prentice-Hall, Inc., 1978–. (Weekly)

This is a six-volume loose-leaf service which is very much the same sort of thing as the *Pension Plan Guide* from Commerce Clearing House (CCH). Users tend to have a favorite between the two, and representatives will summon up tomes of reasons for theirs being the better service. There probably are differences between these services, but I would avoid making a choice if possible. Buy them both, if you can. Librarians should solicit user opinion if they cannot afford both. If a decision between them is necessary, I suggest flipping a coin. There are better ways to spend your energy. (cf. the CCH treatment at *Pension Plan Guide*, entry 391.)

378. *Pension & Profit Sharing Plans.* By Sheldon M. Young. New York: Matthew Bender, 1977?–. 5 vols.

379. *Pension and Profit Sharing Plans for Small & Medium Size Businesses.* Greenvale, NY: Panel Publishers, Inc., 1986–. (Quarterly)

An advertising flier claims quarterly updates and a monthly newsletter with the same title. An earlier edition was authored by Carmine V. Scudere and Kevin J. Moran.

380. *Pension and Profit-Sharing; Sample Plans & Workbook.* Greenvale, NY: Panel Publishers, Inc. 1985–. (Annual)

381. *Pension and Retirement Plans; Issues and Strategies.* Greenvale, NY: Panel Publishers, Inc., 1985–. (Annual)
>When I purchased the first of these, I had no inkling that I was entering a standing order, but the speeches or trendy articles are sufficiently useful that you can easily overcome your irritation with the publisher.

382. *Pension Briefings.* Washington, DC: Federal Publications, Inc., 1986?–. (Monthly)
>I have seen seven issues of this newsletter. Each of them is an extensively footnoted treatment of a single legislative or regulatory issue. The authors are mostly employee benefits attorneys.

383. *Pension Coordinator.* New York: Research Institute of America, Inc., 1987?–. 11 vols.
>This loose-leaf service in 1987. It will include a two-volume forms service from Corbel & Co. RIA has a reputation for making tax law comprehensible to nonlawyers. This service will no doubt be roughly comparable to the Commerce Clearinghouse *Pension Plan Guide* (entry 391) and the Prentice-Hall *Pension and Profit Sharing* (entry 377).

384. *Pension Disputes and Settlements.* By Seymour Goldberg. Greenvale, NY: Panel Publishers, 1978–. 1 vol.

385. *Pension Facts.* Washington, DC: American Council of Life Insurance, 1974–. (Annual?)
>The frequency of appearance of this publication is probably determined on the basis of what resources are available to produce it. It is handy for statistics, and it has a bibliography in some issues.

386. *The Pension Forum.* Itasca, IL: Society of Actuaries, Pension Section, 1985–. (Quarterly)
>The first issue was entitled *The Pension Journal.* The articles could easily be of interest to people outside the actuarial profession. For an understanding of most of them, the reader need only be arithmetically competent.

387. *Pension Investment Reporter.* Charlottesville, VA: Money Market Directories, Inc., 1985–. (Monthly)
>This newsletter targets small- to medium-sized fund sponsors in an endeavor to increase their investment expertise.

388. *Pension Law Today; Course Manual.* Washington, DC: Federal Publications, Inc., 1979?–. (Annual?)
>Prior to 1985, this was entitled *ERISA Today.*

389. *Pension News.* Washington, DC: Association of Private Pension and Welfare Plans, 1979–. (Monthly?)
>This newsletter is probably defunct and possibly folded into the *Legislative and Regulatory Report* which is currently done by APPWP.

390. *Pension Plan Forms with Lurie's Commentaries on Pension Design.* Jacksonville, FL: Corbel & Co., 1978?–.

391. *Pension Plan Guide.* Chicago: Commerce Clearing House, Inc., 1953–. (Weekly)
>This is a seven-volume loose-leaf service which concentrates purely on the legal and taxation aspects of retirement plans. It is accompanied by a weekly newsletter intended for routing. The endeavor is to bring all federal laws, regulations, court decisions, and near-law, such as private letter rulings, which bear on retirement plans into a useable body. The endeavor is quite successful. This or the Prentice-Hall equivalent (*Pension*

and Profit Sharing, entry 377) is indispensable in a library that needs a good collection in this area.

392. *Pension Planning and Deferred Compensation.* By Jeffrey G. Sherman. New York: Matthew Bender, 1985–.

393. *Pension, Profit-Sharing and Other Deferred Compensation Plans; ALI-ABA Course of Study Materials.* Philadelphia, PA: American Law Institute-American Bar Association, Committee on Continuing Professional Education, 198?–. (Irregular)

394. *Pension Reform Handbook; Employee Retirement Income Security Act of 1974 and Later Amendments.* By Martin E. Holbrook. Englewood Cliffs, NJ: Prentice-Hall, Inc., 1982?–. (Annual)

395. *Pension Regulation Manual.* By Robert A. Bildersee. Rev. ed. Boston: Warren, Gorham & Lamont, 1977–.

396. *Pension World.* Atlanta, GA: Communication Channels, Inc., 1964–. (Monthly)
In addition to publishing excellent and authoritative articles, this journal makes awards to outstanding achievers in the retirement area and publishes an annual compliance calendar. Other special features include an annual software directory, listings of master and directed trust services, real estate portfolio managers and third party administrators, and an annual survey of state retirement systems.

397. *Pensions & Investment Age.* Chicago: Crain Communications, Inc., 1973–. (Fortnightly)
Formerly *Pensions and Investments*, this publication serves up general news in addition to a concentration on the investment of pension assets. Its quarterly *PIPER* (*Pensions Investment Performance Evaluation Report*) is a relatively cheap way of following the performance of investment managers. It runs a monthly listing of proprietary capital market indices that are otherwise hard to get at. The Russell 3000, the Ryan Index, and the Shearson Lehman Government/Corporate bond index graced one recent issue. In addition, there are lists of underwriters, large pension funds, GIC rates, largest issuers of securities, financial associations and organizations, largest money mangers, service providers in cash management, investment consultants, and "best" brokers some of which are the only directories of their kind. Many of the articles require some background in finance, but there is a refreshing propensity toward informal English.

398. *Personnel.* New York: American Management Association, 1919–. (Monthly)
There is infrequent but important retirement plan coverage. The "Career Development Calendar" in each issue is a good guide to upcoming educational seminars.

399. *Personnel Administrator.* Alexandria, VA: American Society for Personnel Administration, 1956–. (Monthly)

400. *Personnel Journal.* Costa Mesa, CA: A. C. Croft, Inc., 1922–. (Monthly)

401. *P.I.P.E.R.; Pensions & Investments' Performance Evaluation Report.* Chicago: Pensions & Investments Age, 1979?–. (Quarterly)
This loose-leaf service may be another way to monitor investment managers and make comparisons with one's own plan. PIPER is compiled by Rogers, Casey and Barksdale, Inc. It is sold from a Detroit address that you can get in those issues of *Pensions & Investment Age* which carry an abstract of PIPER.

402. *Plan Administrator's Compliance Manual for All Types of Benefit Plans; Checklists, Forms, Instructions, Calendars, Editorial Explanation.* Englewood Cliffs, NJ: Prentice-Hall, Inc., 1975–. (Monthly)
> This two-volume loose-leaf title is very much the same thing as the *Compliance Guide for Plan Administrators* which is described in entry 256.

403. *The Practical Accountant.* New York: Warren, Gorham & Lamont, Inc., 1968–. (Monthly)
> There is fairly frequent coverage of retirement in a section entitled "ERISA & Compensation."

404. *The Proceedings.* Itasca, IL: The Conference of Actuaries in Public Practice, 1951–. (Annual)
> Each volume is a record of what was said at meetings of the conference. There are also a number of formal papers published.

405. *Profile.* Washington, DC: The Employee Stock Ownership Association of America, n.d. (Monthly)
> This newsletter profiles companies with ESOPs.

406. *Profit Sharing.* Chicago: Profit Sharing Council of America, 1970–. (Monthly)

407. *Public Employee Benefit Plans.* Brookfield, WI: International Foundation of Employee Benefit Plans, 1970–. (Annual)
> A collection of speeches given at an annual conference.

408. *Quadrennial Review of Military Compensation.* Washington, DC: U.S. Department of Defense, 1968–. (Quadrennial)

409. *Qualified Deferred Compensation Plans.* Wilmette, IL: Callaghan & Co., 1984?–.
> This loose-leaf service seemingly attempts to do in two volumes what Commerce Clearing House and Prentice-Hall do in six or seven. A reading of the prefaces discloses that there is coverage of legislation, regulation, and court decisions. Updating is certainly less frequent than CCH and P-H, but the price is less as well. Because the government is constantly tinkering with the retirement field, this title is not going to suffice for the needs of some practitioners.

410. *Qualified Plans; Insurance and Professional Corporations, ALI-ABA Course of Study Materials.* Philadelphia, PA: American Law Institute-American Bar Association, Committee on Continuing Professional Education, 198?–. (Annual?)

411. *Qualified Retirement Plans.* Published in cooperation with the Oregon Society of Certified Public Accountants by Ray R. Benner and Leslie L. Wellman. Owings Mills, MD: National Law Publishing Corp., 1977–.
> This one-volume loose-leaf service is an attempt to explain government requirements with respect to plan design, implementation, administration, amendment, and termination. It targets small accounting and law firms dealing mostly with small plans.

412. *Railroad Retirement Information.* Chicago: U.S. Railroad Retirement Board, Office of Public Affairs, n.d. (Irregular)
> This newsletter is intended for participants and people interested in the Railroad Retirement System.

413. *The Record.* Chicago: American Institute of Actuaries, 1909–1949. (Annual)
> Formal papers and discussions presented at meetings of the institute are published here. Relatively few of them are on retirement topics, but these few are seminal.

414. *Record.* Itasca, IL: Society of Actuaries, 1975–. (Quarterly)
This is a record of speeches and discussions occurring at meetings of the Society of Actuaries.

415. *Research and Statistics Note.* Washington, DC: U.S. Department of Health and Human Services. Social Security Administration, n.d. (Irregular)
This publication may be defunct, but issues were released at a rate of fifteen to twenty per year in the period from 1967 through 1980. Many of them had to do with retirement issues.

416. *RRB Actuarial Studies.* Chicago: U.S. Railroad Retirement Board, Office of the Chief Actuary, n.d. (Irregular)

417. *The RRB Quarterly Review.* Chicago: U.S. Railroad Retirement Board, Information Service, 1968–1981. (Quarterly)

418. *SEC Monthly Statistical Review.* Washington, DC: U.S. Securities and Exchange Commission, 1942–. (Monthly)
Although this is still of some interest, perhaps, to pension fund investment managers, the pension fund asset figures which were once published were discontinued about 1981. Comparable figures are now published by the Federal Reserve.

419. *Sector.* Silver Spring, MD: CDA Investment Technologies, Inc., n.d. (Quarterly)
This comes in two volumes. It covers banks, insurance companies, mutual funds, investment advisors, and internal financial managements. The reader can derive a pretty good idea of what equity sectors the money managers are invested in and whether they are shifting money. The importance to our topic is that much of that money belongs to retirement plans.

420. *Self-Employed Retirement Plans.* Publication 560. Washington, DC: Internal Revenue Service, 19?–. (Irregular?)

421. *Social Security Bulletin.* Washington, DC: U.S. Department of Health and Human Services, Social Security Administration, 1938–. (Monthly with an annual statistical supplement)
A considerable amount of the statistics and writing published in this periodical has application to private and public retirement plans.

422. *Society of Actuaries Yearbook.* Itasca, IL: Society of Actuaries, 1949?–. (Annual)
This is mostly a directory of members, but a considerable part of it has to do with the exams one must pass in order to become an actuary.

423. *SOI Bulletin.* Washington, DC: U.S. Department of the Treasury, Internal Revenue Service, 1981–. (Quarterly)
This is a handy source of statistical data such as that individuals reported $80,447,934,000.00 in taxable pension and annuity income in 1984 and that partnerships deducted $530,116,000.00 for payments to pension, profit sharing, annuity and bond purchase plans in the same year. One does not know whether such figures are pure enough to have significance, but one gets asked for them.

424. *State Tax Guide.* Chicago: Commerce Clearing House, Inc., 1937–. (Biweekly)
This two-volume loose-leaf title is accompanied by a weekly newsletter for routing. It is germane to this book because the states differ in how they tax contributions to and distributions from retirement plans.

425. *Stocks, Bonds, Bills, and Inflation Yearbook.* Chicago: Ibbotson Associates, 197?–. (Annual)
Market results for various securities since 1926.

426. *Survey of Current Business.* Washington, DC: U.S. Department of Commerce, Bureau of Economic Analysis, 1924–. (Monthly)
This is a source of interest rates, statistical indices, and other data frequently used in retirement work.

427. *Tax Facts on Life Insurance.* Cincinnati, OH: NU Law Service, 1951?–. (Annual)
The current edition of the first volume has considerable retirement plan content.

428. *Tax Management Compensation Planning Journal.* Washington, DC: Tax Management, Inc., 1973–. (Monthly)
The Bureau of National Affairs seems to have a problem with how to title this journal. It has been *Compensation Planning Journal, Tax Management Executive Compensation Journal,* and *Executive Compensation Journal.* Under some of these titles, there was little retirement plan coverage, but there is a good deal of it at this writing. Tax Management, Inc., by the way, is a subsidiary of Bureau of National Affairs, Inc.

429. *Tax Management International Journal.* Washington, DC: Tax Management, Inc., 1972–. (Monthly)
Each issue contains an update on the current status of U.S. tax treaties. There are often international tax implications in contributions to and distributions from retirement plans.

430. *Tax News.* Boston: Warren, Gorham & Lamont, Inc., 1979–. (Quarterly)
This quarterly in tabloid format contains occasional retirement plan material.

431. *Taxation for Accountants.* Boston: Warren, Gorham & Lamont, Inc., 1966–. (Monthly)

432. *Taxes; The Tax Magazine.* Chicago: Commerce Clearing House, Inc., 1923–. (Monthly)

433. *Technical Update.* Washington, DC: Pension Benefit Guaranty Corp., 1978?–. (Monthly)
If you can get on their mailing list, PBGC will send you, dated about the 15th of each month, a list of interest rates and factors useful for terminating pension plans. These rates and factors are also available in the *Federal Register* (entry 306). You will also get a quarterly announcement of withdrawal liability interest rates.

434. *Three Budgets for a Retired Couple.* Washington, DC: U.S. Department of Labor, Bureau of Labor Statistics, 1970–1982. (Annual)
First issued as Bulletin 1570–6, although there was a precursor in Bulletin 1570–4, and last issued as news release, USDL 82–266, this title afforded a very important piece of information. It gave target incomes at which retirement planners could aim the designs of their plans. Whatever the form of the original release, an abstract of the data was usually published in a November or December issue of *Monthly Labor Review.* The Bureau of National Affairs also repeated the salient data in its *Daily Labor Report.* Bureau of Labor Statistics ceased publication, for budgetary reasons, with the autumn 1981 budgets as of July 30, 1982.

435. *Topics in Employee Benefits for Association Executives.* Brookfield, WI: International Foundation of Employee Benefit Plans, 198?–. (Annual)

436. *Transactions.* Itasca, IL: Society of Actuaries, 1949–. (Annual)
Formal papers presented at meetings, minutes of meetings, financial reports, and obituary of the most important body of actuaries in the U.S. There is considerable content of interest to retirement practioners.

437. *Transactions.* n.p., Actuarial Society of America, 1892–1949. (Annual)
Formerly entitled *Papers and Transactions*, this was the chief publication of an important predecessor of the Society of Actuaries.

438. *Trusts & Estates.* Atlanta, GA: Communication Channels, Inc., 1904–. (Monthly)
In addition to some important coverage relevant to retirement issues, there is an annual directory issue. The "Directory of Trust Institutions" gives names and addresses of firms that will accept and invest pension money.

439. *Unemployment Insurance Reports with Social Security.* Chicago: Commerce Clearing House, Inc., 1934–. (Weekly)
Two-thirds of this three-volume loose-leaf service are concerned with social security. There is a weekly newsletter accompanying the filings.

440. *Uniformed Services Almanac.* Washington, DC: Uniformed Services Almanac, Inc., 1959–. (Annual)
This has a concise and up-to-date treatment of the military retirement system from the viewpoint of the participant.

441. *U.S. Civil Service Retirement and Disability.* Publication 567. Washington, DC: Internal Revenue Service, 19?–. (Annual)

442. *Wall Street Journal.* New York: Dow Jones & Co., 1889–. (Daily)

443. *What's Ahead in Personnel.* Chicago: Human Resource Management News, Enterprise Publications, 1973–. (Fortnightly)
This would not be a bad newsletter for keeping marketing, production, or finance people abreast of major trends in retirement. Of course only a small proportion of the material published is on retirement issues. I think it may also be useful for keeping people immersed in retirement issues aware of the larger context in which many of them function.

444. *Year Book.* New York: The Actuarial Society of America, 1889?–1948?. (Annual)
Those interested in the early bibliography of retirement plans could examine this title. From 1936 on, the recommended course of reading to pass actuarial examinations is incorporated in its issues.

Monographs

This is a chapter that a good many of the patrons of my library would label as useless. However, there are a lot of other people, inside and outside the pension industry, who might find the chapter a very useful one indeed. In the introduction, I touched upon the disparate backgrounds and tasks that characterize those who toil in this particular vineyard. For many practitioners and their consultants, any information that has undergone the tedious process of being published in book form is likely to be stale at best and already incorrect or misleading at worst.

That is not to say that the monograph is useless even to these leading-edge types. I have often been asked to find "something simple" for someone new to the field, and there are a number of pieces that do the job fairly well. Further, topics tend to recur. Material on the effects of inflation on the pension system was once very popular, and I am certain that it will be in vogue again. There are some writings that are classics. I can think of one piece having to do with the calculation of investment return to a pension fund which I expect to use in answering questions many times in the future. I do not see how it can be outmoded. Finally, there are areas wherein a good knowledge of history is cardinal. For obvious reasons, policymakers must know what has gone before.

It may help the user to know how this material was gathered. I started with the MARC holdings of the Library of Congress and worked my way through the card catalog at LC for pre-1980 imprints. I then incorporated material from the online version of *Books in Print*, and went through the holdings of the library in which I am employed. I checked my data against a number of bibliographies that I found in the latter collection. I found a considerable number of errors in MARC data which makes me certain that there are pagination and series errors throughout this chapter. Finally, I checked the data against a continuing series of book reviews in a publication of the International Foundation of Employee Benefit Plans. When I found that nearly one in ten of those items considered important enough to review were still missing from my data, I resigned myself to producing a less than perfect piece of work.

The criteria for inclusion of monographic material were necessarily subjective. I included material on investment, demography, economic policy, and union-management relations when I knew it to be particularly useful in retirement plan work. I avoided material on social security as much as possible because that topic is being done by another author in this series. Material on retirement counseling did not seem to me to be part of the scope of this book, but a few items crept in because of their retirement plan content. When I came across material that treated employee ownership and profit sharing only from the incentive aspect, I avoided including it. Literature having to do with particular plans was not included unless I could perceive usefulness for larger constituencies. Where there are multiple editions of a work, I included only the most current edition. Where early editions have historical importance, I made an annotation to that effect.

Finally, except where it serves a purpose, as in the case of the Financial Accounting Standards Board, which brings together documents with confusingly similar titles, I eschew the use of "corporate" entries. If I could not find an author, editor, or compiler, I entered the piece under title. This is more a matter of personal taste than anything else. It proceeds from a feeling, grown deeper of late, that organizations do not produce books, people do.

445. Aaron, Benjamin. *Legal Status of Employee Benefit Rights under Private Pension Plans.* Homewood, IL: Published for the Pension Research Council by Richard D. Irwin, Inc., 1961. 130 p.

446. Aaron, Henry J., and Burtless, Gary, eds. *Retirement and Economic Behavior.* Washington, DC: Brookings Institution, 1984. 352 p.

447. Abel, Andrew B. *Capital Accumulation and Uncertain Lifetimes with Adverse Selection.* NBER Working Paper, 1664. Cambridge, MA: National Bureau of Economic Research, 1985. 16 p.

448. *Abolishing Mandatory Retirement; Implications for America and Social Security of Eliminating Age Discrimination in Employment, an Interim Report. . . .* Printed for the use of the Select Committee on Aging. Washington, DC: U.S. Government Printing Office, 1981. 371 p.

449. Abraham, Katherine G., and Farber, Henry S. *Job Duration, Seniority and Earnings.* NBER Working Paper, 1819. Cambridge, MA: National Bureau of Economic Research, 1986. 55 p.

450. *Accounting for Pensions; Results of Applying the FASB's Preliminary Views.* New York?: Coopers & Lybrand, 1983. 256 p.

451. *Accounting for the Cost of Pension Plans; Text and Explanatory Comments on APB Opinion No. 8.* New York: American Institute of Certified Public Accountants, 1968. 109 p.
     The cover title is *Five Articles on Accounting for the Cost of Pension Plans,* and the text of the opinion is included.

452. Accounting Principles Board. *Accounting for the Cost of Pension Plans.* Opinion, 8. New York: American Institute of Certified Public Accountants, Inc., 1966. 103 p.

453. *Action Needed to Reduce, Account for, and Collect Overpayments to Federal Retirees; Report to the Congress.* Washington, DC: U.S. General Accounting Office, 1983. 45 p.

454. *Actuarial and Economic Analysis of State and Local Government Pension Plans.* Washington, DC: U.S. General Accounting Office, 1980. 45 p.

455. *Administration of the Employee Retirement Income Security Act, ERISA; A Report to Congress.* . . . Washington, DC: U.S. Office of Management and the Budget, 1980. 81 p.

456. *Aging America; Trends and Projections, 1985–86 Edition.* Prepared by. . .The U.S. Senate Special Committee on Aging et al. . . . Washington, DC: U.S. Government Printing Office, 1986. 129 p.

457. Alden, Phillip M. *Controlling the Costs of Retirement Income and Medical Care Plans.* An AMA Management Briefing. New York: AMACOM, 1980, 78 p.

458. Alexander, Donald C. *Pension Plans; Qualification.* Washington, DC: Tax Management, 1972. Various pagings.

459. *All You Need to Know about Individual Retirement Plans (IRAs).* Englewood Cliffs, NJ: Prentice-Hall, Inc., 1983. 48 p.

460. Allen, Everett T., Jr.; Melone, Joseph J.; and Rosenbloom, Jerry S. *Pension Planning; Pensions, Profit Sharing and Other Deferred Compensation Plans.* 5th ed. The Irwin Series in Insurance and Economic Security. Homewood, IL: Richard D. Irwin, Inc., 1984. 448 p.

461. Allen, Steven G., and Clark, Robert L. *Unions, Pension Wealth, and Age-Compensation Profiles.* NBER Working Paper, 1677. Cambridge, MA: National Bureau of Economic Research, 1985. 40 p.

462. Allen, Steven G.; Clark, Robert L.; and McDermed, Ann A. *Job Mobility, Older Workers and the Role of Pensions.* Raleigh, NC: North Carolina State University. Center for Economics and Business Studies, 1986. 106 p.

463. Allen, Steven G.; Clark, Robert L.; and Sumner, Daniel A. *Post-Retirement Adjustment of Pension Benefits.* NBER Working Paper, 1364. Cambridge, MA: National Bureau of Economic Research, 1984. 32 p.

464. Ambachtsheer, Keith P. *Pension Funds and the Bottom Line; Managing the Corporate Pension Fund as a Financial Business.* Homewood, IL: Dow Jones-Irwin, 1986. 167 p.

465. Amble, Joan Lordi, and Cassel, Jules M. *A Guide to Implementation of Statement 87 on Employers' Accounting for Pensions; Questions and Answers.* Special Report. Stamford, CT: Financial Accounting Standards Board, 1986. 106 p.

466. *American Academy of Actuaries Factbook.* Washington, DC: American Academy of Actuaries, 198?. Unpaged.
This booklet informs its reader about the actuarial profession.

467. American Bar Association. Committee on Unauthorized Practice of the Law. *Employee Benefit Planning; Informative Opinion A of 1977, May 1, 1977.* Chicago, 1978. 23 p.

468. *Analysis & Application of the 1986 Tax Reform Act; P.L. 99–514, Effective October 22, 1986, A Special Report. . . .* Greenvale, NY: Panel Publishers, Inc., 1986. 326 p.

469. *Analysis of Alternative Vesting Requirements for Private Pensions.* Washington, DC: Employee Benefit Research Institute, 1980. 35 p.

470. *Analysis of Grace Commission Proposals to Change the Civil Service Retirement System.* Washington, DC: U.S. General Accounting Office, 1985. 14 p.

471. *An Analysis of Pension Plan Costs, 1972–1976; Final Report, 1980.* Prepared by ICF Incorporated for the Office of Pension and Welfare Benefit Programs. U.S. Department of Labor. Washington, DC, 1980. 113 p.
Concludes that the limited sample does not permit generalizations about ERISA's effects.

472. *Analysis of Pension Plans/Workers' Compensation Offsets.* Prepared for the Department of Labor by Hay Associates. Washington, DC: National Technical Information Service, 1979. 27 p.

473. *An Analysis of the Provisional, Financial, and Demographic Characteristics of Small and Medium-Sized Employer Sponsored Private Retirement Plans and a Model Comparison of the Benefits and Costs Associated with Alternative Types of Plans and Plan Provisions; Report to the President's Commission on Pension Policy.* Washington, DC: American Society of Pension Actuaries, 1980?. 70 p.

474. Anderson, Arthur W. *Anderson's Complete Guide to Revenue Rulings on Qualified Plans, 1971–1986.* Boston, 1986. 93 p.
This is printed and distributed by the Windsor Press of Wellesley Hills, Massachusetts.

475. Anderson, Arthur W. *Pension Mathematics for Actuaries.* Needham, MA, 1985. 175 p.

476. Andrews, Emily S. *The Changing Profile of Pensions in America.* An EBRI-ERF Policy Study. Washington, DC: Employee Benefit Research Institute, 1985. 234 p.

477. Apfel, Kenneth S. *Seminar Material for the Legal Aspects of Executive Compensation.* Newark, NJ: New Jersey Institute for Continuing Legal Education, 1984. 207 p.

478. Apolinsky, Harold I. *Life Insurance and Executive Compensation in the Closely Held Corporation.* Tax Law and Practice Course Handbook Series, 146. New York: Practising Law Institute, 1980. 520 p.

479. *Are Pension Beneficiaries Harmed by Large Bank Trust Department Sales of Large Common Stock Positions? The Evidence.* Washington, DC: U.S. General Accounting Office, 1978. 37 p.

480. Areson, David C., ed. *Employee Retirement Income Security Act of 1974, Updated through September 1, 1986.* Paramus, NJ: Prentice-Hall, Inc., 1986. 2 vols.
Updated with a "Supplement Reflecting the Tax Reform Act of 1986."

481. Areson, Todd W., and Kossak, Shelley E. *Pension Issues for Local Policymakers.* Washington, DC: National Association of Counties/National League of Cities, 1980. 46 p.

482. *Assessment of Special Rules Exempting Employers Withdrawing from Multiemployer Pension Plans from Withdrawal Liability.* Washington, DC: U.S. General Accounting Office, 1984. 54 p.

483. *Asset Reversions from Defined Benefit Pension Plans; Proposal of the American Society of Pension Actuaries.* Washington, DC: ASPA, 1986. 31 p.

484. Atkins, G. Lawrence. *Spend It or Save It? Pension Lump-Sum Distributions and Tax Reform.* An EBRI-ERF Research Report. Washington, DC: Employee Benefit Research Institute, 1986. 85 p.

485. *Audits of Employee Benefit Plans.* Audit and Accounting Guide. New York: American Institute of Certified Public Accountants. Employee Benefit Plans and ERISA Special Committee, 1983. 184 p.

486. Babson, Stanley M., Jr. *Fringe Benefits; The Depreciation, Obsolescence, and Transience of Man, Costs Strategies, and Trends for Financial Managers, Personnel Directors, and General Management.* New York: John Wiley & Sons, 1974. 178 p.

487. Bachelder, Joseph E., III. *Employee Stock Ownership Plans.* New York: Practising Law Institute, 1979. 788 p.
Updated by an addendum in 1982.

488. Bachelder, Joseph E., III, and Rizzo, Ronald S. *ESOPs, TRASOPs, PAYSOPs and Other Employee Stock Ownership Plans.* Tax Law and Practice Course Handbook Series, 174. New York: Practising Law Institute, 1982. 880 p.

489. Bachman, Arthur, and Marblestone, Kenneth. *The REA's Joint and Survivor Annuity Rules; Coping with the Regulations.* Pension Planning Series. Englewood Cliffs, NJ: Prentice-Hall, Inc., 1986. 24 p.

490. *Background Analysis of the Potential Effects of a Minimum Universal Pension System; Final Report Submitted to the President's Commission on Pension Policy and. . .the Department of Labor.* By ICF Incorporated, April 15, 1981. Washington, DC: ICF Inc., 1981. Various pagings.

491. Baker, David R. *Individual Retirement Arrangements.* Tax Management Portfolios, 355–2nd. Washington, DC: Bureau of National Affairs, Inc., 1986. Various pagings.

492. Baldwin, Stuart A., et al. *Pension Funds & Ethical Investment; A Study of Investment Practices & Opportunities, State of California Retirement Systems.* New York: Council on Economic Priorities, 1985. 191 p.

493. Ball, Robert M. *Pensions in the United States; A Study. . . .* By the National Planning Association. Washington, DC: U.S. Government Printing Office, 1952. 106 p.

494. Bank, Richard M. *Non-Traditional Investment of Pension Funds; A Brief Overview of the Antitrust Question.* Working Papers. Washington, DC: President's Commission on Pension Policy, 1980. 31 p.

495. Barker, Michael, ed. *Financing State and Local Development.* Duke Press Policy Studies. Durham, NC: Duke University Press, 1983. 480 p.

496. Bartell, H. Robert, Jr., and Simpson, Elizabeth T. *Pension Funds of Multiemployer Industrial Groups, Unions and Nonprofit Organizations.* New York: National Bureau of Economic Research, 1968. 52 p.

497. Bartholomew, Herbert A. *Military Compensation Background Papers; Compensation Elements and Related Manpower Cost Items, Their Purposes and Legislative Backgrounds.* 2d ed. Washington, DC: U.S. Government Printing Office, 1983. 402 p.

498. Bassett, Preston C. *Federal Pension Programs.* Working Papers. Washington, DC: President's Commission on Pension Policy, 1980. Unpaged.

499. Bauman, W. Scott. *Guidelines for Communications to Investors; Standards of Disclosure for Investment Managers of Pension Funds, Mutual Funds, Advisory Accounts, and Financial Institutions.* Monograph, 14. Charlottesville, VA: Financial Analysts Research Foundation, 1982. 124 p.

500. Beam, Burton T., Jr., and McFadden, John J. *Employee Benefits.* Homewood, IL: Richard D. Irwin, Inc., 1985. 500 p.

501. Beller, Daniel. *Estimates of Participant and Financial Characteristics of Private Pension Plans.* Washington, DC: U.S. Government Printing Office, 1983. 36 p.

502. Belous, Richard S. *An International Comparison of Fringe Benefits; Theory, Evidence, and Policy Implications.* Washington, DC: Congressional Research Service, 1984. 34 p.

503. Beman, L. T. *Old Age Pensions.* New York: H. W. Wilson Co., 1927. 359 p.

504. *Benefit Levels of Nonfederal Retirement Programs.* Washington, DC: U.S. General Accounting Office, 1985. 28 p.

505. Benna, R. Theodore. *Sec. 401(k) Plans; Flexible Benefits under Tax Reform.* Paramus, NJ: Prentice-Hall, Inc., 1986. 24 p.

506. Bennewitz, Dall, and Garrigan, Richard T. *Pension Fund Investments in Mortgages and Mortgage-Backed Securities; A Focus on State Retirement Systems.* Chicago: United States League of Savings Institutions, 1984. 19 p.

507. Berger, Paul S. *Jointly Managed and Multiemployer Pension Plans.* Corporate Law and Practice Course Handbook Series, 172. New York: Practising Law Institute, 1975. 216 p.

508. Berger, Paul S., and Hester, Stephen L. *Special Problems of Multi-Employer Plans.* Pension and Profit Sharing Plans. Series A, Folio 4. Philadelphia, PA: American Law Institute-American Bar Association. Committee on Continuing Professional Education, 1978. 45 p.

509. Berger, Paul S., and Neal, Philip S. *Executive Compensation and Employee Benefits; Planning in the Light of the Economic Recovery Tax Act of 1981.* New York: Law & Business, Inc., Harcourt Brace Jovanovich, 1982. 183 p.

510. Berger, Paul S., and Siegel, Mayer. *Pensions and Employee Benefits under the 1982 Tax Act.* New York: Law & Business, 1982. 352 p.

511. Bergman, Stanley N., and Reynolds, David L. *Plan Selection; Pension and Profit-Sharing Plans.* Tax Management Portfolios, 350. Washington, DC: Bureau of National Affairs, Inc., 1986. Various pagings.

512. Berin, Barnet N. *The Fundamentals of Pension Mathematics.* New York: William M. Mercer, Inc., 1978. 125 p.
There was an earlier edition sponsored by the Society of Actuaries and published in 1971.

513. Berin, Barnet N. *Pensions; A Guide to the Technical Side.* 2d ed. Chicago: Spencer & Associates, Inc., 1981. 71 p.

514. Bernhcim, B. Douglas. *Dissaving after Retirement; Testing the Pure Life Cycle Hypothesis.* NBER Working Paper, 1409. Cambridge, MA: National Bureau of Economic Research, 1984. 63 p.

515. Bernheim, B. Douglas, and Shoven, John B. *Pension Funding and Saving.* NBER Working Paper, 1622. Cambridge, MA: National Burcau of Economic Research, 1985. 41 p.

516. Bernstein, Merton C. *The Future of Private Pensions.* New York: The Free Press of Glencoe, 1964. 385 p.

517. *Better Management of Private Pension Data Can Reduce Costs and Improve ERISA Administration.* Washington, DC: U.S. General Accounting Office, 1981. 118 p.

518. *A Bibliography of Research; Retirement Income & Capital Accumulation Programs.* Washington, DC: Employee Benefit Research Institute, Education and Research Fund, 1981. 414 p.

519. *A Bibliography of Selected Recent Research on Retirement Income Programs.* Prepared for EBRI under Contract by Mathematica Policy Research, Inc. Washington, DC: Employee Benefit Research Institute, 1979. 2 vols.

520. Biegel, Herman C., et al. *Pensions and Profit Sharing.* 2d ed. Washington, DC: Bureau of National Affairs, Inc., 1956. 296 p.
The first edition, published in 1953, would have been entered under George B. Buck, Jr., because he was the first named of many authors.

521. Bierwag, Gerald O. *Duration Analysis.* Hagerstown, MD: Ballinger Publishing Co., 1987. 384 p.

522. Biles, George E. *Impact of New Withholding Requirements for Pensions, Annuities and Other Deferred Income under TEFRA of 1982.* Research Report 84–4. Brookfield, WI: International Foundation of Employee Benefit Plans, 1984. 23 p.

523. Billman, Brookes D., Jr. *Restricted Property; Section 83.* Tax Management Portfolios, 384. Washington, DC: Bureau of National Affairs, Inc., 1982. Various pagings.

524. Billman, Brookes D., Jr., and Zonana, Victor. *Introduction to Qualified Pension and Profit Sharing Plans.* Tax Law and Practice Course Handbook Series, 129. New York: Practising Law Institute, 1979. 592 p.

525. Binkin, Martin, and Kyriakopoulos, Irene. *Paying the Modern Military.* Studies in Defense Policy. Washington, DC: Brookings Institution, 1981. 83 p.

526. Black, Fischer. *The Tax Advantages of Pension Fund Investment in Bonds.* NBER Working Paper, 533. Cambridge, MA: National Bureau of Economic Research, 1980. 21 p.

527. Bleakney, Thomas P. *Retirement Systems for Public Employees.* Homewood, IL: Published for the Pension Research Council by Richard D. Irwin, Inc., 1972. 205 p.

528. Blinder, Alan S. *Private Pensions and Public Pensions; Theory and Fact.* NBER Working Paper, 902. Cambridge, MA: National Bureau of Economic Research, 1982. 70 p.

529. Blinder, Alan S.; Gordon, Roger H.; and Wise, Donald E. *Reconsidering the Work Disincentive Effects of Social Security.* NBER Working Paper, 562. Cambridge, MA: National Bureau of Economic Research, 1980. 19 p.

530. Bloch, Max. *Lecture Notes for American Pension Fund Actuaries.* New York: Johnson & Higgins, 1977. 373 p.

531. Blodget, Richard. *Conflicts of Interest; Union Pension Fund Asset Management.* New York: The Twentieth Century Fund, 1977. 61 p.

532. Bloom, David E., and Freeman, Richard B. *The "Youth Problem"; Age or Generational Crowding?* NBER Working Paper, 1829. Cambridge, MA: National Bureau of Economic Research, 1986. 60 p.

533. *Blueprinting the Pension Plan.* Chicago: Commerce Clearing House, Inc., 1950. 127 p.

534. Bluestein, Joseph S., and Levy, Jack B. *Owner-Dominated Plans; Top-Heavy and HR 10 Plans.* Tax Management Portfolios, 353–2nd. Washington, DC: Bureau of National Affairs, Inc., 1986. Various pagings.

535. Blum, Robert A., and Kolm, Claude F. *Age and Sex Discrimination and Employee Benefit Plans.* Tax Management Portfolios, 363. Washington, DC: Bureau of National Affairs, Inc., 1984. Various pagings.

536. Blumenthal, William. *Horizontal Mergers; Law & Policy.* Chicago: American Bar Association. Merger Standards Task Force, 1987?. 336 p.

537. Bodie, Zvi. *Investment Strategy in an Inflationary Environment.* NBER Working Paper, 701. Cambridge, MA: National Bureau of Economic Research, 1981. 31 p.

538. Bodie, Zvi. *Purchasing-Power Annuities; Financial Innovation for Stable Real Retirement Income in an Inflationary Environment.* NBER Working Paper, 442. Cambridge, MA: National Bureau of Economic Research, 1980. 27 p.

539. Bodie, Zvi, and Pesando, James E. *Retirement Annuity Design in an Inflationary Climate.* NBER Reprint, 765. Cambridge, MA: National Bureau of Economic Research, 1986. 26 p.

540. Bodie, Zvi, and Shoven, John B., eds. *Financial Aspects of the United States Pension System.* A National Bureau of Economic Research Project Report. Chicago: University of Chicago Press, 1983. 452 p.

541. Bodie, Zvi, et al. *Funding and Asset Allocation in Corporate Pension Plans; An Empirical Investigation.* NBER Working Paper, 1315. Cambridge, MA: National Bureau of Economic Research, 1984. 33 p.

542. Bodie, Zvi; Marcus, Alan J.; and Merton, Robert C. *Defined Benefit versus Defined Contribution Pension Plans; What Are the Real Tradeoffs?* NBER Working Paper, 1719. Cambridge, MA: National Bureau of Economic Research, 1985. 35 p.

543. Bodie, Zvi; Shoven, John B.; and Wise, David A. *Issues in Pension Economics.* An NBER Project Report. Chicago: University of Chicago Press, 1987. 376 p.

544. Boettcher, Barbara. *Summary Plan Descriptions.* Pension and Profit Sharing Plans. Series C, Folio 11. Philadelphia, PA: American Law Institute-American Bar Association. Committee on Continuing Professional Education, 1979. 42 p.

545. Bomar, Fleming, et al. *Handbook for Pension Planning.* Washington, DC: Bureau of National Affairs, Inc., 1949. 373 p.

546. Borjas, George J. *Union Control of Pension Funds; Will the North Rise Again?* San Francisco, CA: Institute for Contemporary Studies, 1979. 41 p.

547. Borzilleri, Thomas C. *In-Kind Benefit Programs and Retirement Income.* Washington, DC: President's Commission on Pension Policy, 1980. 77 p.

548. Boskin, Michael J., and Hurd, Michael D. *Are Inflation Rates Different for the Elderly?* NBER Working Paper, 943. Cambridge, MA: National Bureau of Economic Research, 1982. 20 p.

549. Boskin, Michael J., and Hurd, Michael D. *The Effect of Social Security on Early Retirement.* NBER Working Paper, 204. Cambridge, MA: National Bureau of Economic Research, 1977.

550. Boskin, Michael J., and Puffert, Douglas J. *Social Security and the American Family.* NBER Working Paper, 2117. Cambridge, MA: National Bureau of Economic Research, 1987. 35 p.

551. Boskin, Michael J., and Shoven, John B. *Concepts and Measures of Earnings Replacement during Retirement.* NBER Working Paper, 1360. Cambridge, MA: National Bureau of Economic Research, 1984. 36 p.

552. Boskin, Michael J.; Kotlikoff, Laurence J.; and Knetter, Michael. *Changes in the Age Distribution of Income in the United States, 1968–1984.* NBER Working Paper, 1766. Cambridge, MA: National Bureau of Economic Research, 1985. 46 p.

553. Boyce, Byrl N., et al. *An Evaluation of the Reverse Annuity Mortgage.* Real Estate Report, 25. Storrs, CT: University of Connecticut. Center for Real Estate and Urban Economic Studies, 1978. 42 p.

554. Boyce, Carroll W. *How to Plan Pension; A Guidebook for Business and Industry.* New York: McGraw-Hill, 1950. 479 p.

555. Boyers, Judith T. *Pensions in Perspective; A Guide to Qualified Retirement Plans.* Cincinnati, OH: NU Law Services, 1986. 227 p.

556. Brady, James; Essner, Warren; and Upbin, Sol. *Accounting and Auditing Problems in Employee Benefit Plans.* Pension and Profit-Sharing Plans. Series D, Folio 5. Philadelphia, PA: American Law Institute-American Bar Association. Committee on Continuing Professional Education, 1978. 29 p.

557. Brannon, Thurza. *Outline of Federal Retirement Systems.* Bureau Report, 15. Washington, DC: U.S. Federal Security Agency, Social Security Administration, Bureau of Research and Statistics, 1948. 145 p.

558. Bronson, Dorrance C. *Concepts of Actuarial Soundness in Pension Plans.* Homewood, IL: Published for the Pension Research Council by Richard D. Irwin, Inc., 1957. 183 p.

559. Brooks, John. *Conflicts of Interest; Corporate Pension Fund Asset Management.* New York: The Twentieth Century Fund, 1975. 61 p.

560. Brown, Leo, and Mamorsky, Jeffrey D. *Rules against Discrimination.* Pension and Profit-Sharing Plans. Series C, Folio 2. Philadelphia, PA: American Law Institute-American Bar Association. Committee on Continuing Professional Education, 1978. 6 p.

561. Buechner, Robert W., and Manzler, David L. *Accumulating Wealth with Before-Tax Dollars; The Use of Qualified Plans to Maximize Personal Wealth in a Tax-Favored, Low Risk Way.* Cincinnati, OH: National Underwriter Co., 1982.

562. Bullock, Paul A., and Kautter, William H. *Executive Wealth-Building Plans.* Rockville Center, NY: Farnsworth Publishing Co., 1983. 240 p.

563. Bulow, Jeremy I. *Analysis of Pension Funding under ERISA.* NBER Working Paper, 402. Cambridge, MA: National Bureau of Economic Research, 1979. 69 p.

564. Bulow, Jeremy I. *Early Retirement Pension Benefits.* NBER Working Paper, 654. Cambridge, MA: National Bureau of Economic Research, 1981. 21 p.

565. Bulow, Jeremy I. *Tax Aspects of Corporate Pension Funding Policy.* NBER Working Paper, 724. Cambridge, MA: National Bureau of Economic Research, 1981. 24 p.

566. Bulow, Jeremy I., and Scholes, Myron S. *Who Owns the Assets in a Defined Benefit Pension Plan?* NBER Working Paper, 924. Cambridge, MA: National Bureau of Economic Research, 1982. 30 p.

567. Bulow, Jeremy I.; Morck, Randall; and Summers, Lawrence. *How Does the Market Value Unfunded Pension Liabilities?* NBER Working Paper, 1602. Cambridge, MA: National Bureau of Economic Research, 1985. 41 p.

568. Bulow, Jeremy I.; Scholes, Myron S.; and Menel, Peter. *Economic Implications of ERISA.* NBER Working Paper, 927. Cambridge, MA: National Bureau of Economic Research, 1982. 32 p.

569. Burkhauser, Richard V., and Warlick, Jennifer L. *Disentangling the Annuity from the Redistributive Aspects of Social Security.* Discussion Paper. Madison, WI: University of Wisconsin. Institute for Research on Poverty, 1979. 30 p.

570. Burtless, Gary, and Hausman, Jerry. *Double Dipping; The Combined Effects of Social Security and Civil Service Pensions on Employee Retirement.* NBER Working Paper, 800. Cambridge, MA: National Bureau of Economic Research, 1981. 28 p.

571. *Cafeteria Compensation; Present Status and Future Potential, A TPF/C Research Study.* New York: Towers, Perrin, Forster & Crosby, 1973. 16 p.

572. Calvert, Geoffrey, N. *Portable Police Pensions; Improving Inter-Agency Transfers.* Washington, DC: National Institute of Law Enforcement and Criminal Justice, 1972. 83 p.

573. Campbell, John Y. *Does Saving Anticipate Declining Labor Income? An Alternative Test of the Permanent Income Hypothesis.* NBER Working Paper, 1805. Cambridge, MA: National Bureau of Economic Research, 1986. 36 p.

574. Canan, Michael J., and Baker, David R. *Qualified Retirement Plans.* West's Handbook Series. St. Paul, MN: West Publishing Co., 1987. 937 p.

575. Casey, William J. *How to Invest Pension and Profit-Sharing Funds.* New York: Institute for Business Planning, Inc., 1960. 189 p.

576. Casey, William J. *How to Run a Pension or Profit-Sharing Plan.* New York: Institute for Business Planning, Inc., 1960.

577. *CCH Guide to Employee Benefits under 1986 Tax Reform; Explanation, Law, Committee Reports.* Chicago: Commerce Clearing House, Inc., 1986. 507 p. 183 p.

578. Cerny, Marsha. *Private Pensions and Retirement Planning; Bibliography in Brief, 1982–1985.* Washington, DC: Congressional Research Service, 1985. 4 p.
  I think this is something in the nature of a placebo to quiet the ravening hordes. There may be others like it and more recent vintages.

579. Chadwick, William J. *Regulation of Employee Benefits; ERISA and the Other Federal Laws.* Brookfield, WI: International Foundation of Employee Benefit Plans, 1978. 315 p.

580. Chadwick, William J., and Hass, Lawrence J., comps. *The Annotated Fiduciary; Materials on Fiduciary Responsibility and Prohibited Transactions under ERISA.* 2d ed. Brookfield, WI: International Foundation of Employee Benefit Plans, 1980. 487 p.

581. Cheeks, James E. *How to Compensate Executives.* 3d ed. Homewood, IL: Dow Jones-Irwin, 1982. 347 p.

582. Cheeks, James E. *Keoghs; Keys to Security and Wealth.* New York: F. Watts, 1986. 248 p.

583. Chingos, Peter T.; Cronquist, Neil R.; and Gill, Charles W. *Financial Considerations of Executive Compensation and Retirement Plans; Accounting, Actuary, Tax and Plan Design.* The Wiley/Ronald Series in Professional Accounting and Business. New York: Wiley, 1984. 236 p.

584. *Citizens' Guide to the President's Commission on Pension Policy Interim Report, 1980.* Washington, DC: Citizens' Commission on Pension Policy, 1980. 38 p.

585. *Civil Service Retirement; Financing and Costs.* Washington, DC: U.S. Congressional Budget Office, 1981. 43 p.

586. Clark, Robert L. *The Role of Private Pensions in Maintaining Living Standards in Retirement.* NPA Report, 154. Washington, DC: National Planning Association, 1977. 49 p.

587. Clark, Robert L. *Cost-Effective Pension Planning.* Work in America Institute. Studies in Productivity. Highlights of the Literature, 20. New York: Pergamon Press, 1982. 38 p.

588. Clark, Robert L., ed. *Retirement Policy in an Aging Society.* Durham, NC: Duke University Press, 1980. 215 p.

589. Clark, Robert L., and Barker, David T. *Reversing the Trend toward Early Retirement.* Washington, DC: American Enterprise Institute for Public Policy Research, 1981. 64 p.

590. *CLE and Ski; March 2 & 3, 1984, Sugarloaf USA.* Sponsored by The Maine State Bar Association, Continuing Legal Education. Augusta, ME: MSBA, 1984. 72 p.

591. Cloud, A. S. *Pensions in Modern Industry.* Chicago: Hawkins and Loomis Co., 1930. 531 p.

592. Cohen, Kalman J., et al. *Measuring the Investment Performance of Pension Funds for the Purpose of Inter-Fund Comparison.* Park Ridge, IL: Bank Administration Institute, 1968. 288 p.
   This is still perfectly valid and, I believe, in print.

593. Coleman, Barbara J. *Primer on the Employee Retirement Income Security Act of 1974.* Washington, DC: BNA Books, 1985. 150 p.

594. Coleman, Jill P., and Kemp, Robert S., Jr. *Issues in Unfunded Pension Liabilities; Accounting Treatment & Investor's Perceptions of Risk.* Brookfield, WI: International Foundation of Employee Benefit Plans, 1981. 61 p.

595. The Commission on Federal Paperwork. *Special Study Report on ERISA; Staff Report. . .to the Commission.* Washington, DC, 1976. 68 p.

596. *Communications and Public Relations for ESOP Companies.* Washington, DC: The ESOP Association, n.d. 12 p.

597. *Comparing and Appraising Investment Performance of Pension Plans.* Elm Grove, WI: National Foundation of Health Welfare and Pension Plans, Inc., 1967. 80 p.

598. *Comparison of Federal and Private Sector Pay and Benefits.* Washington, DC: U.S. General Accounting Office, 1985. 19 p.

599. *Comparison of Retirement Benefits for W. R. Grace & Company and Civil Service Employees.* Washington, DC: U.S. General Accounting Office, 1984. 10 p.

600. *A Complete Guide to the Tax Reform Act of 1986; Explanation, Code Sections as Amended, Committee Reports, Index.* Paramus, NJ: Prentice-Hall Information Services, 1986. Various pagings.

601. *Comprehensive Tax Guide to U.S. Civil Service Retirement Benefits.* Publication 721. Washington, DC: Internal Revenue Service, 1986. 48 p.

602. Conant, Luther, Jr. *A Critical Analysis of Industrial Pension Systems.* NY: The Macmillan Co., 1922. 262 p.
This book contains a fifteen-page survey of pension systems found by the author in 1922.

603. *Concentrated Course in Pension Reform; Course Manual.* Washington, DC: Federal Publications, 1977. 438 p.

604. *Concise Explanation of the Economic Recovery Tax Act of 1981.* Englewood Cliffs, NJ: Prentice-Hall, Inc., 1981. 79 p.

605. *Concise Explanation of the Multiemployer Pension Plan Amendments Act.* Englewood Cliffs, NJ: Prentice-Hall, Inc., 1983. 64 p.

606. *Conference on ERISA Simplification; ALI-ABA Invitational Conference Papers.* Philadelphia, PA: American Law Institute-American Bar Association. Committee on Continuing Professional Education, 1979. 359 p.

607. *Conference on Life Insurance Company Products; Current Securities and Tax Issues, ALI-ABA Course of Study Materials.* Philadelphia, PA: American Law Institute-American Bar Association. Committee on Continuing Professional Education, 1982. 388 p.

608. *Conference Report on H.R. 4961, "Tax Equity and Fiscal Responsibility Act of 1982," Including Compromise Bill and Conferees Explanatory Statement.* Washington, DC: Bureau of National Affairs, Inc., 1982. 188 p.

609. *Contractor Pension Costs; More Control Could Save Department of Defense Millions.* Washington, DC: U.S. General Accounting Office, 1977. 83 p.

610. Cook, Earleen H., and Cook, Joseph Lee. *Employee Stock Option Plans and Trusts*. Public Administration Series; Bibliography, P-471. Monticello, IL: Vance Bibliographies, 1980. 25 p.

611. Cooper, Robert D., ed. *Issues in Unfunded Pension Liabilities; Accounting Treatment and Investors' Perceptions of Risk*. Brookfield, WI: International Foundation of Employee Benefit Plans, 1981. 61 p.

612. Cooper, Robert D., and Caswell, Cheryl A. *A Study of Current Collection Practices, Procedures and Problems*. Brookfield, WI: International Foundation of Employee Benefit Plans, 1978. 54 p.

613. *A Corporate Guide to Pension & Retirement Planning*. Chicago: Dartnell Corp., 1982.

614. Corwin, Thomas M., et al. *Changing Retirement Policies*. 1978 National Conference Series. Washington, DC: American Association for Higher Education, 1978. 25 p.

615. *Cost Accounting Standard 414; Its Relationship to DOD Profit Policy*. Washington, DC: U.S. General Accounting Office, 1986. 29 p.

616. *Cost of Living Adjustments for New Federal Retirees; More Rational and Less Costly Processes Are Needed*. Washington, DC: U.S. General Accounting Office, 1977. 6 p.

617. *The Cost of Mandating Pension Accruals for Older Workers; An Information Paper*. Washington, DC: U.S. Government Printing Office, 1986. 61 p.

618. Costa, Michael L. *Master Trust; Simplifying Employee Benefits Trust Fund Administration*. New York: AMACOM, 1980. 213 p.

619. Cottle, Sidney. *Pension Asset Management; The Corporate Decisions, A Research Study*. Prepared for the Financial Executives Research Foundation by FRS Associates. New York: FERF, 1980. 285 p.

620. Couper, Walter J., and Vaughan, Roger. *Pension Planning; Experience and Trends*. Industrial Relations Monograph, 16. New York: Industrial Relations Counselors, Inc., 1954. 245 p.

621. Cowan, Paul C. *Association Retirement Plans*. Washington, DC: Chamber of Commerce of the United States, 1961. 30 p.

622. Cowdrick, E. S. *Pensions; A Problem of Management*. New York: American Management Association, 1928. 40 p.

623. Coy, Robert W. *Pennsylvania Public Pension Funds for Economic Development*. Harrisburg, PA: MILRITE Council, 1983. 28 p.

624. *A CPI for Retirees Is Not Needed Now but Could Be in the Future*. Washington, DC: U.S. General Accounting Office, 1982. 95 p.

625. Cramer, Joe J., Jr. *Accounting and Reporting Requirements of the Private Pension Trust*. Indiana Business Information Bulletin, 55. Bloomington, IN: Indiana University, Bureau of Business Research, 1965. 111 p.

626. Creed, Barbara B. *ERISA Compliance; Reporting and Disclosure.* New York: Practising Law Institute, 1981. 477 p.

627. Crocker, Thomas F., Jr.; Sarason, Harry M.; and Straight, Byron W. *The Actuary's Pension Handbook.* Los Angeles: Pension Publications, 1955–1957. 2 vols.
The second volume is entitled *Retirement Plan Mathematics.*

628. Cummings, Frank, and Kershaw, Alice M. *Multiemployer Plans; Special Rules.* Tax Management Portfolios, 359–2nd. Washington, DC: Bureau of National Affairs, Inc., 1983. Various pagings.

629. Cummins, J. David, ed. *Investment Activities of Life Insurance Companies.* Huebner Foundation Lectures. Homewood, IL: Richard D. Irwin, Inc., 1977. 356 p.

630. Cummins, J. David; Percival, John; and Westerfield, Randolph. *The Impact of ERISA on the Investment Policies of Private Pension Funds and Capital Market Efficiency.* Prepared for the U.S. Department of Labor. Philadelphia, PA: University of Pennsylvania, Wharton School, 1980. 272 p.

631. *Current Developments in Pension Law; Program Materials.* Washington, DC: Georgetown University Law Center. Continuing Legal Education Division, 1986. Various pagings.

632. Damico, Nicholas P. *Qualified Plans; Taxation of Distributions.* Tax Management Portfolios, 370. Washington, DC: Bureau of National Affairs, Inc., 1983. Various pagings.

633. Dankner, Harold; Friedman, Kenneth L.; and Goldstein, Murray H. *Accounting for Pensions; Results of Applying the FASB's Preliminary Views.* Morristown, NJ: Financial Executives Research Foundation, 1983. 256 p.

634. Darley, Michael R. *The Effects of Social Security on Income and the Capital Stock.* Washington, DC: American Enterprise Institute for Public Policy Research, 1979. 90 p.

635. Davey, Patrick J. *Current Directions in Pension Fund Management.* Information Bulletin, 39. New York: Conference Board, 1978. 13 p.

636. Davey, Patrick J. *Financial Management of Company Pension Plans.* Conference Board Report, 611. New York: Conference Board, 1973. 117 p.

637. Davie, Bruce F. *Investment Practices of Public Employee Retirement Systems; State and Local Government Systems in the United States and New England.* Boston: Federal Reserve Bank of Boston, 1959. 33 p.

638. *Deficit Reduction Act of 1984; Tax Provisions.* New York: Peat Marwick & Mitchell & Co., 1984. 90 p.

639. *Defined Contribution Plans; Issues & Answers.* New York?: Buck Consultants, Inc., 1984. 31 p.

640. Delquadro, David M. *The Railroad Retirement System; Benefits and Financing.* A CBO Study. Washington, DC: Congressional Budget Office, 1982. 43 p.

641. De Mong, Richard F.; Gray, William S., III; and Milne, Robert D. *Broader Perspectives on the Interest of Pension Plan Participants.* FARF Monograph Series, 22. Charlottesville, VA: Financial Analysts Research Foundation, 1985. 43 p.

642. Denero, Walter A., and Stakes, Mary E. *Public Pension Plans; State and National Issues.* Athens, GA: University of Georgia, Institute of Government, 1978. 59 p.

643. Dennis, Charles N., and Hamwi, Iskandar S. *Tax-Sheltered Annuities; Selection Criteria.* Occasional Paper, 14. Hattiesburg, MS: University of Southern Mississippi, Bureau of Business Research, 1977. 37 p.

644. Denzau, Arthur T. and Hardin, Clifford M. *Company Retirement Plans Eight Years after ERISA.* St. Louis, MO: Center for the Study of American Business, 1983. 23 p.

645. *The Department of Labor's Enforcement of the Employee Retirement Income Security Act (ERISA); A Report.* Washington, DC: U.S. Government Printing Office, 1986. 71 p.

646. *Description of S. 19 (Retirement Equity Act of 1983) and S888 (Economic Equity Act of 1983) Scheduled for Hearings. . . .* Washington, DC: U.S. Government Printing Office, 1983. 37 p.

647. *Designing a Retirement Program for Federal Workers Covered by Social Security.* Prepared by the Congressional Research Service. Washington, DC: U.S. Government Printing Office, 1985. 350 p.

648. *Designing Qualified Plans to Meet the 1982–1984 Statutory Requirements; Model Plans and Provisions, ALI-ABA Video Law Review Study Materials.* Philadelphia, PA: American Law Institute-American Bar Association. Committee on Continuing Professional Education, 1984. 58 p.

649. Dexter, Michael K. *Replacement Ratios; A Major Issue in Employee Pension Systems.* Washington, DC: National Committee on Public Employee Pension Systems, 1984. 67 p.

650. Dicks-Mireaux, Louis, and King, Mervyn A. *Pension Wealth and Household Savings; Tests of Robustness.* NBER Working Paper, 962. Cambridge, MA: National Bureau of Economic Research, 1982. 27 p.

651. Dicks-Mireaux, Louis, and King, Mervyn A. *Portfolio Composition and Pension Wealth; An Econometric Study.* NBER Working Paper, 903. Cambridge, MA: National Bureau of Economic Research, 1982. 31 p.

652. Dietz, Peter O. *Pension Funds; Measuring Investment Performance.* New York: Graduate School of Business, Columbia University, 1966. 166 p.

653. *Disclaimer of Opinion on the Financial Statements of the Pension Benefit Guaranty Corporation for the Fiscal Year Ended September 30, 1980.* Washington, DC: U.S. General Accounting Office, 1982. 55 p.

654. *Discrimination against Minorities and Women in Pensions and Health, Life and Disability Insurance.* By the U.S. Commission on Civil Rights. Washington, DC: U.S. Government Printing Office, 1978. 1,288 p.

655. *Diskette Reporting; Submitting FICA Wage and Tax Data to the Social Security Administration.* SSA Pub. No. 42–003. Washington, DC: Social Security Administration, 1984. 32 p.

656. Downey, Sheridan. *Pensions or Penury?* New York: Harper, 1939. 113 p.

657. Drucker, Peter F. *The Unseen Revolution; How Pension Fund Socialism Came to America.* New York: Harper & Row, 1976. 214 p.

658. Dunctz, Martin R. *How to Finance Your Retirement.* Reston, VA: Reston Publishing Co., 1979. 227 p.

659. Dunkle, David S. *Guide to Pension and Profit Sharing Plans; Taxation Selection and Design.* Tax and Estate Planning Series. Colorado Springs, CO: Shepherds/McGraw-Hill, 1984. 500 p.

660. Eaton, Jonathan, and Rosen, Harvey S. *Agency, Delayed Compensation and the Structure of Executive Remuneration.* NBER Working Paper, 777. Cambridge, MA: National Bureau of Economic Research, 1981. 30 p.

661. *Effects of Liabilities Assessed Employers Withdrawing from Multiemployer Pension Plans.* Washington, DC: U.S. General Accounting Office, 1985. 74 p.

662. *The Effects of the Employee Retirement Income Security Act on the Collective Bargaining Process.* Prepared for the Department of Labor. Washington, DC: Kramer Associates, Inc., 1978. 2 vols.

663. *Effects of the 1980 Multiemployer Pension Plan Amendments Act on Plan Participants' Benefits.* Washington, DC: U.S. General Accounting Office, 1985. 49 p.

664. Einhorn, Madeline W. *The Guaranteed Investment Contract.* New York: BEA Associates, Inc., 1976. 18 p.

665. Ekman, Lennart G., and Fuller, James W. *U.S. Private Pension Funds.* Research Report, 578. Menlo Park, CA: SRI Business Intelligence Program, 1976. 20 p.

666. *Elements of Industrial Pension Plans.* New York: National Industrial Conference Board, 1931. 48 p.

667. Elkin, Jack M. *Qualified Joint and Survivor Annuities.* Pension and Profit-Sharing Plans. Series C, Folio 9. Philadelphia, PA: American Law Institute-American Bar Association. Committee on Continuing Professional Education, 1978. 11 p.

668. Ellig, Bruce R. *Compensation & Benefits; Design and Analysis.* Phoenix, AZ: American Compensation Association, 1985. 192 p.

669. Ellig, Bruce R. *Executive Compensation; A Total Pay Perspective.* New York: McGraw-Hill, 1981. 343 p.

670. Ellis, Charles D. *Investment Policy; How to Win the Loser's Game.* Homewood, IL: Dow Jones-Irwin, Inc., 1986. 81 p.

671. Elston, James S. *Sources and Characteristics of the Principal Mortality Tables.* 2d ed. Actuarial Studies, 1. New York: The Actuarial Society of America, 1932. 170 p.

672. *Employee Benefit Plans.* New York: Research Institute of America, 1945. 60 p.

673. *Employee Benefit Plans; A Glossary of Terms.* 6th ed. Brookfield, WI: International Foundation of Employee Benefit Plans, 1987. 157 p.
A very useful, but not encyclopedic, book which can help in coping with the jargon that infests the industry. It gets more useful with every edition.

674. *Employee Benefit Plans in Corporate Acquisitions and Dispositions.* Chicago: American Bar Association. Division for Professional Education, 1986. 420 p.

675. *Employee Benefit Plans; Sources of Information.* Publication 1251. Washington, DC: Internal Revenue Service, 1984. 9 p.

676. *Employee Benefit Provisions of the Tax Equity and Fiscal Responsibility Act of 1982.* New York?: Coopers & Lybrand, 1982. 26 p.

677. *Employee Ownership; Resource Guide.* Arlington, VA: National Center for Employee Ownership, 1986. 25 p.

678. *Employee Pension Systems in State and Local Government.* Research Publication, 33. New York: Tax Foundation, 1976. 68 p.
A 1969 edition was entitled *State and Local Employee Pension Systems.*

679. *The Employee Retirement Income Security Act.* Washington, DC: Employee Benefit Research Institute, 1979. 8 p.

680. *The Employee Retirement Income Security Act; A Report of the Commission on Federal Paperwork.* Washington, DC: U.S. Government Printing Office, 1976. 68 p.

681. *Employee Retirement Income Security Act, 1974; Public Law 93–406 (H.R. 2), Text of Public Law, Statement on the Part of Managers, and Summary of the Legislation.* Washington, DC: U.S. Government Printing Office, 1974. 370 p.

682. *The Employee Retirement Income Security Act of 1974; The First Decade, an Information Paper.* Prepared for use by the Special Committee on Aging, United States Senate. Washington, DC: U.S. Government Printing Office, 1984. 207 p.

683. *Employee Retirement Systems of State and Local Governments.* Census of Governments, 1962. v. VI, 1. Washington, DC: Bureau of the Census, 1963. 53 p.

684. *Employee Retirement Systems of State and Local Governments.* Washington, DC: Bureau of the Census, 1978. 55 p.

685. *The Employee Stock Ownership Plan.* Washington, DC: Employee Benefit Research Institute, 1979. 4 p.

686. *Employee Stock Ownership Plans; An Employer Handbook.* Washington, DC: U.S. Government Printing Office, 1980. 63 p.

687. *Employee Stock Ownership Plans; Benefits and Costs of ESOP Tax Incentives for Broadening Stock Ownership.* Washington, DC: U.S. General Accounting Office, 1987. 72 p.

688. *Employee Stock Ownership Plans; Who Benefits Most in Closely Held Companies? Report. . . .* Washington, DC: U.S. General Accounting Office, 1980. 52 p.

689. *Employees' Retirement Annuities.* Washington, DC: Chamber of Commerce of the United States, 1932. 45 p.

690. *Employer Accounting for Pension Costs & Other Post-Retirement Benefits.* New York: Coopers & Lybrand, 1981.

691. *Employers' Accounting for Pensions; Understanding and Implementing FASB Statement No. 87.* Financial Reporting Developments. Cleveland, OH: Ernst & Whinney, 1986. 153 p.

692. *The Encyclopedia of Employee Fringe Benefit Programs.* Old Saybrook, CT: Institute For Management, 1975. 320 p.

693. *ERISA and Its Interpretations until May 30, 1976; Texts of Laws and Official Interpretations with CCH Index.* Chicago: Commerce Clearing House, Inc., 1976. 442 p.

694. *ERISA Enforcement Guide.* Chicago: Commerce Clearing House, Inc., 1978. 255 p.
This is a CCH republishing of Part III of the Department of Labor's Pension and Welfare Benefits Program Compliance Manual. It deals with enforcement programs.

695. *ERISA; Selected Legislative History, 1974–1985.* Washington, DC: Bureau of National Affairs, Inc., 1986. 253 p.

696. *ERISA; Text of the Law as Amended through 1980.* Washington, DC: Bureau of National Affairs, Inc., 1981. 312 p.

697. *ESOPs and the 1986 Tax Reform Act.* Washington, DC: The ESOP Association, 1986. 321 p.
Contains a bibliography of booklets and audiovisuals produced by the association.

698. *ESOPs Updated.* Chicago: Commerce Clearing House, Inc., 1978.

699. *Explanation of Employee Benefit Provisions; Tax Reform Act of 1984.* Chicago: Commerce Clearing House, Inc., 1984. 64 p.

700. *Explanation of H.R. 3904. . .Relating to Multiemployer Pension Plan Amendments Scheduled for a Markup by the Committee on Ways and Means. . . .* Washington, DC: U.S. Government Printing Office, 1980. 68 p.

701. *Explanation of Tax Reform Act of 1984 as Signed by the President on July 18, 1984.* Chicago: Commerce Clearing House, Inc., 1984. 448 p.

702. *Explanation of Tax Reform Act of 1986 as Signed by the President on October 22, 1986.* Chicago: Commerce Clearing House, Inc., 1986. 671 p.

703. Faber, Joseph F. *Life Tables for the United States, 1900–2050.* Actuarial Study, 87. Baltimore, MD: U.S. Social Security Administration, Office of the Actuary, 1982. 86 p.

704. Faircloth, Charlotte P. *Limitations on Benefits and Contributions on Behalf of Individual Plan Participants.* Pension and Profit-Sharing Plans. Series C, Folio 8. Philadelphia, PA: American Law Institute-American Bar Association. Committee on Continuing Professional Education, 1978. 18 p.

705. *The Fairness Issue in Reforming Federal COLAs.* Washington, DC: Chamber of Commerce of the United States, 1983. 57 p.

706. Falk, Murray H. *Tax Court Declaratory Judgment Proceedings.* Pension and Profit-Sharing Plans. Series G, Folio 3. Philadelphia, PA: American Law Institute-American Bar Association. Committee on Continuing Professional Education, 1978. 13 p.

707. Fama, Eugene F. *Risk and the Evaluation of Pension Fund Portfolio Performance.* Park Ridge, IL: Bank Administration Institute, 1969. 36 p.

708. Farber, Lawrence. *Estate Planning Strategies for Physicians.* Oradell, NJ: Medical Economics Books, 1986. 174 p.

709. Farney, Kathleen. *Collective Bargaining Implications of the FASB Proposals on Pension Accounting.* Research Report, 84–6. Brookfield, WI: International Foundation of Employee Benefit Plans, 1984. 17 p.

710. Farrell, Peter B. *Planning for Military Retirement.* Alexandria, VA: Retired Officers Association, 1983. 48 p.

711. *FAS 87 and Single Employer Defined Benefit Pension Plans; A Road Map for Actuaries and Other Mere Mortals, an Outline.* Prepared by the staff of the Pentad Corp. Waltham, MA: Pentad Corp., 1986. 37 p.

712. *Favorable Determination Letter.* Publication 794. Washington, DC: Internal Revenue Service, 1985. 1 p.

713. *Features of Nonfederal Retirement Programs.* Washington, DC: U.S. General Accounting Office, 1984. 28 p.

714. *Federal Compensation: Effects of Proposed Retirement Changes on a Typical Federal Retiree.* Washington, DC: U.S. General Accounting Office, 1986. 2 p.

715. *Federal Employee Retirement Systems.* Research Publication, 34. New York: Tax Foundation, 1978. 57 p.

716. *Federal Retirement; Records Processing Is Better, Can Be Further Improved.* Washington, DC: U.S. General Accounting Office, 1986. 36 p.

717. *Federal Retirement; Retirement Data for Selected Agencies.* Washington, DC: U.S. General Accounting Office, 1986. 3 p.

718. *Federal Retirement Systems; Unrecognized Costs, Inadequate Funding, Inconsistent Benefits, Report to the Congress.* Washington, DC: U.S. General Accounting Office, 1977. 74 p.

719. *Federal Workforce; Retirement Credit Has Contributed to Reduced Sick Leave Usage.* Washington, DC: U.S. General Accounting Office, 1986. 5 p.

720. Feldman, Charles F., ed. *Executive Compensation Planning.* New York: Practising Law Institute, 1982.

721. Feldstein, Martin. *Do Private Pensions Increase National Saving?* NBER Working Paper, 186. Cambridge, MA: National Bureau of Economic Research, 1977.

722. Feldstein, Martin. *The Effect of Social Security on Private Saving; The Time Series Evidence.* NBER Working Paper, 314. Cambridge, MA: National Bureau of Economic Research, 1979. 11 p.

723. Feldstein, Martin. *The Effect of Social Security on Saving.* NBER Working Paper, 334. Cambridge, MA: National Bureau of Economic Research, 1979.

724. Feldstein, Martin. *The Optimal Level of Social Security Benefits.* NBER Working Paper, 970. Cambridge, MA: National Bureau of Economic Research, 1982. 22 p.

725. Feldstein, Martin. *Private Pensions and Inflation.* NBER Working Paper, 568. Cambridge, MA: National Bureau of Economic Research, 1980. 16 p.

726. Feldstein, Martin. *Private Pensions as Corporate Debt.* NBER Working Paper, 703. Cambridge, MA: National Bureau of Economic Research, 1981. 25 p.

727. Feldstein, Martin. *Should Private Pensions Be Indexed?* NBER Working Paper, 787. Cambridge, MA: National Bureau of Economic Research, 1981. 31 p.

728. Feldstein, Martin. *Should Social Security Be Means Tested?* NBER Working Paper, 1775. Cambridge, MA: National Bureau of Economic Research, 1985. 39 p.

729. Feldstein, Martin. *Social Security Benefits and the Accumulation of Preretirement Wealth.* NBER Working Paper, 477. Cambridge, MA: National Bureau of Economic Research, 1980. 31 p.

730. Feldstein, Martin. *Social Security, Induced Retirement, and Aggregate Capital Accumulation; A Correction and Update.* NBER Working Paper, 579. Cambridge, MA: National Bureau of Economic Research, 1980.

731. Feldstein, Martin. *The Welfare Cost of Social Security's Impact on Private Saving.* NBER Working Paper, 969. Cambridge, MA: National Bureau of Economic Research, 1982. 16 p.

732. Feldstein, Martin, and Morck, Randall. *Pension Funding Decisions, Interest Rate Assumptions and Share Prices.* NBER Working Paper, 938. Cambridge, MA: National Bureau of Economic Research, 1982. 44 p.

733. Feldstein, Martin, and Pellechio, Anthony. *Social Security and Household Wealth Accumulation; New Microeconomic Evidence.* NBER Working Paper, 206. Cambridge, MA: National Bureau of Economic Research, 1977.

734. Feldstein, Martin, and Seligman, Stephanie. *Pension Funding, Share Prices and National Saving.* NBER Working Paper, 509. Cambridge, MA: National Bureau of Economic Research, 1980. 44 p.

735. Fellers, William W., and Jackson, Paul H. *Non-Insured Pension Mortality; The UP-1984 Table.* Washington, DC: The Wyatt Co., 1976. 36 p.
This set of tables was also published in *Proceedings of the Conference of Actuaries in Public Practice* (PCAPP XXV, pp. 456–507). There are two reasons for saying that this is an important table. The first is that it takes its experience from the larger segment of pensions, that segment wherein the benefits are paid from a trust. The second is that it is a unisex table. Its issuance anticipated government regulation by years.

736. Ferrara, Peter J. *Social Security Rates of Return for Today's Young Workers.* Washington, DC: National Chamber Foundation, 1986. 41 p.

737. Fields, Gary S., and Mitchell, Olivia S. *Economic Determinants of the Optimal Retirement Age; An Empirical Investigation.* NBER Working Paper, 876. Cambridge, MA: National Bureau of Economic Research, 1982. 27 p.

738. Fields, Gary S., and Mitchell, Olivia S. *The Effects of Social Security Reforms on Retirement Ages and Retirement Incomes.* NBER Working Paper, 1348. Cambridge, MA: National Bureau of Economic Research, 1984. 26 p.

739. Fields, Gary S., and Mitchell, Olivia S. *Retirement, Pensions and Social Security.* Cambridge, MA: MIT Press, 1984. 192 p.

740. Fifth National Forum on Jobs, Money and People. Washington, DC, October 13, 1981. *Social Security and Pension Systems; Turning Liabilities into Assets.* Arlington, VA: Fiscal Policy Council, 1982. 42 p.

741. Figlewski, Stephen; John, Kose; and Merrick, John. *Hedging with Financial Futures for Institutional Investors.* Hagerstown, MD: Ballinger Publishing Co., 1985. 200 p.

742. *Final Report; Assessment of the Impact of ERISA on the Administrative Costs of Small Retirement Plans.* Prepared for the Department of Labor. Washington, DC: Price Waterhouse & Co. 1977. Various pagings.

743. Financial Accounting Standards Board. *Accounting and Reporting by Defined Benefit Pension Plans.* Exposure Draft (Revised). Stamford, CT, 1979. 133 p.

744. Financial Accounting Standards Board. *Accounting and Reporting by Defined Benefit Pension Plans.* Statement of Financial Accounting Standards, 35. Stamford, CT, 1980. 145 p.

745. Financial Accounting Standards Board. *An Analysis of Additional Issues Related to Employers' Accounting for Pensions and Other Postemployment Benefits.* Discussion Memorandum. Stamford, CT, 1983. 87 p.

746. Financial Accounting Standards Board. *An Analysis of Issues Related to Accounting and Reporting for Employee Benefit Plans.* Stamford, CT, 1975. 159 p.

747. Financial Accounting Standards Board. *An Analysis of Issues Related to Employers' Accounting for Pensions and Other Postemployment Benefits.* Discussion Memorandum. Stamford, CT, 1981. 211 p.

748. Financial Accounting Standards Board. *Analysis of Issues Related to Employers' Accounting for Pensions and Other Postemployment Benefits.* Stamford, CT, 1982. 2 v. in 6.

749. Financial Accounting Standards Board. *Disclosure of Pension Information; An Amendment of APB Opinion No. 8.* Statement of Financial Accounting Standards, 36. Stamford, CT, 1980. 11 p.

750. Financial Accounting Standards Board. *Employers' Accounting for Pensions.* Statement of Financial Accounting Standards, 87. Stamford, CT, 1985. 132 p.

751. Financial Accounting Standards Board. *Employers' Accounting for Settlements and Curtailments of Defined Benefit Pension Plans and for Termination Benefits.* Statement of Financial Accounting Standards, 88. Stamford, CT, 1985. 43 p.

752. Financial Accounting Standards Board. *Preliminary Views; A Field Test, Employers' Accounting for Pensions.* Special Report. Stamford, CT, 1983. 192 p.

753. *Financing Work-Related Entitlement Programs; An Update.* A report prepared by the Congressional Research Service for the Committee on the Budget of the U.S. Senate. Washington, DC: U.S. Government Printing Office, 1985. 126 p.

754. Finston, Irving L., and Mehr, Robert I. *Pension Funds and Insurance Reserves; A Resource for Financial Officers.* Homewood, IL: Dow Jones-Irwin, 1986. 229 p.

755. Fisher, Carl H. *Vesting and Termination Provisions in Private Pension Plans.* Washington, DC: American Enterprise Institute for Public Policy Research, 1970. 39 p.

756. *Flexible Benefits; How to Set Up a Plan When Your Employees Are Complaining, Your Costs Are Rising and You're Too Busy to Think about It.* New York: Catalyst, 1986. 139 p.

757. *The Flexible Compensation Plan.* Washington, DC: Employee Benefit Research Institute, 1981. 7 p.

758. *Flexible Compensation Sourcebook.* Washington, DC: Employers Council on Flexible Compensation, 1986. 598 p.

759. *Flexible Compensation under Section 125 of the Internal Revenue Code; Background and Overview, September, 1983.* Washington, DC: Employee Benefits Research Institute, 1983. 25 p.

760. Fogelson, James H., and Ludwig, Ronald L. *The New Role of Employee Ownership in Corporate Acquisitions.* New York: Law & Business, Inc., 1985. 395 p.

761. Fogelson, Robert M. *Pensions; The Hidden Costs of Public Safety.* New York: Columbia University Press, 1984.

762. *Food Industry Benefit Plans, 1984.* Brookfield, WI: International Foundation of Employee Benefit Plans, 1984. 41 p.

763. *Foreign Pension Plans, 1985; The New Section Rules under IRC Section 404A.* New York: Practising Law Institute, 1985. 319 p.

764. *Forums on Federal Pensions.* Committee Print 598-159 Washington, DC: U.S. Government Printing Office, 1984–1985. 5 vols.

765. Fosler, Charles W. *Public Pension Reform; An Overview.* Research Notes. Washington, DC: National Governors Association, 1978. 24 p.

766. Foster, Ronald M. *The Manager's Guide to Employee Benefits; How to Select and Administer the Best Program for Your Company.* New York: Facts on File, 1986. 248 p.

767. Francis, Bion H. *Employee Savings Plans; The Coming Trend in Retirement Planning.* Chicago: Advertising Publications, Inc., 1969. 330 p.

768. Freeman, Richard B. *Unions, Pensions and Union Pension Funds.* NBER Working Paper, 1226. Cambridge, MA: National Bureau of Economic Research, 1983. 56 p.

769. Friedman, Benjamin M. *Pension Funding, Pension Asset Allocation, and Corporate Finance; Evidence from Individual Company Data.* NBER Working Paper, 957. Cambridge, MA: National Bureau of Economic Research, 1982. 42 p.

770. Friedman, Benjamin M., and Warshawsky, Mark. *Annuity Prices and Saving Behavior in the United States.* NBER Working Paper, 1683. Cambridge, MA: National Bureau of Economic Research, 1985. 26 p.

771. Friedman, Benjamin M., and Warshawsky, Mark. *The Cost of Annuities; Implications for Saving Behavior and Bequests.* NBER Working Paper, 1682. Cambridge, MA: National Bureau of Economic Research, 1985. 22 p.

772. Frisch, Robert A. *ESOP for the 80's; The Fabulous New Instrument of Corporate Finance Comes of Age.* Rockville Center, NY: Farnsworth Publishing Co., 1982. 323 p.

773. Frisch, Robert A. *The Magic of ESOPs and LBOs; The Definitive Guide to Employee Stock Ownership Plans and Leveraged Buyouts.* Rockville Center, NY: Farnsworth Publishing Co., 1985. 310 p.

774. *Fund Administration and the Administrative Manager; Abstracts from Foundation Sources.* Brookfield, WI: International Foundation of Employee Benefit Plans, 1975. 74 p.

775. *Fundamentals of Employee Benefit Programs.* 3d ed. Washington, DC: Employee Benefit Research Institute, 1987. 304 p.
This is composed of the various pamphlets on each benefit that have been published by EBRI.

776. *Funding of State and Local Government Pension Plans; A National Problem, Report to the Congress.* Washington, DC: U.S. General Accounting Office, 1979. 125 p.

777. *The Funding Status of Multiemployer Pension Plans and Implications for Collective Bargaining; Report of the Secretary of Labor to Congress.* Washington, DC: U.S. Department of Labor, 1985. 194 p.

778. *Future Aspects of Benefit Plan Bargaining; Papers Presented at an IMLR Conference, 11/29/67.* New Brunswick, NJ: Rutgers University. Institute of Management and Labor Relations, 1968?. 27 p.

779. *The Future of State and Local Pensions.* Washington, DC: The Urban Institute, 1981. Various pagings.

780. *Future Retirement Benefits under Employer Retirement Plans; Final Report.* Prepared for the American Council of Life Insurance by ICF Incorporated. Washington, DC: ICF Incorporated, 1984. 64 p.

781. Gardner, Esmond B., and Weber, C. Jerome. *Pension, Bonus, and Profit-Sharing Plans.* New York: The Chase National Bank of the City of New York, 1943. 92 p.

782. Gass, Sylvester F. *Ecclesiastical Pensions; An Historical Synopsis and Commentary.* Canon Law Studies. Washington, DC: The Catholic University of America Press, 1942. 206 p.

783. *General Explanation of the Economic Recovery Tax Act of 1981; HR 4242; . . .Public Law 97–34.* Prepared by the staff of the Joint Committee on Taxation. Washington, DC: U.S. Government Printing Office, 1981. 411 p.

784. *General Explanation of the Revenue Provisions of the Deficit Reduction Act of 1984 (HR 4170, PL 98–369).* Prepared by the staff of the Joint Committee on Taxation. Washington, DC: U.S. Government Printing Office, 1985. 1255 p.

785. *General Explanation of the Revenue Provisions of the Tax Equity and Fiscal Responsibility Act of 1982, (HR 4961, PL 97–248).* Prepared by the staff of the Joint Committee on Taxation. Washington, DC: U.S. Government Printing Office, 1983. 465 p.

786. Gersh, Harry, and Paul, Robert D., eds. *Employee Benefits FactBook, 1972.* New York: Martin E. Segal Co., 1972. 531 p.

787. Gersovitz, Mark. *Economic Consequences of Unfunded Vested Pension Benefits.* NBER Working Paper, 480. Cambridge, MA: National Bureau of Economic Research, 1980. 23 p.

788. Ghilarducci, Teresa. *Pensions and Collective Bargaining; Toward a Comprehensive Retirement Income Security Policy.* Research Report, 85–1. Brookfield, WI: International Foundation of Employee Benefit Plans, 1985. 27 p.

789. Gilbert, Geoffrey M.; Lachowicz, Gregory J.; and Zid, James F. *Accounting and Auditing for Employee Benefit Plans.* Boston: Warren, Gorham & Lamont, Inc., 1978. Various pagings.

790. Gilbert, Richard A.; Homer, Barry W.; and Smith, Carolyn E. *Attorney's Guide to Pension & Profit-Sharing Plans.* 3d ed. Berkeley, CA: California Continuing Education of the Bar, 1985.

791. Gillen, James R. *Life Insurance Company Investments and the Prohibited Transactions Provisions of ERISA; Paper. . . .* New York: The Association of Life Insurance Counsel, 1980. 67 p.

792. Glasser, Stephen A. *Pension Plans, Deferred Compensation and Executive Benefits.* Corporate Law and Practice Transcript Series, 6. New York: Practising Law Institute, 1969. 253 p.

793. Glasson, William Henry. *History of Military Pension Legislation in the United States.* Columbia University Studies in the Social Sciences, 32. New York: AMS Press, 1968. 135 p.
   Reprint of a 1900 edition.

794. Gody, Celia Star. *The IRA Rollover as Tax Shelter.* Washington, DC: Foster Associates, Inc., 1980. 230 p.

795. Goetz, Raymond. *Tax Treatment of Pension Plans; Preferential or Normal?* Washington, DC: American Enterprise Institute for Public Policy Research, 1969. 79 p.

796. Goldberg, Steven S. *Pension Plans and Executive Compensation.* Tax Law and Practise Course Handbook Series, 8. New York: Practising Law Institute, 1974. 764 p.

797. Goldberg, Steven S. *Pension Plans under ERISA.* New York: Practising Law Institute, 1976. 697 p.

798. Golden, Howard J. *The Norris Case and Benefit Planning.* Tax Law and Practice Course Handbook Series, 193. New York: Practising Law Institue, 1983. 160 p.

799. Goldfarb, Steve. *Benefits for the Future; An Employee Perspective.* New York?: Johnson & Higgins, 1985. 17 p.

800. Goldfield, Carl. *Employee Plans; Deductions, Contributions and Funding.* Tax Management Portfolios, 371. Washington, DC: Bureau of National Affairs, Inc., 1986. Various pagings.

801. Goldstein, William M., and Meilman, Roy K. *Life Insurance; Corporate Business Use.* Revised by Edward M. Burgh and Charlotte S. Liptak. Tax Management Portfolios, 34–4th. Washington, DC: Bureau of National Affairs, Inc., 1983. Various pagings.

802. Gollin, James. *The Star Spangled Retirement Dream; Why It's Going Sour & What You Can Do about It.* New York: Scribner, 1981. 218 p.

803. Goodman, Hortense. *Illustrations and Analysis of Disclosures of Pension Information; A Survey of the Application of the Requirements of FASB Statement No. 36, an Amendment of APB Opinion No. 8.* Financial Report Survey, 22. New York: American Institute of Certified Public Accountants, 1981. 258 p.

804. Goodman, Hortense, and Lorensen, Leonard. *Illustrations of Accounting for Employee Benefits.* New York: American Institute of Certified Public Accountants, 1977. 122 p.

805. Goodman, Isidore. *Assured Pensions.* Chicago: Commerce Clearing House, Inc., 1983. 23 p.

806. Goodman, Isidore. *Choice of Plan under ERISA.* Chicago: Commerce Clearing House, Inc., 1979. 24 p.

807. Goodman, Isidore. *The Compensation Package*. Chicago: Commerce Clearing House, 1982. 21 p.

808. Goodman, Isidore. *Contributory Retirement Plans*. Chicago: Commerce Clearing House, Inc., 1985. 23 p.

809. Goodman, Isidore. *Coping with the Rising Costs of Employee Benefits*. Chicago: Commerce Clearing House, Inc., 1984. 23 p.

810. Goodman, Isidore. *Declaratory Judgment Remedy in Retirement Plan Cases*. Chicago: Commerce Clearing House, Inc., 1980. 23 p.

811. Goodman, Isidore. *Defined Contribution Plans in the Employee Benefit Structure*. Chicago: Commerce Clearing House, Inc., 1986. 24 p.

812. Goodman, Isidore. *Employee Benefit Plans in Business Reorganizations*. Chicago: Commerce Clearing House, Inc., 1984. 24 p.

813. Goodman, Isidore. *Employee Benefit Plans under TRA of 1984*. Chicago: Commerce Clearing House, Inc., 1984. 24 p.

814. Goodman, Isidore. *Employee Plan Investments under ERISA*. Chicago: Commerce Clearing House, Inc., 1978. 23 p.

815. Goodman, Isidore. *Employee Turnover under Tax-Qualified Plans*. Chicago: Commerce Clearing House, Inc., 1984. 23 p.

816. Goodman, Isidore. *Equitable Treatment of Retirement Benefits*. Chicago: Commerce Clearing House, Inc., 1984. 23 p.

817. Goodman, Isidore. *ESOPs since ERISA*. Chicago: Commerce Clearing House, Inc., 1980. 23 p.

818. Goodman, Isidore. *Establishing a TRASOP*. Chicago: Commerce Clearing House, Inc., 1979. 23 p.

819. Goodman, Isidore. *Exempt Employees' Trusts under ERISA*. Chicago: Commerce Clearing House, Inc., 1980. 23 p.

820. Goodman, Isidore. *Funding under ERISA*. Chicago: Commerce Clearing House, Inc., 1978. 23 p.

821. Goodman, Isidore. *Future Changes in Employee Benefits*. Chicago: Commerce Clearing House, Inc., 1985. 23 p.

822. Goodman, Isidore. *H.R. 10 Plans under ERISA*. Chicago: Commerce Clearing House, Inc., 1978. 24 p.

823. Goodman, Isidore. *Impact of Investment Yields on Employees' Trusts*. Chicago: Commerce Clearing House, Inc., 1981. 23 p.

824. Goodman, Isidore. *The Impact of Security Fluctuations on Employee Benefit Plans*. Chicago: Commerce Clearing House, Inc., 1983. 23 p.

825. Goodman, Isidore. *Incidental and Supplemental Benefits.* Chicago: Commerce Clearing House, Inc., 1986. 24 p.

826. Goodman, Isidore. *Individual Account Plans.* Chicago: Commerce Clearing House, Inc., 1981. 23 p.

827. Goodman, Isidore. *Individual Retirement Plans.* Chicago: Commerce Clearing House, Inc., 198?–. 48 p.

828. Goodman, Isidore. *Industry-Geared Retirement Plans.* Chicago: Commerce Clearing House, Inc., 1983. 23 p.

829. Goodman, Isidore. *Innovations in Employee Plan Designs.* Chicago: Commerce Clearing House, Inc., 1982. 23 p.

830. Goodman, Isidore. *Innovative Compensation Plans.* Chicago: Commerce Clearing House, Inc., 1986. 24 p.

831. Goodman, Isidore. *Integrated Pension and Profit-Sharing Plans.* Chicago: Commerce Clearing House, Inc., 1980. 31 p.

832. Goodman, Isidore. *Interest of Spouse in Employee Retirement Benefits.* Chicago: Commerce Clearing House, Inc., 1982. 21 p.

833. Goodman, Isidore. *Investments of Exempt Employees' Trusts in the 1980's.* Chicago: Commerce Clearing House, Inc., 1982. 23 p.

834. Goodman, Isidore. *Investments of Retirement Plans in the Mid 80's.* Chicago: Commerce Clearing House, Inc., 1985. 23 p.

835. Goodman, Isidore. *Isidore Goodman on Qualified Pension and Profit-Sharing Plans under the Internal Revenue Code; Speeches Delivered between October 20, 1955 and October 5, 1970.* Englewood Cliffs, NJ: Prentice-Hall, Inc., 1970?. 778 p.

836. Goodman, Isidore. *Lump-Sum Distributions; A Target of New Tax Proposals.* Chicago: Commerce Clearing House, Inc., 1985. 23 p.

837. Goodman, Isidore. *Lump-Sum Distributions under ERISA.* Chicago: Commerce Clearing House, Inc., 1978. 23 p.

838. Goodman, Isidore. *Minimum Participation Standards under ERISA.* Chicago: Commerce Clearing House, Inc., 1978. 23 p.

839. Goodman, Isidore. *Multiemployer Plans under ERISA.* Chicago: Commerce Clearing House, Inc., 1978. 24 p.

840. Goodman, Isidore. *Multi-Plan Retirement Programs.* Chicago: Commerce Clearing House, Inc., 1982. 23 p.

841. Goodman, Isidore. *New Employee Benefit Plan Rules.* Chicago: Commerce Clearing House, Inc., 1987. 24 p.

842. Goodman, Isidore. *New Employee Benefit Rules under TEFRA.* Chicago: Commerce Clearing House, Inc., 1982. 23 p.

843. Goodman, Isidore. *The New TRASOPs*. Chicago: Commerce Clearing House, Inc., 1979. 23 p.

844. Goodman, Isidore. *Nondiscriminatory Employee Benefit Plans*. Chicago: Commerce Clearing House, Inc., 1979. 23 p.

845. Goodman, Isidore. *Pending Employee Benefit Changes*. Chicago: Commerce Clearing House, Inc., 1986. 23 p.

846. Goodman, Isidore. *Pension Issues Ten Years after ERISA*. Chicago: Commerce Clearing House, Inc., 1985. 23 p.

847. Goodman, Isidore. *Pensions in an Inflationary Era*. Chicago: Commerce Clearing House, Inc., 1981. 23 p.

848. Goodman, Isidore. *Plan Terminations under ERISA*. Chicago: Commerce Clearing House, Inc., 1978. 31 p.

849. Goodman, Isidore. *Portable Retirement Benefits*. Chicago: Commerce Clearing House, Inc., 1980. 23 p.

850. Goodman, Isidore. *Preemption under ERISA and the Effect of the Taft-Hartley Act*. Chicago: Commerce Clearing House, Inc., 1979. 23 p.

851. Goodman, Isidore. *The Prospects for Keogh Plans after TEFRA*. Chicago: Commerce Clearing House, Inc., 1983. 21 p.

852. Goodman, Isidore. *Protection of Employee Benefit Rights under ERISA*. Chicago: Commerce Clearing House, Inc., 1979. 31 p.

853. Goodman, Isidore. *Providing for Retirement*. Chicago: Commerce Clearing House, Inc., 1982. 23 p.

854. Goodman, Isidore. *Recovery of Retirement Plan Contributions*. Chicago: Commerce Clearing House, Inc., 1985. 23 p.

855. Goodman, Isidore. *Recovery of Retirement Plan Funds*. Chicago: Commerce Clearing House, Inc., 1984. 23 p.

856. Goodman, Isidore. *Reorganizations under ERISA*. Chicago: Commerce Clearing House, Inc., 1979. 23 p.

857. Goodman, Isidore. *Retirement Distributions*. Chicago: Commerce Clearing House, Inc., 1982. 23 p.

858. Goodman, Isidore. *Retirement Plans for Employees in Foreign Service*. Chicago: Commerce Clearing House, Inc., 1979. 24 p.

859. Goodman, Isidore. *Retirement Plans for Retail Establishments*. Chicago: Commerce Clearing House, Inc., 1980. 23 p.

860. Goodman, Isidore. *Retirement Plans in Reorganizations and Liquidations*. Chicago: Commerce Clearing House, Inc., 1985. 23 p.

861. Goodman, Isidore. *Rollovers and Constructive Receipt.* Chicago: Commerce Clearing House, Inc., 1978. 23 p.

862. Goodman, Isidore. *Salary Reduction Arrangements.* Chicago: Commerce Clearing House, Inc., 1985. 23 p.

863. Goodman, Isidore. *Selecting a Retirement Plan.* Chicago: Commerce Clearing House, Inc., 1986. 24 p.

864. Goodman, Isidore. *Some Ins and Outs of ERISA.* Chicago: Commerce Clearing House, Inc., 1980. 24 p.

865. Goodman, Isidore. *Special Categories of Employee Benefit Plans under the Tax Reform Act.* Chicago: Commerce Clearing House, Inc., 1987. 24 p.

866. Goodman, Isidore. *Tax Deductible Employer Contributions under ERISA.* Chicago: Commerce Clearing House, Inc., 1979. 23 p.

867. Goodman, Isidore. *Tax Objectives of Employee Benefit Plans.* Chicago: Commerce Clearing House, Inc., 1985. 23 p.

868. Goodman, Isidore. *Tax Savings on Lump Sum Distributions.* Chicago: Commerce Clearing House, Inc., 1983. 24 p.

869. Goodman, Isidore. *Tax-Sheltered Employee Benefit Programs.* Chicago: Commerce Clearing House, Inc., 1980. 24 p.

870. Goodman, Isidore. *Tax-Sheltered Retirement Programs for Professionals.* Chicago: Commerce Clearing House, Inc., 1981. 23 p.

871. Goodman, Isidore. *Tax Treatment of Participants in Employee Benefit Plans.* Chicago: Commerce Clearing House, Inc., 1980. 23 p.

872. Goodman, Isidore. *Top-Heavy Plans under TEFRA.* Chicago: Commerce Clearing House, Inc., 1983. 21 p.

873. Goodman, Isidore. *Towards a Minimum Universal Pension System.* Chicago: Commerce Clearing House, Inc., 1981. 24 p.

874. Goodman, Isidore. *Trends in Employee Benefit Plans.* Chicago: Commerce Clearing House, Inc., 1983. 23 p.

875. Goodman, Isidore. *Types of Distribution under Employee Benefit Plans.* Chicago: Commerce Clearing House, Inc., 1981. 23 p.

876. Goodman, Isidore. *Universal Pension Coverage.* Chicago: Commerce Clearing House, Inc., 1980. 23 p.

877. Goodman, Isidore. *Variable Annuities in an Erratic Economy.* Chicago: Commerce Clearing House, Inc., 1980. 23 p.

878. Goodman, Isidore. *Variations in Employee Benefit Patterns.* Chicago: Commerce Clearing House, Inc., 1984. 23 p.

879. Goodman, Isidore. *Vesting in Plans with Rapid Employee Turnover*. Chicago: Commerce Clearing House, Inc., 1980. 23 p.

880. Goodman, Isidore. *Vesting under ERISA*. Chicago: Commerce Clearing House, Inc., 1978. 24 p.

881. Gordon, Roger H. *Social Security and Labor Supply Incentives*. NBER Working Paper, 986. Cambridge, MA: National Bureau of Economic Research, 1982. Various pagings.

882. Gordus, Jeanne P. *Leaving Early; Perspectives and Problems in Current Retirement Practice and Policy*. Kalamazoo, MI: W. E. Upjohn Institute for Employment Research, 1980. 88 p.

883. Government Accounting Standards Board. *Applicability of FASB Statement No. 87, Employers' Accounting for Pensions, to State and Local Governmental Employers*. Exposure Draft. Stamford, CT, 1986. 8 p.

884. Government Accounting Standards Board. *Applicability of FASB Statement No. 87, Employers' Accounting for Pensions, to State and Local Governmental Employers*. Statement, 4. Stamford, CT, 1986. 10 p.

885. Government Accounting Standards Board. *Disclosure of Defined Benefit Pension Information for Public Employee Retirement Systems and State and Local Governmental Employers*. Exposure Draft. Stamford, CT, 1985. 88 p.

886. Government Accounting Standards Board. *Disclosure of Pension Information by Public Employee Retirement Systems and State and Local Governmental Employers*. Statement, 5. Stamford, CT, 1986. 95 p.

887. Government Accounting Standards Board. *Financial Reporting of Deferred Compensation Plans Adopted under the Provisions of Internal Revenue Code Section 457*. Statement, 2. Stamford, CT, 1986. 16 p.

888. Government Accounting Standards Board. *Financial Reporting of Deferred Compensation Plans Adopted under the Provisions of Internal Revenue Code Section 457 for State and Local Government Employees*. Discussion Memorandum. Stamford, CT, 1985.

889. Government Accounting Standards Board. *Financial Reporting of Deferred Compensation Plans Adopted under the Provisions of Internal Revenue Code Section 457 for State and Local Government Employees*. Exposure Draft. Stamford, CT, 1985. 16 p.

890. Graham, Sharon S., and Marshall, S. Brooks. *Pension Fund Decision Making; A Questionnaire to Corporate Managers*. Research Report, 84–9. Brookfield, WI: International Foundation of Employee Benefit Plans, 1984. 9 p.

891. Gray, Hillel. *New Directions in the Investment and Control of Pension Funds*. Washington, DC: Investor Responsibility Research Center, 1983. 120 p.

892. Grayck, Marcus D. *Tax Aspects of Distributions of Pension and Profit Sharing Plans*. New York: Dornost Publishing Co., Inc., 1964. 19 p.

893. Green, Paul A., and Beyer, William G. *The Single Employer Pension Plan Amendments of 1986; An Overview.* Chicago: C. D. Spencer & Associates, 1986. 36 p.

894. Greenough, William C. *College Retirement and Insurance Plans.* New York: Columbia University Press, 1948. 274 p.

895. Greenough, William C., and King, Francis P. *Benefit Plans in American Colleges.* New York: Columbia University Press, 1969. 481 p.

896. Greenough, William C., and King, Francis P. *Pension Plans and Public Policy.* New York: Columbia University Press, 1976. 311 p.

897. Greenough, William C., and King, Francis P. *Retirement and Insurance Plans in American Colleges.* New York: Columbia University Press, 1959. 480 p.

898. Griffes, Ernest J. *Employee Benefit Programs; Management Planning and Control.* Homewood, IL: Dow Jones-Irwin, 1983. 318 p.

899. Griffes, Ernest J. *Organizing & Managing; The Responsibilities of a Pension & Welfare Plan Administrator.* Greenvale, NY: Panel Publishers, Inc., 1976.

900. Griffin, Frank L., and Trowbridge, Charles L. *Status of Funding under Private Pension Plans.* Homewood, IL: Published for the Pension Research Council by R. D. Irwin, 1969. 106 p.

901. Gronau, Reuben. *Sex-Related Wage Differentials and Women's Interrupted Labor Careers; The Chicken or the Egg.* NBER Working Paper, 1002. Cambridge, MA: National Bureau of Economic Research, 1982. 65 p.

902. Grubbs, Donald S., Jr. *Funding.* Pension and Profit-Sharing Plans. Series D, Folio 1. Philadelphia, PA: American Law Institute-American Bar Association. Committee on Continuing Professional Education, 1978. 35 p.

903. Grubbs, Donald S., Jr. *Integration of Plans with Social Security.* Pension and Profit-Sharing Plans. Series C, Folio 5. Philadelphia, PA: American Law Institute-American Bar Association, 1978. 32 p.

904. Gruber, Martin, and Sachs, Reynold. *Pension Funds, 1966.* New York: Investors Publishing Co., Inc., 1966. 295 p.
This contains financial information for several hundred pension funds in 1963 and 1964.

905. *A Guarantee That Isn't; The Impossible Concept of Multiemployer Withdrawal Liability.* Washington, DC: Council on Multiemployer Pension Security, 1981?. 8 p.

906. *A Guide to Pension Negotiations and Planning.* Prepared by Research Department, International Association of Machinists. Washington, DC: IAM, 1960. 106 p.

907. *A Guide to Public Finance, Employment, & Pension Statistics.* Legislative Finance Papers Series. Denver, CO: National Conference of State Legislators, 1985. 45 p.

908. *A Guide to Understanding Your Pension Plan.* Washington, DC: Pension Rights Center, 1982. 32 p.

909. *Guidebook to Pension Planning.* Chicago: Commerce Clearing House, Inc., 1983. Various pagings.
Contents are reprinted from the CCH *Pension Plan Guide.*

910. Gujarati, Damodar. *Pensions and New York City's Fiscal Crisis.* AEI Studies, 212. Washington, DC: American Enterprise Institute for Public Policy Research, 1978. 72 p.

911. Gustman, Alan L., and Steinmeier, Thomas L. *A Disaggregated Structural Analysis of Retirement by Race, Difficulty to Work and Health.* NBER Working Paper, 1585. Cambridge, MA: National Bureau of Economic Research, 1985. 59 p.

912. Gustman, Alan L., and Steinmeier, Thomas L. *Minimum Hours Constraints and Retirement Behavior.* NBER Working Paper, 940. Cambridge, MA: National Bureau of Economic Research, 1982. 40 p.

913. Gustman, Alan L., and Steinmeier, Thomas L. *Partial Retirement and the Analysis of Retirement Behavior.* NBER Working Paper, 763. Cambridge, MA: National Bureau of Economic Research, 1981. 41 p.

914. Gustman, Alan L., and Steinmeier, Thomas L. *Partial Retirement and Wage Profiles of Older Workers.* NBER Working Paper, 1000. Cambridge, MA: National Bureau of Economic Research, 1982. 31 p.

915. Gustman, Alan L., and Steinmeier, Thomas L. *Pensions, Unions and Implicit Contracts.* NBER Working Paper, 2036. Cambridge, MA: National Bureau of Economic Research, 1986. 25 p.

916. Gustman, Alan L., and Steinmeier, Thomas L. *Retirement Flows.* NBER Working Paper, 1069. Cambridge, MA: National Bureau of Economic Research, 1983. 30 p.

917. Gustman, Alan L., and Steinmeier, Thomas L. *Social Security Reform and Labor Supply.* NBER Working Paper, 1212. Cambridge, MA: National Bureau of Economic Research, 1984. 62 p.

918. Hack, Stuart. *Retirement Planning for Professionals.* Wiley Tax and Business Guides for Professionals. New York: Wiley, 1987.

919. Hakala, Donald J. *The Complete Guide to Tax-Free Rollovers.* Portland, OR: D. J. Hakala, 1983. 195 p.

920. Hale, Robert F. *Retirement Accounting Changes; Budget and Policy Impacts.* Congressional Budget Office Background Paper. Washington, DC: U.S. Government Printing Office, 1977. 17 p.

921. Hall, Challis A., Jr. *Executive Compensation and Retirement Plans.* Boston: Harvard University. Graduate School of Business Administration. Division of Research, 1951. 365 p.

922. Hall, Harold R. *Some Observations on Executive Retirement.* Boston: Harvard University. Graduate School of Business Administration. Division of Research, 1953. 298 p.

923. Hall, William D., and Landsittel, David L. *A New Look at Accounting for Pension Costs.* Homewood, IL: Published for the Pension Research Council by Richard D. Irwin, Inc., 1977. 183 p.

924. Hamermesh, Daniel S. *Consumption during Retirement; The Missing Link in the Life Cycle.* NBER Working Paper, 930. Cambridge, MA: National Bureau of Economic Research, 1982. 27 p.

925. Hamermesh, Daniel S. *Expectations; Life Expectancy and Economic Behavior.* NBER Working Paper, 835. Cambridge, MA: National Bureau of Economic Research, 1982. 28 p.

926. Hamermesh, Daniel S. *Life-Cycle Effects on Consumption and Retirement.* NBER Working Papers, 976. Cambridge, MA: National Bureau of Economic Research, 1982. 32 p.

927. Hamilton, James A., and Bronson, Dorrance C. *Pensions.* New York: McGraw-Hill, 1958. 410 p.

928. Hammaker, Paul M., ed. *The Pension Reform Law of 1974; Impact on American Society.* Charlottesville, VA: University of Virginia. Colgate Darden Graduate School of Business Administration. Center for the Study of Applied Ethics, 1975. 121 p.

929. *Handbook; Jointly Administered Labor Management (Multi-Employer) Pension Plans.* 2d ed. New York: Institute of Life Insurance, 1970?. 64 p.
Cover title: *Multi-Employer Pension Plans.* Title of previous edition: *Handbook on Negotiated Multi-Employer Pension Plans.*

930. *Handbook on Multiemployer Pension Plan Amendments Act of 1980; Complete Explanation, ERISA Sections as Amended, Code Sections as Amended, Committee Reports, Index, Date of Enactment, September 26, 1980, Public Law 96–364.* Englewood Cliffs, NJ: Prentice-Hall, Inc., 1980. 216 p.

931. *Handbook on the Economic Recovery Tax Act of 1981; Concise Explanation, Code Sections as Amended, Committee Reports, Index.* Englewood Cliffs, NJ: Prentice-Hall, Inc., 1981. Various pagings.

932. Hansman, Robert J., and Larrabee, John W. *Deferred Compensation; The New Methodology for Executive Reward.* Lexington, MA: Lexington Books, 1983. 126 p.

933. Harbrecht, Paul P. *Pension Funds and Economic Power.* New York: The Twentieth Century Fund, 1959. 319 p.

934. Hardy, C. Colburn. *ABCs of Investing Your Retirement Funds.* 2d ed. Oradell, NJ: Medical Economics Books, 1982. 241 p.

935. Hardy, C. Colburn, and Wiener, Howard J. *Personal Pension Plan Strategies for Physicians.* Oradell, NJ: Medical Economics Books, 1985. 132 p.

936. Hargrove, John O., and Daly, Charles D., eds. *Attorney's Guide to Pension and Profit-Sharing Plans.* 3d ed. Berkeley, CA: California Continuing Education of the Bar, 1985.

937. Harker, Carlton. *Pension Plan Partial Terminations.* Brookfield, WI: International Foundation of Employee Benefit Plans, 1982. 92 p.

938. Harper, F. S. *Unified Mathematics of Finance.* Washington, DC: American Society of Pension Actuaries, 1976.

939. Harrell, Karen Fair. *The Administration of Public Pension Plans at the State and Local Level.* Public Administration Series. Bibliography, P-807. Monticello, IL: Vance Bibliographies, 1981. 5 p.

940. Harris, Robert, ed. *Does Retirement Have a Future? Three Views.* An Urban Institute Paper. Washington, DC: Urban Institute Press, 1980. 25 p.

941. Harrison, J. Michael, and Sharpe, William F. *Optimal Funding and Asset Allocation Rules for Defined-Benefit Pension Plans.* NBER Working Paper, 935. Cambridge, MA: National Bureau of Economic Research, 1982. 26 p.

942. Hartman, Robert W. *Pay and Pensions for Federal Workers.* Washington, DC: Brookings Institution, 1983. 118 p.

943. Hartman, Robert W., and Weber, Arnold R. *The Rewards of Public Service; Compensating Top Federal Officials.* Washington, DC: Brookings Institution, 1980. 238 p.

944. *Harvard Business Review; Pension Management.* Boston: Harvard Business Review, 198?–. 95 p.
Texts of articles appearing in HBR from 1966 through 1980.

945. Harvey, Ernest C., and Friedly, Phillip H. *Containment of Pension Plan Costs; The Management Role.* Business Intelligence Program, 1063. Menlo Park, CA: SRI International, 1981. 12 p.

946. Hausman, Jerry A. and Burtless, Gary. *Double Dipping; The Combined Effects of Social Security and Civil Service Pensions on Employee Retirement.* NBER Reprint, 381. Cambridge, MA: National Bureau of Economic Research, 1982. 21 p.

947. Henss, John L. *Professional Incorporation and the Employee Stock Ownership Plan.* n.p., 1977. 88 p.

948. Herman, Edward S. *Conflicts of Interest; Commercial Bank Trust Departments.* New York: The Twentieth Century Fund, 1975. 166 p.

949. Hibbert, Jack. *Measuring the Effects of Inflation on Income, Saving and Wealth.* Paris: Organization for Economic Cooperation and Development, 1983. 170 p.

950. Hicks, Ernest L. *Accounting for the Cost of Pension Plans.* Accounting Research Study, 8. New York: American Institute of Certified Public Accountants, 1965. 159 p.

951. Hicks, Ernest L., and Trowbridge, C. L. *Employer Accounting for Pensions; An Analysis of the Financial Accounting Standards Board's Preliminary Views and Exposure Draft.* Homewood, IL: Published for the Pension Reserach Council by R. D. Irwin, 1985. 89 p.

952. *The Hidden Costs of ESOPs.* Portland, OR: Triad Financial Reports, 1975. 25 p.

953. *Highlights of the New Pension Reform Law; Text of Act, Statement of the Managers, Editorial Analysis.* Washington, DC: Bureau of National Affairs, Inc., 1974. 365 p.

954. Hildebrandt, David A., and Goldberg, Steven S. *ERISA; Qualified Plans, IRS Determination Letter Procedures.* Tax Management Portfolios, 360. Washington, DC: Bureau of National Affairs, Inc., 1986. Various pagings.

955. Hoffner, Thomas A., and Windmuller, Paul R. *Understanding & Using Pensions.* Eau Claire, WI: Professional Education Systems, 1984. 146 p.

956. Holden, James P., and Suwalsky, A. L., Jr. *Reasonable Compensation.* Tax Management Portfolios, 202–3rd. Washington, DC: Bureau of National Affairs, Inc., 1985. Various pagings.

957. Holland, Daniel M. *Private Pension Funds; Projected Growth.* Occasional Paper, 97. New York: National Bureau of Economic Research, 1966. 146 p.

958. Holzman, Robert S. *Guide to Pension and Profit-Sharing Plans under the Employee Retirement Income Security Act of 1974.* Edited by Bernhart R. Snyder. 4th ed. Rockville Center, NY: Farnsworth Publishing Co., 1975. 210 p.

959. Holzman, Robert S. *Tax-Free Reorganizations after the Pension Reform Act of 1974.* Rev. ed. Rockville Center, NY: Farnsworth Publishing Co., 1977. 350 p.

960. Hommel, Dennis. *The Employee Benefit Communications Handbook.* Redwood City, CA: Dennis Hommel Associates, 1980. 31 p.

961. *How the 1980 Multiemployer Amendments to ERISA Affect the Construction Industry.* Washington, DC: Associated General Contractors of America, 1981. 65 p.

962. *How to Cope with ERISA's Reporting & Disclosure Rules.* Englewood Cliffs, NJ: Prentice-Hall, Inc., 1983. 48 p.

963. *How to Integrate a Retirement Plan with Social Security.* Englewood Cliffs, NJ: Prentice-Hall, Inc., 1982. 32 p.

964. *How to Make the Most of Keogh Plans.* Pension Planning Series. West Nyack, NY: Prentice-Hall, Inc., 1985. 39 p.

965. *How to Make the Most of Keogh Plans under the Economic Recovery Tax Act of 1981.* Englewood Cliffs, NJ: Prentice-Hall, Inc., 1983. 32 p.

966. *How to Save Taxes on Your Lump-Sum Distribution.* Englewood Cliffs, NJ: Prentice-Hall, Inc., 1982. 40 p.

967. Howard, Bion B., and Dietz, Peter O. *A Study of the Financial Significance of Profit Sharing.* Chicago: Council of Profit Sharing Industries, 1969. 130 p.

968. Hubbard, R. Glenn. *Uncertain Lifetimes, Pensions, and Individual Saving.* NBER Working Paper, 1363. Cambridge, MA: National Bureau of Economic Research, 1984. 47 p.

969. Hughes, Gary E., and Mason, Paul J. *Insurance Products under the Securities Laws; New Regulatory Initiatives.* Corporate Law and Practice Course Handbook Series, 493. New York: Practising Law Institute, 1985. 328 p.

970. Huling, Ronald L. *Study of Multi-Employer Plans.* Prepared for Labor Management Services Administration by Towers, Perrin, Forster and Crosby, Inc. Springfield, VA: National Technical Information Service, 1979. Various pagings.

971. Hurd, Michael D., and Boskin, Michael J. *The Effect of Social Security on Retirement in the Early 1970's.* NBER Working Paper, 659. Cambridge, MA: National Bureau of Economic Research, 1981. 48 p.

972. Hurd, Michael D., and Shoven, John B. *The Distributional Impact of Social Security.* NBER Working Paper, 1155. Cambridge, MA: National Bureau of Economic Research, 1983. 37 p.

973. Hurd, Michael D., and Shoven, John B. *The Economic Status of the Elderly.* NBER Working Paper, 914. Cambridge, MA: National Bureau of Economic Research, 1982. 61 p.

974. Ibbotson, Roger G., and Sinquefield, Rex A. *Stocks, Bonds, Bills, and Inflation; Historical Returns, 1926–1978.* 2d ed. Charlottesville, VA: Financial Analysts Research Foundation, 1979. 85 p.

975. *Impact of ERISA on Small-Scale Pension Plans.* Boca Raton, FL: Reymont Associates, 1979.

976. *The Implications of Past Investment Performance for Future Investment Policy of Multiemployer Pension Funds.* Brookfield, WI: National Foundation of Health, Welfare and Pension Plans, 1970. 76 p.

977. *Improved Retirement Financing; Recommendations. . . .* Washington, DC: U.S. Civil Service Commission, 1967. 23 p.

978. *Individual Retirement Accounts; A Guide to Personal Retirement Savings.* New York: Peat, Marwick, Mitchell & Co., 1982. 21 p.

979. *Individual Retirement Plans.* Washington, DC: American Consulting Engineers Council, 1985. 48 p.

980. *Individual Retirement Plans after Tax Reform; Individual Retirement Accounts, Individual Retirement Annuities, Simplified Employee Pensions.* Chicago: Commerce Clearing House, Inc., 1987. 48 p.

981. *Individual Retirement Plans under 1981 Tax Law.* Chicago: Commerce Clearing House, Inc., 1981. 40 p.

982. *Industrial Pensions in the United States.* New York: National Industrial Conference Board, 1925. 157 p.

983. *Initial Recommendations to the Treasury Department Regarding the Tax Reform Act of 1986, December 10, 1986.* Washington, DC: The ERISA Industry Committee, 1986. 39 p.

984. *Initial Results of a Survey on Employee Stock Ownership Plans and Information on Related Economic Trends.* Washington, DC: U.S. General Accounting Office, 1985. 46 p.

985. Inman, Robert P. *The Funding Status of Teacher Pensions; An Econometric Approach.* NBER Working Paper, 1727. Cambridge, MA: National Bureau of Economic Research, 1985. 29 p.

986. *Institutional Investor Study Report of the Securities and Exchange Commission.* Washington, DC: U.S. Government Printing Office, 1971. 2 vols.

987. *Integrating Pension Plans with Social Security.* Washington, DC: Employee Benefits Research Institute, 1981. 5 p.

988. *Internal Revenue Service Efforts and Plans to Enforce the Employee Retirement Income Security Act.* Washington, DC: U.S. General Accounting Office, 1979. 12 p.

989. *Investing Pension Funds in Home Mortgages; The Connecticut Experience.* Lexington, KY: The Council of State Governments, 1984. 6 p.

990. *Investment of Union Pension Funds.* Washington, DC: AFL-CIO Committee on the Investment of Union Pension Funds, 1980. 133 p.

991. *Investment Performance of Multiemployer Pension Funds; Measurement and Reporting, Comparison and Evaluation, Implications for Future Policy.* Brookfield, WI: International Foundation of Employee Benefit Plans, 1976. 21 p.

992. *Investment Policy Guidebook for Corporate Pension Plan Trustees.* Brookfield, WI: International Foundation of Employee Benefit Plans, 1984. 185 p.

993. *Investment Policy Guidebook for Trustees; An Introduction to Drafting the Written Investment Statement for a Labor-Management Employee Benefit Trust Fund.* Rev. ed. Brookfield, WI: International Foundation of Employee Benefit Plans, 1981. 92 p.

994. Ippolito, Richard A. *Pensions, Economics and Public Policy.* Homewood, IL: Published for the Pension Research Council by Dow Jones-Irwin, 1986. 267 p.

995. Ippolito, Richard A., and Kolodrubetz, Walter W., eds. *The Handbook of Pension Statistics, 1985.* Chicago: Commerce Clearing House, Inc., 1986. 469 p.

996. *IRA Basics.* Chicago: Institute of Financial Education, 1984. 173 p.

997. *The IRA Book; The Complete Guide to IRAs & Retirement Planning.* Washington, DC: Center for the Study of Services, n.d.

998. *The IRA Plus Report, 1984.* Los Angeles: E. F. Baumer & Co., 1983. 68 p.

999. Irish, Leon E., and McClure, William B., Jr., eds. *The 1984 Flexible Compensation Conference.* New York: Law & Business, Inc., 1984. 767 p.

1000. Jacobson, Simon. *The "Controlled Group of Employers" Concept and Its Application to Qualified Plans.* Pension and Profit-Sharing Plans. Series C, Folio 10. Philadelphia, PA: American Law Institute-American Bar Association. Committee on Continuing Professional Education, 1978. 25 p.

1001. Jarrett, James, and Hicks, Jimmy E. *Retirement System Consolidation.* Lexington, KY: Council of State Governments, 1976. 46 p.

1002. Jenny, Hans H.; Heim, Peggy; and Hughes, Geoffrey C. *Another Challenge; Age 70 Retirement in Higher Education.* New York: TIAA-CREF, 1979. 80 p.

1003. Jessup, Libby F. *Law of Retirement.* 2d ed. Legal Almanac Series, 53. Dobbs Ferry, NY: Oceana Publications, 1979. 120 p.

1004. Joanette, Francois P. *Funding and Asset Allocation Decisions in Corporate Pension Plans.* Research Report, 86–1. Brookfield, WI: International Foundation of Employee Benefit Plans, 1986. 17 p.

1005. Jochim, Timothy C. *Employee Stock Ownership and Related Plans; Analysis and Practice.* Westport, CT: Quorum Books, 1982. 334 p.

1006. Johnson, Richard E. *Flexible Benefits; A How-to Guide.* Brookfield, WI: International Foundation of Employee Benefit Plans, 1986. 163 p.

1007. *Jointly Trusteed Funds; Responsibilities, Operations and Benefits, a Subject Bibliography.* Brookfield, WI: International Foundation of Employee Benefit Plans, 1975. 65 p.

1008. Jorgensen, James A. *The Graying of America; Retirement and Why You Can't Afford It.* New York: Dial Press, 1980. 245 p.

1009. Jost, Lee F., and Sutherland, C. Bruce. *Guide to Professional Benefit Plan Management and Administration.* Brookfield, WI: International Foundation of Employee Benefit Plans, 1980. 405 p.

1010. Kalish, Gerald I. *Compensating Yourself; Personal Income, Benefits, and Tax Strategies for Business Owners.* Chicago: Probus Publishing Co., 1985. 203 p.

1011. Kaplan, Jared; Brown, Gregory K.; and Ludwig, Ronald L. *ESOPs.* Tax Management Portfolios, 354–3rd. Washington, DC: Bureau of National Affairs, Inc., 1986. Various pagings.

1012. Kaster, Lewis R., and Nellis, Noel W. *Pension Trust Investments in Realty; Banks, Insurance Companies, Wall Street, Developers.* Real Estate Law and Practice Course Handbook Series, 203. New York: Practising Law Institute, 1981. 992 p.

1013. Kaster, Lewis R., and Nellis, Noel W. *Realty Joint Ventures; Pension Funds, Institutional Investors, Developers.* Real Estate Law and Practice Course Handbook Series, 186. New York: Practising Law Institute, 1980. 520 p.

1014. Katona, George. *Private Pensions & Individual Saving.* Ann Arbor, MI: Institute for Social Research, 1965. 114 p.

1015. Kavanaugh, James E. *Industrial Pensions or the Care of Faithful Workers.* Washington, DC: Chamber of Commerce of the United States, 1924. 17 p.

1016. Kearl, J. R., and Pope, Clayne L. *Life-Cycles in Income and Wealth.* Cambridge, MA: National Bureau of Economic Research, 1983. 25 p.
The period under study is 1850 to 1900, so this item is theoretical or historical depending on your viewpoint.

1017. Kelso, Louis O., and Kelso, Patricia Hetter. *Democracy and Economic Power; Extending the ESOP Revolution.* Cambridge, MA: Ballinger Publishing Co., 1986.

1018. Kemp, Robert S., Jr. *Firm Life Cycle Effects on Pension Funding Decisions.* Research Report, 84–10. Brookfield, WI: International Foundation of Employee Benefit Plans, 1984. 21 p.

1019. Kenty, David E. *Tax-Deferred Annuities; Section 403(b).* Tax Management Portfolios, 388–2nd. Washington, DC: Bureau of National Affairs, Inc., 1986. Various pagings.

1020. King, Francis P. *Benefit Plans in Junior Colleges.* Washington, DC: American Association of Junior Colleges, 1971. 636 p.

1021. King, Francis P., and Cook, Thomas J. *Benefit Plans in Higher Education.* New York: Columbia University Press, 1980. 385 p.

1022. Kinzel, Robert K. *Retirement; Creating Promise out of Threat.* New York: AMACOM, 1979. 131 p.

1023. Kleiler, Frank M. *Can We Afford Early Retirement?* Policy Studies in Employment and Welfare, 32. Baltimore, MD: Johns Hopkins University Press, 1978. 163 p.

1024. Klein, James P. *Flexible Compensation Plans, 1984. Cash or Deferred 401(k) and Cafeteria (125) Arrangements.* Tax Law and Practice Course Handbook Series, 204. New York: Practising Law Institute, 1984. 320 p.

1025. Klein, James P. *Foreign Pension Plans; Handling the New Elections.* Tax Law and Practice Course Handbook Series, 160. New York: Practising Law Institute, 1981. 408 p.

1026. Klein, James P. *Foreign Pension Plans, 1985; The New Rules under IRC Section 404A.* Tax Law and Practice Course Handbook Series, 119. New York: Practising Law Institute, 1985. 328 p.

1027. Klevan, Morton, and Pitt, Harvey L. *ERISA, Securities Laws and Banking Regulation; Effects on Employee Benefit Plans, Corporate Sponsors and Investment Managers.* Tax Law and Practice Course Handbook Series, 122. New York: Practising Law Institute, 1978. 824 p.

1028. Klimkowsky, Beverly M. *Evaluating ERISA.* Research Report, 84–1. Brookfield, WI: International Foundation of Employee Benefit Plans, 1984. 9 p.

1029. *Know Your Pension Plan.* By the U.S. Department of Labor, Labor-Management Services Administration. Washington, DC: U.S. Government Printing Office, 1973. 34 p.

1030. Koehler, Paul D. *Selecting & Managing Tax-Qualified Retirement Plans.* Denver, CO: Center for Research in Ambulatory Health Care Administration, 1984. 52 p.

1031. Kohlmeier, Louis M. *Conflicts of Interest; State and Local Pension Fund Asset Management.* New York: The Twentieth Century Fund, 1976. 69 p.

1032. Koitz, David, and Miller, Nancy L. *Summary of Recommendations and Surveys on Social Security and Pension Policies; An Information Paper.* Prepared by the Congressional Research Service. Washington, DC: U.S. Government Printing Office, 1980. 48 p.

1033. Korczyk, Sophie M. *Retirement Income Opportunities in an Aging America; Pensions and the Economy.* Washington, DC: Employee Benefit Research Institute, 1982. 150 p.

1034. Korczyk, Sophie M. *Retirement Security and Tax Policy.* An EBRI-ERF Policy Study. Washington, DC: Employee Benefit Research Institute, 1984. 136 p.

1035. Kordus, Claude L. *Trustee's Handbook; A Basic Text on Labor-Management Employee Benefit Plans.* 3d ed. Brookfield, WI: International Foundation of Employee Benefit Plans, 1979. 545 p.

1036. Kotlikoff, Laurence J., and Smith, Daniel E. *Pensions in the American Economy.* A National Bureau of Economic Research Monograph. Chicago: University of Chicago Press, 1983. 449 p.

1037. Kotlikoff, Laurence J., and Summers, Lawrence H. *The Contribution of Intergenerational Transfers to Total Wealth; A Reply.* NBER Working Paper, 1827. Cambridge, MA: National Bureau of Economic Research, 1986. 24 p.

1038. Kotlikoff, Laurence J., and Wise, David A. *The Incentive Effects of Private Pension Plans.* NBER Working Paper, 1510. Cambridge, MA: National Bureau of Economic Research, 1984. 72 p.

1039. Kotlikoff, Laurence J.; Shoven, John B.; and Spivak, Avia. *Annuity Markets, Savings, and the Capital Stock.* NBER Working Paper, 1250. Cambridge, MA: National Bureau of Economic Research, 1983. 31 p.

1040. Kotlikoff, Laurence J.; Shoven, John B.; and Spivak, Avia. *The Impact of Annuity Insurance on Savings and Inequality.* NBER Working Paper, 1403. Cambridge, MA: National Bureau of Economic Research, 1984. 40 p.

1041. Krass, Stephen J., and Keschner, Richard L. *The Pension Answer Book.* 3d ed. Greenvale, NY: Panel Publishers, 1984. 432 p.
This is updated by supplements. The 1987 supplement has 371 pages.

1042. Kravitz, William N. *Employee Benefit Plans; Mergers and Acquisitions.* New York: Practising Law Institute, 1981. 240 p.

1043. Kravitz, William N. *Introduction to Qualified Pension and Profit Sharing Plans.* Tax Law and Practice Course Handbook Series, 149. New York: Practising Law Institue, 1980. 392 p.

1044. Kravitz, William N. *Qualified Plans Which Invest in Employer Securities.* Tax Law and Practice Course Handbook Series, 206. New York: Practising Law Institute, 1984. 288 p.

1045. Kravitz, William N., and Smith, Charles R. *ESOPs and ESOP Transactions.* Tax Law and Practice Course Handbook Series, 231. New York: Practising Law Institute, 1985. 488 p.

1046. Kreps, Juanita, and Clark, Robert. *Sex, Age, and Work; The Changing Composition of the Labor Force.* Baltimore, MD: The Johns Hopkins University Press, 1975. 95 p.

1047. Krislov, Joseph. *State and Local Government Retirement Systems . . . 1965; A Survey of Systems Covering Employees Also Covered by the Federal Old-Age, Survivors, Disability, and Health Insurance Program.* Research Report, 15. Washington, DC: Social Security Administration, 1966. 82 p.

1048. Kroll, Arthur H. *Deferred Compensation Arrangements.* Tax Management Portfolios, 385. Washington, DC: Bureau of National Affairs, Inc., 1986. Various pagings.

1049. Kroll, Arthur H. *The ERISA Evolution Continues; The Tax Reform Act's Impact on Employee Benefits.* Paramus, NJ: Prentice-Hall Information Services, 1986. 40 p.

1050. Kroll, Arthur H. *Reporting and Disclosure under ERISA.* Tax Management Portfolios, 361–2nd. Washington, DC: Bureau of National Affairs, Inc., 1986. Various pagings.

1051. Kumata, Hideya. *Communication Dynamics for Employee Benefit Plans.* Brookfield, WI: International Foundation of Employee Benefit Plans, 1978. 113 p.

1052. Kurz, Mordecai, and Avrin, Marcy. *Private Pensions and Capital Formation.* Working Papers. Washington, DC: President's Commission on Pension Policy, 1980?. 10 p.

1053. Kurz, Mordecai, and Avrin, Marcy. *Social Security and Capital Formation; The Funding Controversy.* Working Papers. Washington, DC: President's Commission on Pension Policy, 1979. 16 p.

1054. Kurz, Mordecai, and Avrin, Marcy. *Technical Paper; The Funding Issue and Modern Growth Theory.* Working Papers. Washington, DC: President's Commission on Pension Policy, 1980?. 46 p.

1055. Kushner, Michael G. *ERISA; Qualified Plans and Fringe Benefits.* Corporate Practice Series, 45. Washington, DC: Bureau of National Affairs, Inc., 1985. Various pagings.

1056. Laarman, Linda M., and Hildebrandt, David A. *Plan Terminations and Mergers.* Tax Management Portfolios, 357. Washington, DC: Bureau of National Affairs, Inc., 1986. Various pagings.

1057. Lake, Robert G.; Rubin, Donald B. and Wiseman, Frederick. *Evaluation Study of the Formation of New Pension Plans.* Cambridge, MA: ABT Associates, Inc., 1979. 2 vols.
    This study was done for the Department of Labor to descry the effect of ERISA on the formation of new plans.

1058. Lapkoff, Shelley, and Fierst, Edith. *Working Women, Marriage and Retirement.* Working Papers. Washington, DC: President's Commission on Pension Policy, 1980. 50 p.

1059. Latimer, Murray W. *Industrial Pension Systems in the United States and Canada.* New York: Industrial Relations Counselors, Inc., 1932. 2 vols.

1060. Latimer, Murray W. *Trade Union Pension Systems.* New York: Industrial Relations Counselors, Inc., 1932. 205 p.

1061. Latta, Geoffrey. *Profit Sharing, Employee Stock Ownership, Savings and Asset Formation Plans in the Western World.* Philadelphia, PA: University of Pennsylvania. Wharton School. Industrial Research Unit, 1981. 192 p.

1062. Lawrence, Sharon. *The Status of State Mandatory Retirement Laws.* State Legislative Report vol. 10, no. 11. Denver, CO: National Conference of State Legislatures, 1985. 15 p.

1063. Lazear, Edward P. *Incentive Effects of Pensions.* NBER Working Paper, 1126. Cambridge, MA: National Bureau of Economic Research, 1983. 38 p.

1064. Lazear, Edward P. *Pensions as Severance Pay.* NBER Working Paper, 944. Cambridge, MA: National Bureau of Economic Research, 1982. 46 p.

1065. Lazear, Edward P. *Severance Pay, Pensions and Efficient Mobility.* NBER Working Paper, 854. Cambridge, MA: National Bureau of Economic Research, 1982. 36 p.

1066. Lazear, Edward P. *Social Security and Pensions.* NBER Working Papers, 1322. Cambridge, MA: National Bureau of Economic Research, 1984. 47 p.

1067. Lazear, Edward P., and Rosen, Sherwin. *Pension Inequality.* NBER Working Paper, 1477. Cambridge, MA: National Bureau of Economic Research, 1984. 28 p.

1068. Leavitt, Thomas D. *Early Retirement Incentive Programs.* Waltham, MA: Policy Center on Aging, 1983. 25 p.

1069. Lecht, Leonard A. *Expenditures for Retirement and Other Age Related Programs; A Major Shift in National Priorities.* New York: Academy for Educational Development, 1981. 64 p.

1070. Lee, John W. *ERISA; Fiduciary Responsibilities and Prohibited Transactions.* Tax Management Portfolios, 308. Washington, DC: Bureau of National Affairs, Inc., 1975. Various pagings.

1071. Lee, M. Mark. *ESOPs and the Smaller Employer.* An AMA Management Briefing. New York: AMACOM, 1979. 79 p.

1072. Lee, M. Mark. *ESOPs in the 80's.* An AMA Management Briefing. New York: American Management Association, 1985. 47 p.

1073. *Legal Issues in Pension Investment, 1985.* New York: Practising Law Institute, 1985. 483 p.

1074. *Legislative Changes Needed to Financially Strengthen Single Employer Pension Plan Insurance Program.* Washington, DC: U.S. General Accounting Office, 1983. 73 p.

1075. *Legislative History of the Employee Retirement Income Security Act of 1974, Public Law 93-406.* Prepared by the Subcommittee on Labor and Public Welfare, United States Senate. Washington, DC: U.S. Government Printing Office, 1976. 3 vols.

1076. *Legislative History of Welfare & Pension Plans Disclosure Act of 1958.* Buffalo, NY: W. S. Hein, 1978. 568 p.
Reprint of the 1962 edition emanating from the Department of Labor.

1077. Lehman, June M. *Handbook for Benefit Plan Professionals, 1985.* Brookfield, WI: International Foundation of Employee Benefit Plans, 1985. 62 p.

1078. Leimberg, Stephan R. *A Comparison; Life Insurance Inside or Outside a Qualified Retirement Plan.* A Market Builder Library Selection. Indianapolis, IN: R&R Newkirk, 1982. 116 p.

1079. Leo, Mario. *Financial Aspects of Private Pension Plans.* Morristown, NJ: Financial Executives Research Foundation, 1975.

1080. Leonard, Herman B. *The Federal Civil Service Retirement System; An Analysis of Its Financial Condition and Current Reform Proposals.* NBER Working Paper, 1258. Cambridge, MA: National Bureau of Economic Research, 1984. 80 p.

1081. Levin, Noel Arnold. *ERISA and Labor-Management Benefit Funds.* 2d ed. rev. New York: Practising Law Institute, 1975. 561 p.
First edition entitled *Labor-Management Benefit Funds.*

1082. Levin, Noel Arnold. *Guidelines for Fiduciaries of Taft-Hartley Trusts; An ERISA Manual.* Brookfield, WI: International Foundation of Employee Benefit Plans, 1980. 137 p.

1083. Levin, Noel Arnold. *Negotiating Fringe Benefits.* New York: AMACOM, 1973. 39 p.

1084. Levin, Noel Arnold, and Brossman, Mark E. *Social Investing for Pension Funds; For Love or Money.* Brookfield, WI: International Foundation of Employee Benefit Plans, 1982. 113 p.

1085. Levine, Sumner N. *Investment Manager's Handbook.* Homewood, IL: Dow Jones-Irwin, 1980. 1,037 p.

1086. Levy, Robert A. *What You Should Know about Performance Measurement.* Silver Spring, MD: Computer Directions Advisors, Inc., 198?–. 15 p.

1087. *Limited Period Early Retirement Incentive Programs.* New York: Towers, Perrin, Forster & Crosby, 1982. 24 p.

1088. *Linkages between Private Pensions and Social Security Reform; An Information Paper.* Prepared for use by the Special Committee on Aging. Washington, DC: U.S. Government Printing Office, 1982. 33 p.

1089. *List of References on the Pension Systems of Corporation and Firms.* Washington, DC: U.S. Library of Congress, Division of Bibliography, 1921. 11 p.

1090. Lister, Harry J. *Your Guide to IRAs and Fourteen Other Retirement Plans.* Glenview, IL: Scott Foresman & Co., 1985. 224 p.

1091. Litvak, Lawrence. *Pension Funds & Economic Renewal.* Studies in Development Policy, 12. Washington, DC: The Council of State Planning Agencies, 1981. 185 p.

1092. Litvak, Lawrence, and Barker, Michael. *Pension Funds & Economic Development; How Public and Private Pension Funds Can Contribute to the Pennsylvania Economy.* Harrisburg, PA: Pennsylvania MILRITE Council, 1983. 92 leaves.

1093. Litvak, Lawrence; Estrella, Julia; and McTigue, Kathleen. *Divesting from South Africa; A Prudent Approach for Pension Funds.* Oakland, CA: Community Economics, Inc., 1981. 53 p.

1094. *Living with ERISA; A Transcript of a MAPI Conference, December 11–12, 1975.* Washington, DC: Machinery and Allied Products Institute, 1976. 246 p.

1095. LoCicero, Joseph A. *Multiemployer Pension Plans; What Employers Should Know.* Morristown, NJ: Financial Executives Research Foundation, 1985. 21 p.

1096. Logue, Dennis E. *Legislative Influence on Corporate Pension Plans.* Washington, DC: American Enterprise Institute for Public Policy Research, 1979. 109 p.

1097. Logue, Dennis E. *Pension Plans at Risk; A Potential Hazard of Deficit Reduction and Tax Reform.* Dallas, TX: National Center for Policy Analysis, 1985. 17 p.

1098. Logue, Dennis E., and Rogalski, Richard J. *Managing Corporate Pension Plans; The Impacts of Inflation.* AEI Studies, 355. Washington, DC: American Enterprise Institute for Public Policy Research, 1984. 68 p.

1099. Lorne, Simon M. *Securities Law Considerations Affecting Employee Benefit Plans.* Tax Management Portfolios, 362. Washington, DC: Bureau of National Affairs, Inc., 1982. Various pagings.

1100. Lorne, Simon M., and Morgan, R. Gregory. *Securities Law Considerations Affecting Employee Benefit Plans.* Corporate Practice Series, 44. Washington, DC: Bureau of National Affairs, Inc., 1985. Various pagings.

1101. Louis Harris & Associates, Inc. *Retirement and Income; A National Research Report of Behavior and Opinion Concerning Retirement, Pensions and Social Security.* Garland Reference Library of Social Science, 142. New York: Garland, 1984. 121 p.

1102. Lucas, Harry. *Pensions & Industrial Relations; A Practical Guide for All Involved in Pensions.* Elmsford, NY: Pergamon Press, 1977.

1103. Lucas, Ronald J. *Pension Planning within a Major Company.* Elmsford, NY: Pergamon Press, 1979.

1104. Ludwig, Ronald L., and Reichler, Richard. *Employee Stock Ownership Plans under the 1984 Tax Law.* New York: Law and Business, 1984. 417 p.

1105. *Lump-Sum Distributions to Employees under Tax Reform Act.* Chicago: Commerce Clearing House, Inc., 1970. 24 p.

1106. Lutz, Carl F. *How to Develop, Conduct and Use a Pay/Fringe Benefit Survey.* Crete, IL: Abbott Langer & Associates, 1986. 211 p.

1107. Lynn, Robert J. *The Pension Crisis.* Lexington, MA: Lexington Books, 1983. 175 p.

1108. MacDonald, Jeffrey A., and Bingham, Anne. *Pension Handbook for Union Negotiators.* Washington, DC: Bureau of National Affairs, Inc., 1986. 189 p.

1109. Mackin, John P. *Protecting Purchasing Power in Retirement; A Study of Public Employee Retirement Systems.* New York: Fleet Academic Editions, Inc., 1971. 249 p.

1110. *A Macroeconomic-Demographic Model of the U.S. Retirement Income System; Final Report to the National Institute on Aging and the President's Commission on Pension Policy, September, 1981.* By ICF Incorporated. Washington, DC: ICF Incorporated, 1981. 2 vols.

1111. Maginn, John L., and Tuttle, Donald L. *Managing Investment Portfolios; A Dynamic Process.* Sponsored by the Institute of Chartered Financial Analysts. Boston: Warren, Gorham & Lamont, 1983. 712 p.

1112. *Magnetic Tape Reporting; Submitting Annuity, Pension, Retired Pay or IRA Payments to the Social Security Administration.* SSA Pub. No. 42–034. Washington, DC: Social Security Administration, 1984. 28 p.

1113. Malca, Edward. *Bank-Administered Commingled Pension Funds; Performance and Characteristics, 1962–1970.* Lexington, MA: Lexington Books, 1973. 93 p.

1114. Malca, Edward. *Pension Funds and Other Institutional Investors; Performance and Evaluation.* Lexington, MA: Lexington Books, 1975. 140 p.

1115. Mamorsky, Jeffrey D. *Employee Benefits Law; ERISA and Beyond.* New York: Law Journal Seminars-Press, 1980. Various pagings.

1116. Mamorsky, Jeffrey D. *Pension and Profit-Sharing Plans; A Basic Guide.* New York: Executive Enterprises Publications, Co., 1977. 301 p.

1117. Mamorsky, Jeffrey D., ed. *Employee Benefits Handbook.* Rev. ed. Editorial Advisor, Fred K. Foulkes. Boston: Warren, Gorham & Lamont, 1987. Various pagings.

1118. Marcus, Alan J. *Corporate Pension Policy and the Value of PBGC Insurance.* NBER Working Paper, 1217. Cambridge, MA: National Bureau of Economic Research, 1983. 34 p.

1119. Mares, Judith W. *The Use of Pension Fund Capital; Its Social and Economic Implications, Some Background Issues.* Working Papers. Washington, DC: President's Commission on Pension Policy, 1980?. 32 p.

1120. *The Market for Employee Benefits; Patterns of Purchasing Administration and Responsibility.* Costa Mesa, CA: A. C. Croft, 1986. 40 p.

1121. Markus, Bruce W. *The Prudent Man; Making Decisions under ERISA.* New York: Pensions and Investments, 1978. 110 p.

1122. Marples, William F. *Actuarial Aspects of Pension Security.* Homewood, IL: Published for the Pension Research Council by Richard D. Irwin, Inc., 1965. 210 p.

1123. Marshall, Ray. *The Multiemployer Pension Plan Amendments Act of 1980; A Report to the Council on Multiemployer Pension Security.* 1985. 80 p.

1124. Martin, Linda J. *Pension Obligations, Subordination and Bond Ratings.* Research Report 84–7. Brookfield, WI: International Foundation of Employee Benefit Plans, 1984. 7 p.

1125. Martorana, R. George. *Your Pension & Your Spouse; The Joint & Survivor Dilemma.* Brookfield, WI: International Foundation of Employee Benefit Plans, 1985. 28 p.

1126. Matthews, Joseph L., and Berman, Dorothy Matthews. *Social Security, Medicare & Pensions; A Sourcebook for Older Americans.* Berkeley, CA: Nolo Press, 1987. 275 p.

1127. McCarthy, David. *Findings from the Survey of Private Pension Benefit Amounts.* Washington, DC: U.S. Department of Labor, Office of Pension and Welfare Benefit Programs, 1985. 77 p.

1128. McClanahan, Donald Townes. *Pension Plans & Pension Funding Simplified for Non-Actuaries.* St. Louis, MO: Pension Service Publishing Co., 1980. 453 p.

1129. McCord, Thomas I., and Dorelan, Raymond W. *ERISA Plan Administrator's Desk Book with Checklists and Guidelines for Successful Communications.* 2d ed. Englewood Cliffs, NJ: Institute for Business Planning, 1979. 528 p.

1130. McDonald, Maurice E. *Reciprocity among Private Multiemployer Pension Plans.* Homewood, IL: Published for the Pension Research Council by Richard D. Irwin, Inc., 1975. 283 p.

1131. McGee, Robert W. *Employee Stock Ownership Plans; A Guide to ESOPs under the Latest Rules.* Englewood Cliffs, NJ: Prentice-Hall, Inc., 1985. 44 p.

1132. McGee, Robert W. *How Tax Reform Would Affect Profit Sharing.* Pension Planning Series. Paramus, NJ: Prentice-Hall, Inc., 1986. 23 p.

1133. McGill, Dan M. *Employer Guarantee of Pension Benefits.* Homewood, IL: Published for the Pension Research Council by Richard D. Irwin, Inc., 1974. 49 p.

1134. McGill, Dan M. *Financing the Civil Service Retirement System; A Threat to Fiscal Integrity.* Homewood, IL: Published for the Pension Research Council by Richard D. Irwin, Inc., 1979. 170 p.

1135. McGill, Dan M. *Fulfilling Pension Expectations.* Homewood, IL: Published for the Pension Research Council by Richard D. Irwin, Inc., 1962. 314 p.

1136. McGill, Dan M. *Guaranty Fund for Private Pension Obligations.* Homewood, IL: Published for the Pension Research Council by Richard D. Irwin, Inc., 1970. 190 p.

1137. McGill, Dan M. *Pensions; Problems and Trends.* Homewood, IL: Published for the S.S. Huebner Foundation for Insurance Education by Richard D. Irwin, Inc., 1955. 211 p.

1138. McGill, Dan M. *Preservation of Pension Benefit Rights.* Homewood, IL: Published for the Pension Research Council by Richard D. Irwin, Inc., 1971. 382 p.

1139. McGill, Dan M. *Social Security and Private Pension Plans; Competitive or Complementary?* Homewood, IL: Richard D. Irwin, 1977. 175 p.

1140. McGill, Dan M., ed. *Social Investing of Pension Plan Assets.* Homewood, IL: Published for the Pension Research Council by Richard D. Irwin, Inc., 1984. 162 p.

1141. McGill, Dan M., and Grubbs, Donald S., Jr. *Fundamentals of Private Pensions.* Homewood, IL: Published for the Pension Research Council by Richard D. Irwin, Inc., 1984. 754 p.
This is the most often used basic text in the retirement plan area. Its resemblance to the first edition of 1955 is minute.

1142. McGinn, Daniel F. *Actuarial Fundamentals for Multiemployer Plans.* Brookfield, WI: International Foundation of Employee Benefit Plans, 1982. 122 p.
I have what appears to be a 1975 edition entitled *Actuarial Primer for Trustees.*

1143. McGinn, Daniel F. *Joint Trust Pension Plans; Understanding and Administering Collectively Bargained Multiemployer Plans under ERISA.* Homewood, IL: Published for the Pension Research Council by Richard D. Irwin, Inc., 1978. 351 p.

1144. McKelvy, Natalie. *Pension Fund Investments in Real Estate; A Guide for Plan Sponsors and Real Estate Professionals.* Westport, CT: Quorum Books, 1983. 299 p.

1145. McNulty, James E. *Decision & Influence Processes in Private Pension Plans.* Homewood, IL: Richard D. Irwin, Inc., 1961.

1146. *Measuring and Reporting Investment Performance of Pension Funds.* Elm Grove, IL: National Foundation of Health Welfare and Pension Plans, 1966. 36 p.

1147. Meier, Elizabeth L. *Employment of Older Workers; Disincentives and Incentives.* Washington, DC: President's Commission on Pension Policy, 1980. 60 p.

1148. Meier, Elizabeth L. *Portability of Pensions.* Working Papers. Washington, DC: President's Commission on Pension Policy, 1981.

1149. Meier, Elizabeth L., and Bremberg, Helen K. *ERISA; Progress and Problems, An Early Assessment of the Pension Reform Law and Its Impact on Older Workers.* Washington, DC: The National Council on the Aging, Inc., 1977. 58 p.

1150. Meier, Elizabeth L., and Dittmar, Cynthia C. *Income of the Retired; Levels and Sources.* Washington, DC: President's Commission on Pension Policy. 1980. 87 p.

1151. Meier, Elizabeth L., and Dittmar, Cynthia C. *Varieties of Retirement Ages.* Working Papers. Washington, DC: President's Commission on Pension Policy, 1979. 117 p.

1152. Meier, Elizabeth L.; Dittmar, Cynthia C.; and Torrey, Barbara Boyle. *Retirement Income Goals.* Working Papers. Washington, DC: President's Commission on Pension Policy, 1980. 60 p.

1153. Meier, Joseph B., ed. *Profit Sharing Manual.* 2d ed. Chicago: Council of Profit Sharing Industries, 1957. 463 p.

1154. Melone, Joseph J. *Collectively Bargained Multi-Employer Pension Plans.* Homewood, IL: Published for the Pension Research Council by Richard D. Irwin, Inc., 1963. 191 p.

1155. Meriam, Lewis. *Principles Governing the Retirement of Public Employees.* New York: D. Appleton and Co., 1918. 450 p.

1156. Merkle, Ned. *Do's and Don'ts of Pension Fund Management.* AMA Management Briefing. New York: AMACOM, 1981. 55 p.

1157. Merton, Robert C. *On Consumption-Indexed Public Pension Plans.* NBER Working Paper, 910. Cambridge, MA: National Bureau of Economic Research, 1982. 32 p.

1158. Merton, Robert C.; Bodie, Zvi; and Marcus, Alan J. *Pension Plan Integration as Insurance against Social Security Risk.* NBER Working Paper, 1370. Cambridge, MA: National Bureau of Economic Research, 1984. 35 p.

1159. Metzger, Bert L. *Employee Investment Choice in Deferred Profit Sharing.* Evanston, IL: Profit Sharing Research Foundation, 1975. 22 p.

1160. Metzger, Bert L. *Investment Practices, Performance, and Management of Profit Sharing Trust Funds.* Evanston, IL: Profit Sharing Research Foundation, 1969. 620 p.

1161. Metzger, Bert L. *Pension, Profit Sharing or Both? Profit Sharing, Thrift and Stock Plans, Viable Supplements or Alternatives to Pension Plans.* Evanston, IL: Profit Sharing Research Foundation, 1975. 56 p.

1162. Metzger, Bert L., ed. *The Future of Profit Sharing.* Evanston, IL: Profit Sharing Research Foundation, 1979. 38 p.

1163. Meuche, Arthur J. *Successful Pension Planning.* New York: Prentice-Hall, Inc., 1949. 77 p.

1164. Meyer, Mitchell, and Fox, Harland. *Early Retirement Programs; A Research Report.* Conference Board Report, 532. New York: The Conference Board, 1971. 42 p.

1165. *Military Retirement Accounting Changes; The Administration's Proposals.* Staff Working Paper. Washington, DC: Congressional Budget Office, 1978. 25 p.

1166. *Military Retirement; The Administration's Plan and Related Proposals.* Legislative Analysis; 96th Congress, 19. Washington, DC: American Enterprise Institute for Public Policy Research, 1980. 86 p.

1167. Miller, Bruce Alan. *Employee Benefits; Mergers and Acquisitions.* New York: Practising Law Institute, 1985. 334 p.

1168. Miller, Elliott I. *Pension Reform Act of '74.* Tax Law and Practice Course Handbook Series, 78. New York: Practising Law Institute, 1974. 600 p.

1169. Miller, Elliott I. *Pension Reform Update.* Tax Law and Practice Course Handbook Series, 116. New York: Practising Law Institute, 1977. 528 p.

1170. Miller, Elliott I. *Pension Reform Update, 1978.* Tax Law and Practice Course Handbook Series, 128. New York: Practising Law Institute, 1978. 536 p.

1171. Miller, Harvey R., and Ordin, Robert L. *Labor & ERISA Law; In and out of the Bankruptcy Courts.* New York: Law & Business, Inc., 1984. 421 p.

1172. Miller, Meredith. *The Collective Bargaining Process for Fringe Benefits in the Private Sector.* Research Report, 84–8. Brookfield, WI: International Foundation of Employee Benefit Plans, 1984. 19 p.

1173. Miller, Ned A. *Nonsalary Compensation for Employees of Independent Schools.* Boston: National Association of Independent Schools, 1985. 38 p.

1174. Mitchell, Olivia S. *The Labor Market Impact of Federal Regulation: OSHA, ERISA, EEO and Minimum Wage.* NBER Working Paper, 844. Cambridge, MA: National Bureau of Economic Research, 1982. 51 p.

1175. Mitchell, Olivia S., and Fields, Gary S. *Economic Incentives to Retire; A Qualitative Choice Approach.* NBER Working Paper, 1096. Cambridge, MA: National Bureau of Economic Research, 1983. 19 p.

1176. Mitchell, Olivia S., and Fields, Gary S. *The Economics of Retirement Behavior.* NBER Working Paper, 1128. Cambridge, MA: National Bureau of Economic Research, 1983. 28 p.

1177. Mitchell, Olivia S., and Fields, Gary S. *The Effects of Pensions and Earnings on Retirement; A Review Essay.* NBER Working Paper, 772. Cambridge, MA: National Bureau of Economic Research, 1981. 55 p.

1178. Mitchell, Olivia S., and Fields, Gary S. *Rewards to Continued Work; The Economic Incentives for Postponing Retirement.* NBER Working Paper, 1204. Cambridge, MA: National Bureau of Economic Research, 1983. 24 p.

1179. Monfried, Thomas S., and Karas, James N., Jr. *Reporting and Disclosure Requirements.* Pension and Profit-Sharing Plans. Series D, Folio 3. Philadelphia, PA: American Law Institute-American Bar Association. Committee on Continuing Professional Education, 1979. 41 p.

1180. Monroe, Stuart A. *Nonqualified Salary Continuation Plans.* New York: Farnsworth Publishing Co., 1979?. Various pagings.

1181. Montana, Patrick J. *Retirement Plans; How to Develop and Implement Them.* Englewood Cliffs, NJ: Prentice-Hall, Inc., 1985. 126 p.

1182. Montanaro, Edward. *Strategic Investment of the Florida Retirement System Trust Fund; An Examination of the Legal, Economic and Programmatic Considerations.* Tallahassee, FL: Florida Advisory Council on Intergovernmental Relations, 1982. 41 p.

1183. Mortimer, Terry J. *Accounting for Pensions by Employers; A Background Paper.* Stamford, CT: Financial Accounting Standards Board, 1980. 12 p.

1184. *Multiemployer Pension Plan Amendments Act of 1980; PL 96–364 as Signed by the President on September 26, 1980, Law and Explanation.* CCH Editorial Staff Publication. Chicago: Commerce Clearing House, Inc., 1980. 256 p.

1185. *The Multiemployer Pension Plan Amendments Act of 1979; Report Together with Separate and Individual Views.* Report 96–869 Part I. Washington, DC: n.p., 1980. 225 p.

1186. *Multiemployer Pension Plan Data Are Inaccurate and Incomplete.* Washington, DC: U.S. General Accounting Office, 1982. 10 p.

1187. *Multiemployer Pension Plans under Collective Bargaining, Spring 1960.* Bulletin, 1326. Washington, DC: U.S. Department of Labor, 1962. 131 p.

1188. *Multiemployer Pension Plans; What Employers Should Know.* New York?: Buck Consultants, Inc., 1985. 25 p.

1189. *The Multiemployer Plan.* Washington, DC: Employee Benefit Research Institute, 1981. 8 p.

1190. Munnell, Alicia H. *The Economics of Private Pensions.* Studies in Social Economics. Washington, DC: Brookings Institution, 1982. 240 p.

1191. Munnell, Alicia H., and Connolly, Ann M. *Pensions for Public Employees.* Washington, DC: National Planning Association, 1979. 102 p.

1192. Murray, Donald X., ed. *Representative Forms and Records for the Administration of Profit Sharing Plans.* Chicago: Council of Profit Sharing Industries, 1970. 182 p.

1193. Murray, Donald X., ed. *Successful Profit Sharing Plans; Theory and Practice.* Chicago: Council of Profit Sharing Industries, 1968. 157 p.

1194. Murray, Roger F. *Economic Aspects of Pensions; A Summary Report.* General Series, 85. New York: National Bureau of Economic Research, 1968. 132 p.

1195. Murray, Samuel H. *Analysis of the Pension Reform Act of 1974, P.L. 93-406.* New York: Matthew Bender, 1974. 138 p.

1196. Myers, Robert J. *Indexation of Pension and Other Benefits.* Homewood, IL: Published for the Pension Research Council by Richard D. Irwin, Inc., 1978. 153 p.

1197. Myles, John. *Old Age in the Welfare State; The Political Economy of Public Pensions.* Little Brown Series on Gerontology. Boston: Little, Brown, 1984. 140 p.

1198. Nader, Ralph, and Blackwell, Kate. *You and Your Pension.* Washington, DC?: Center for Responsive Law, 1973. 215 p.

1199. Nalebuff, Barry, and Zeckhauser, Richard. *Pensions and the Retirement Decision.* NBER Working Paper, 1285. Cambridge, MA: National Bureau of Economic Research, 1984. 40 p.

1200. National Council on Governmental Accounting. *Pension Accounting and Financial Reporting; Public Employee Retirement Systems and State and Local Government Employers.* Statement, 6. Chicago, 1983. 35 p.

1201. *National Directory of Pension Funds That Invest in Real Estate Investments and Mortgages.* Brooklyn, NY: Communication Network International, Inc., n.d.

1202. *Need for Overall Policy and Coordinated Management of Federal Retirement Systems; Report.* Washington, DC: U.S. General Accounting Office, 1978. 2 vols.

1203. Nektarios, Miltiades. *Public Pensions, Capital Formation and Economic Growth.* Boulder, CO: Westview Press, 1982. 184 p.

1204. Nestingen, Carolyn S., and Glassman, Arthur J. *Estate and Retirement Planning for Employee Benefits.* St. Paul, MN: Advanced Legal Education. Hamline University School of Law, 1984. 69 p.

1205. *New Directions in the Investment & Control of Pension Funds.* Washington, DC: Investor Responsibility Research Center, 1983. 120 p.

1206. *New Employee Benefits under Tax Reform Act of 1986; Law and Explanation.* Chicago: Commerce Clearing House, Inc., 1986. 227 p.

1207. *New 1986 Mandatory Retirement and Maximum Age Benefit Rules; Law and Explanation.* Chicago: Commerce Clearing House, Inc., 1986. 62 p.

1208. *New Pension and Employee Benefits Provisions; Including Revenue Act of 1978; Pregnancy Discrimination Amendment, ERISA Reorganization Plan.* Chicago: Commerce Clearing House, Inc., 1978. Various pagings.

1209. *New Pension Legislation; ALI-ABA Course of Study Materials.* Philadelphia, PA: American Law Institute-American Bar Association. Committee on Continuing Professional Education, 1982. 429 p.

1210. *New Pension Legislation; ALI-ABA Video Law Review Study Materials.* Philadelphia, PA: American Law Institute-American Bar Association. Committee on Continuing Professional Education, 1982. 413 p.

1211. *New Pension Rules under 1982 Tax Law, As Signed by the President on September 3, 1982.* Chicago: Commerce Clearing House, Inc., 1982. 32 p.

1212. *1980 Multiemployer Pension Amendments; Overview of Effects and Issues.* Washington, DC: U.S. General Accounting Office, 1986. 33 p.

1213. *The 1980 Multiemployer Pension Plan Admendments Act; An Assessment of Funding Requirement Changes.* Washington, DC: U.S. General Accounting Office, 1985. 75 p.

1214. *1986 Tax Reform Act; Summary of Employee Benefit Provisions and Required Action.* New York: Martin E. Segal Co., 1986. 19 p.

1215. *The 1974 Pension Reform Act; A Reference.* New York: Ernst & Ernst, 1974. 158 p.

1216. Nix, William, and Nix, Susan. *The Dow Jones-Irwin Guide to Stock Index Futures and Options.* Homewood, IL: Dow Jones-Irwin, 1984. 255 p.

1217. Novikoff, Harold S., and Susko, Richard. *ERISA and Bankruptcy.* Commercial Law and Practice Course Handbook Series, 296. New York: Practising Law Institute, 1983. 656 p.

1218. Obrentz, Bert N., and Woodward, Arthur F. *ERISA; The Multiemployer Pension Plan Amendments Act of 1980.* Tax Law and Practice Course Handbook Series, 208. New York: Practising Law Institute, 1984. 112 p.

1219. O'Connell, Marjorie A., and Kittrell, Steven D. *Retirement Equity Act; Divorce & Pensions.* Washington, DC: Divorce Taxation Education, 1985.

1220. O'Connell, Michael J. *Early Retirement in Public Safety Organizations.* Working Papers. Washington, DC: President's Commission on Pension Policy, 1981.

1221. O'Farrell, Brendan. *Pensions and Divorce; The Rights of Divorced Spouses as They Pertain to Pension Benefits Earned in the Course of Employment during Marriage.* Working Papers. Washington, DC: President's Commission on Pension Policy, 1981. 41 p.

1222. *Official ERISA Guidelines for the Adoption or Amendment of Employee Benefit Plans.* Issued jointly by the Internal Revenue Service and the Department of Labor. Englewood Cliffs, NJ: Prentice-Hall, Inc., 1976. 212 p.

1223. *Often-Asked Questions about the Employee Retirement Income Security Act of 1974.* Washington, DC: U.S. Department of Labor, 1975?. 28 p.

1224. Ohio Retirement Study Commission. *The Divestment of Ohio Public Pension Funds in U.S. Companies Which Do Business in South Africa.* Columbus, OH, 1983. 40 p.

1225. Older, Jack S. *Individual Retirement Accounts.* Pension and Profit Sharing Plans. Series A, Folio 7. Philadelphia, PA: American Law Institute-American Bar Association. Committee on Continuing Professional Education, 1978. 47 p.

1226. Olian, Judy D.; Carroll, Stephen J., Jr.; and Schneier, Craig E. *Pension Plans; The Human Resource Management Perspective.* Key Issues, 28. Ithaca, NY: ILR Press, 1985. 49 p.

1227. Olian, Judy D.; Carroll, Stephen J., Jr.; and Schneier, Craig E. *Pensions and Personnel/Human Resource Management; Documented and Potential Impacts of Pensions on Human Resource Management Systems and Individual Work Behaviors.* Working Papers. Washington, DC: President's Commission on Pension Policy, 1981.

1228. Ollinger, W. James. *Multiemployer Pension Plans.* Tax Law and Practice Course Handbook Series, 136. New York: Practising Law Institute, 1979. 632 p.

1229. *On Your Retirement; Tax and Benefit Considerations.* Chicago: Commerce Clearing House, Inc., 1982. 96 p.

1230. Orenstein, Melvin. *Taxation of Fringe Benefits under the Latest Rules.* Paramus, NJ: Prentice-Hall Information Services, 1986. 39 p.

1231. Osgood, Russell K. *The Law of Pensions and Profit-Sharing; . . . 1986 Supplement.* Boston: Little, Brown, 1986. 160 p.

1232. Osgood, Russell K. *The Law of Pensions and Profit-Sharing; Qualified Retirement Plans and Other Deferred Compensation Arrangements.* Boston: Little, Brown, 1984. 454 p.

1233. *Our Town out of South Africa; A Key to Gaining Community Control of Public Pension Funds.* New York: Africa Fund, 1982. 125 p.

1234. *Overfunded Pension Plans; Considering Your Options.* New York?: Ernst & Whinney, 1985. 28 p.

1235. *Oversight Inquiry of the Department of Labor's Investigation of the Teamsters Central States Pension Fund.* Washington, DC: U.S. Government Printing Office, 1981. 191 p.

1236. *Overview of Tax-Favored Retirement Arrangements.* Prepared by the staff of the Joint Committee on Taxation. Washington, DC: U.S. Government Printing Office, 1985. 31 p.

1237. Owen, E. H., and Werner, L. *Accounting for Pension Costs.* New York?: Peat, Marwick, Mitchell & Co. 1967. 41 p.

1238. Paley, Stephen H. *Advising Professional Corporations after TEFRA; An Advanced Tax and Business Planning Program.* Tax Law and Practice Course Handbook Series, 183. New York: Practising Law Institute, 1983. 616 p.

1239. Paley, Stephen H. *Professional Corporations and Small Businesses after the Tax Reform Act of 1984.* New York: Practising Law Institute, 1984. 664 p.

1240. Pancheri, Michael P., and Flynn, David H. *The IRA Handbook; A Complete Guide.* Piscataway, NJ: New Century, 1984. 192 p.

1241. Parkington, John J., and Schiemann, William A., eds. *Employee Benefits; Regaining Control, a Hands-on Resource for the Human Resource Executive.* New York: Opinion Research Corp., 1985. 212 p.

1242. Parnes, Herbert S., et al. *Retirement among American Men.* Lexington, MA: Lexington Books, 1985. 233 p.

1243. Parsons, R. David. *Employers Accounting for Pensions; A Basic Guide to FASB Statement No. 87.* Atlanta, GA: The Hazlehurst Group, 1986. 29 p.

1244. *Participant-Directed Pension and Profit-Sharing Plans and Defined Benefit HR 10 Plans; ALI-ABA Course of Study Materials.* Philadelphia, PA: American Law Institute-American Bar Association. Committee on Continuing Professional Education, 1981. 129 p.

1245. Patten, Thomas H., Jr. *A Bibliography of Compensation Planning and Administration Publications, 1975–1985.* 3d ed. Scottsdale, AZ: American Compensation Association, 1987. 105 p.
    In the ten pages on retirement plans, there are exemplary journal articles.

1246. Patterson, Archibald L. *Public Pension Administration.* Athens, GA: University of Georgia, Institute of Government, 1982. 108 p.

1247. Patterson, Edwin W. *Legal Protection of Private Pension Expectations.* Homewood, IL: Published for the Pension Research Council by Richard D. Irwin, Inc., 1960. 286 p.

1248. Paul, Carolyn E., et al. *The Costs and Benefits of Deferred Retirement; A Case Study at the City of Los Angeles, Executive Summary.* Los Angeles, CA: University of Southern California. Ethel Percey Andrus Retirement Center, 1982. 28 p.

1249. Peckman, David A. *Employee Stock Ownership Plans; A Decision Maker's Guide.* An EBRI Issue Report. Washington, DC: Employee Benefits Research Institute, 1983. 55 p.

1250. Pellechio, Anthony J. *The Effect of Social Security on Retirement.* NBER Working Paper, 260. Cambridge, MA: National Bureau of Economic Research, 1978.

1251. Pellechio, Anthony J. *Social Security and the Decision to Retire.* NBER Working Paper, 734. Cambridge, MA: National Bureau of Economic Research, 1981. 45 p.

1252. *Pension and Profit-Sharing; Plans and Clauses.* Chicago: Commerce Clearing House, Inc., 1958. 459 p.

1253. *Pension and Profit-Sharing Plans and Trusts; Explanatory Digests of the Internal Revenue Code and Regulations.* New York: Prentice-Hall, Inc., 1943. 40 p.

1254. *Pension and Profit-Sharing Trusts.* New York: Research Institute of America, 1941. 15 p.

1255. *Pension and Retirement Planning for Small Businesses and Professionals; ALI-ABA Course of Study Materials.* Philadelphia, PA: American Law Institute-American Bar Association. Committee on Continuing Professional Education, 1985. 403 p.
    Previous editions came out in 1983 and 1984.

1256. *Pension Asset Management; The Corporate Decision.* Prepared by FRS Associates for the Financial Executives Research Foundation. New York: 1980. 285 p.

1257. Pension Benefit Guaranty Corp. *Actuarial Tables Effective for Terminations from October 1, 1975 through August 31, 1976.* PBGC, 504. Washington, DC, 1977. 165 p.

1258. Pension Benefit Guaranty Corp. *Actuarial Tables Effective for Terminations from September 1, 1976 through February 28, 1978.* PBGC, 506. Washington, DC, 1978. 125 p.

1259. Pension Benefit Guaranty Corp. *Actuarial Tables Effective for Terminations from September 2, 1974 through September 30, 1975.* PBGC, 502. Washington, DC, 1977. 43 p.

1260. Pension Benefit Guaranty Corp. *Actuarial Tables Effective for Terminations March 1, 1978 through November 30, 1980.* PBGC, 508. Washington, DC, 1980. Various pagings.

1261. Pension Benefit Guaranty Corp. *An Analysis of Issues Related to Contingent Employer Liability Insurance and the Role of the Pension Benefit Guaranty Corporation in the Private Pension System.* Washington, DC, 1978. 27 p.

1262. Pension Benefit Guaranty Corp. *Analysis of Single Employer Defined Benefit Plan Terminations, 1976.* PBGC, 505. Washington, DC, 1977. 17 p.

1263. Pension Benefit Guaranty Corp. *Analysis of Single Employer Defined Benefit Plan Terminations, 1977.* PBGC, 507. Washington, DC, 1978.

1264. Pension Benefit Guaranty Corp. *Analysis of Single Employer Defined Benefit Plan Terminations, 1978.* Washington, DC, 1981. 46 p.

1265. Pension Benefit Guaranty Corp. *Contingent Employer Liability Insurance; Status Report to Congress.* Washington, DC, 1978. 57 p.

1266. Pension Benefit Guaranty Corp. *Guidelines on Voluntary Termination.* PBGC, 503. Washington, DC, 1977. 8 p.

1267. Pension Benefit Guaranty Corp. *Mortality Tables.* PBGC, 501. Washington, DC, 1977. 10 p.

1268. Pension Benefit Guaranty Corp. *Multiemployer Study Required by P.L. 95–214. July 1, 1978.* Washington, DC, 1978. 164 p.

1269. Pension Benefit Guaranty Corp. *Potential Multiemployer Plan Liabilities under the Title IV of ERISA.* Washington, DC, 1977. 12 p.

1270. Pension Benefit Guaranty Corp. *Prospective Actuarial and Mortality Tables.* PBGC, 509. Washington, DC, 1985. 978 p.

1271. Pension Benefit Guaranty Corp. *Recommendations to Congress for Revising Multiemployer Plan Termination Insurance.* Washington, DC, 1979. 18 p.

1272. *Pension Book Reserves in West Germany; Their Application to Other Countries, Their Potential Applicability to the United States; A Research Study.* Prepared for the Financial Executives Research Foundation by Towers, Perrin, Forster and Crosby. Morristown, NJ: FERF, 1983. 110 p.

1273. *Pension Cost Method Analysis.* Washington, DC: American Academy of Actuaries. Committee on Pension Actuarial Principles and Practices, 1985. 14 vols.
> The principal purpose is to provide the FASB a basis for evaluating the degree to which expense for defined benefit plans may vary when based upon one of five actuarial cost methods. Two volumes and several pages of other volumes were revised in 1986.

1274. *Pension Costs and Active Bond Management.* New York: Bankers Trust Co., 1974. 36 p.

1275. *Pension Costs; Oversight of Contractor Pension Costs Could Be Improved.* Washington, DC: U. S. General Accounting Office, 1986. 18 p.

1276. *Pension Coverage and Expected Retirement Benefits; Final Report.* Prepared for the American Council of Life Insurance by ICF Incorporated. Washington, DC: ICF Incorporated, 1982. 2 vols.

1277. *Pension Directory.* Washington, DC: President's Commission on Pension Policy, 1979. 116 p.

1278. *Pension Fund Investment in Agricultural Land.* Washington, DC: U.S. General Accounting Office, 1981. 32 p.

1279. *The Pension Game; The American Pension System from the Viewpoint of the Average Woman.* Washington, DC: U.S. Government Printing Office, 1979. 78 p.

1280. *Pension Integration; How Large Defined Benefit Plans Coordinate Benefits with Social Security.* Washington, DC: U.S. General Accounting Office, 1986. 28 p.

1281. *Pension Investments; A Social Audit, A CDE Handbook.* New York: Corporate Data Exchange, Inc., 1979. 125 p.

1282. *Pension Law and Practice Update; ALI-ABA Video Law Review Study Materials.* Philadelphia, PA: American Law Institute-American Bar Association. Committee on Continuing Professional Education, 1985. 234 p.

1283. *The Pension Plan.* Washington, DC: Employee Benefit Research Institute, 1980. 8 p.

1284. *Pension Plan Terminations with Asset Reversions; Final Report.* To the U.S. Department of Labor by Hay/Huggins Co., Inc. Washington, DC?: Hay/Huggins Co., Inc., 1986. 64 p.

1285. *Pension Planning; Terms & Topics.* Chicago: Commerce Clearing House, Inc., 1985. 32 p.

1286. *Pension Plans and Compensation for the Small Employer; ALI-ABA Course of Study Materials.* Philadelphia, PA: American Law Institute-American Bar Association. Committee on Continuing Professional Education, 1981. 263 p.

1287. *Pension Plans at Risk; A Potential Hazard of Deficit Reduction and Tax Reform.* Dallas, TX: National Center for Policy Analysis, 1985. 17 p.

1288. *Pension Plans under Collective Bargaining.* 2d ed. Publication, 132. Washington, DC: American Federation of Labor and Congress of Industrial Organizations, n.d. 131 p.

1289. *Pension Plans under Collective Bargaining; Benefits for Survivors, 1960–61.* Bulletin, 1334. Washington, DC: Bureau of Labor Statistics, 1962. 26 p.

1290. *Pension Provisions of the Tax Equity and Fiscal Responsibility Act of 1982.* Englewood Cliffs, NJ: Prentice-Hall, Inc., 1982. 25 p.

1291. *Pension Reform Act of 1974; Law and Explanation.* Chicago: Commerce Clearing House, Inc., 1974. 399 p.

1292. *The Pension System in the United States.* New York?: Haskins & Sells, 1964. 67 p.

1293. *Pension Task Force Report on Public Employee Retirement Systems.* By the Committee on Education and Labor of the House of Representatives. Washington, DC: U.S. Government Printing Office, 1978. 858 p.

1294. *Pension Terminology; Final Report by the Joint Committee on Pension Terminology.* Washington, DC: American Academy of Actuaries et al., 1981. 14 p.

1295. *Pensioner Cost-of-Living Increases; Who Needs Them?* A Towers, Perrin, Forster & Crosby Special Report. New York: TPF&C, 1981. 20 p.

1296. *Pensions; A Study of Benefit Fund Investment Policies.* Washington, DC: AFL-CIO Industrial Union Department, 1980. 106 p.

1297. *Pensions and Mortgages; Housing Investment Opportunities for the 80's.* Washington, DC: U.S. Department of Housing and Urban Development, 1984. 211 p.

1298. *Pensions and Retirement Plans; Issues and Strategies.* Greenvale, NY: Panel Publishers, 1986. 194 p.

1299. *Pensions and Taxes; Who Wins, Who Loses? Private Sector Retirement Security and U.S. Tax Policy.* Issues Book. Washington, DC: Government Research Corp., 1984. 34 p.

1300. *Pensions; Fundamentals in the Development of Pension and Other Retirement Plans.* Washington, DC: Chamber of Commerce of the United States, 1929. 54 p.

1301. Pesando, James E. *Discontinuities in Pension Benefit Formulas and the Spot Model of the Labor Market; Implications for Financial Economists.* NBER Working Paper, 1795. Cambridge, MA: National Bureau of Economic Research, 1986. 37 p.

1302. Pesando, James E. *Employee Valuation of Pension Claims and the Impact of Indexing Initiatives.* NBER Working Paper, 767. Cambridge, MA: National Bureau of Economic Research, 1981. 30 p.

1303. Pesando, James E. *The Usefulness of the Wind-Up Measure of Pension Liabilities; A Labour Market Perspective.* NBER Working Paper, 1559. Cambridge, MA: National Bureau of Economic Research, 1985. 15 p.

1304. Pesando, James E. *Valuing Pensions (Annuities) with Different Types of Inflation Protection in Total Compensation Comparisons.* NBER Working Paper, 956. Cambridge, MA: National Bureau of Economic Research, 1982. 25 p.

1305. Peterson, John E. *Public Pension Fund Financial Disclosure.* n.p.: Municipal Financial Officers Association, 1980. Various pagings.

1306. Phillips, Howard M. *All You Need to Know about Defined Benefit Keogh Plans.* Wayne, NJ: Avery Publishing Group, 1981. 132 p.

1307. Pianko, Howard. *Legal Issues in Pension Investment.* Tax Law and Practice Course Handbook Series, 156. New York: Practising Law Institute, 1981. 400 p.

1308. Pianko, Howard. *Legal Issues in Pension Investment.* Tax Law and Practice Course Handbook Series, 185. New York: Practising Law Institute, 1983. 352 p.

1309. Pianko, Howard. *Legal Issues in Pension Investment, 1982.* Tax Law and Practice Course Handbook Series, 169. New York: Practising Law Institute, 1982. 832 p.

1310. *Planning and Compliance under ERISA.* Palo Alto, CA: California Certified Public Accountants Foundation for Education and Research, 1977. 134 p.

1311. *Planning for Your Retirement; IRAs & Keogh Plans.* Chicago: Commerce Clearing House, Inc., 1983. 96 p.

1312. *Plans with Excess Assets.* Washington, DC: U.S. General Accounting Office, 1986. 19 p.

1313. Pomeranz, Felix; Ramsey, Gordon P.; and Steinberg, Richard M. *Pensions; An Accounting and Management Guide.* New York: The Ronald Press, 1976. 329 p.

1314. Pound, John, and Shiller, Robert J. *Speculative Behavior of Institutional Investors.* NBER Working Paper, 1964. Cambridge, MA: National Bureau of Economic Research, 1986. 27 p.

1315. Pozzelbon, Silvana, and Mitchell, Olivia S. *Married Women's Retirement Behavior.* NBER Working Paper, 2104. Cambridge, MA: National Bureau of Economic Research, 1986. 23 p.

1316. *Prentice-Hall's Explanation of the Tax Reform Act of 1986; P.L. 99–514.* Paramus, NJ: Prentice-Hall Information Services, 1986. Various pagings.

1317. *Prentice-Hall's Guide to Effective Communication; On Pay and Employee Benefits.* Paramus, NJ: Prentice-Hall Information Services, 1986. 116 p.

1318. *The Pre-Retirement Years; A Longitudinal Study of the Labor Market Experience of Men.* Manpower R&D Monograph, 15. Washington, DC: U.S. Department of Labor, 1970. 4 vols. ?

1319. *Present Law and Background Relating to Funding and Deductions for Defined Benefit Pension Plans.* Washington, DC: Joint Committee on Taxation, 1986. 18 p.

1320. President's Commission on Pension Policy. *An Interim Report.* Washington, DC, 1980. 51 p.
This covers the retirement system, income goals, government policy, treatment of spouses, Social Security coverage, disability, retirement age, asset ownership and control, and employment of older workers.

1321. President's Commission on Pension Policy. *An Interim Report.* Washington, DC, 1980. 54 p.
This covers the retirement system, Social Security integration, and the minimum universal pension system.

1322. President's Commission on Pension Policy. *Coming of Age; Toward a National Retirement Income Policy.* Washington, DC, 1981. 130 p.
This covers the retirement system and makes recommendations for future government policy with regard to MUPs (Minimum Universal Pension System), vesting, portability, integration, spouse benefits, retirement age, public plans, asset ownership and control, Social Security, savings and retirement income.

1323. President's Commission on Pension Policy. *Coming of Age; Toward a National Retirement Income Policy, Technical Papers.* Washington, DC, 1981. 2,033 p.

1324. President's Commission on Pension Policy. *Federal Pension Programs.* Working Papers. Washington, DC, 1981. 11 p.

1325. President's Commission on Pension Policy. *Pension Coverage in the United States.* Working Papers. Washington, DC, 1981?. 12 p.

1326. *Primer on Pensions.* Sponsored by Advanced Legal Education, Hamline University School of Law. St. Paul, MN, 1986. 288 p.
There were 1983 and 1985 editions.

1327. Pritchett, Henry S. *The Social Philosophy of Pensions with a Review of Existing Pension Systems for Professional Groups.* Bulletin, 25. New York: Carnegie Foundation for the Advancement of Teaching, 1930. 85 p.

1328. Pritchett, S. Travis, et al. *Individual Annuities as a Source of Retirement Income.* Rev. ed. FMLI Insurance Education Program Series. Atlanta, GA: Life Office Management Association, 1982. 94 p.

1329. *Private and Public Pension Plans in the United States.* 2d ed. New York: Institute of Life Insurance, 1967. 28 p.

1330. *A Private Pension Forecasting Model; Final Report, October 1979.* Submitted to the Office of Pension and Welfare Benefit Plans. U.S. Department of Labor. Prepared by ICF Incorporated. Washington, DC: ICF Incorporated, 1979. 118 p. and extensive appendices.

1331. *Private Pension Plans; Which Way Are They Headed?* A paper by the Congressional Research Service. Washington, DC: U.S. Government Printing Office, 1985. 32 p.

1332. *Private Pensions and the Public Interest; A Symposium.* Sponsored by American Enterprise Institute for Public Policy Research. Washington, DC: American Enterprise Institute, 1970. 253 p.

1333. *Private Pensions; Their Economic, Political and Social Realities and Expectations.* Washington, DC: American Council on Life Insurance, 1979. 95 p.

1334. *Profit Sharing Benefits to Business, Labor and Capital Markets.* Evanston, IL: Profit Sharing Council of America, 1979?. 39 p.

1335. *Profit Sharing Design Manual.* Englewood Cliffs, NJ: Prentice-Hall, Inc., 1976.

1336. *Profit Sharing for Workers.* Studies in Personnel Policy, 97. New York: National Industrial Conference Board, Inc., 1948. 56 p.
Includes a survey of fifty-seven then existing plans showing their major features.

1337. *The Profit Sharing Plan.* Washington, DC: Employee Benefit Research Institute, 1979. 8 p.

1338. *Providing Retirement Income Security; Social & Economic Considerations.* An EBRI Research Review, III. Washington, DC: Employee Benefit Research Institute, 1980. 58 p.

1339. *Public Pension Plans; A Bibliography, Review Draft.* Washington, DC: U.S. Department of Labor Library, 1977. 89 p.

1340. *Public Pensions; A Legislator's Guide.* Denver, CO: National Conference of State Legislators, 1985. 47 p.

1341. *Public Policy and Private Pension Programs; A Report to the President on Private Employee Retirement Plans.* By President's Committee on Corporate Pension Funds and Other Private Retirement and Welfare Programs. Washington, DC: U.S. Government Printing Office, 1965. 82 p.

1342. *Public Retirement Systems; Summaries of Public Retirement Plans Covering Colleges and Universities, 1985.* New York: Teachers Insurance and Annuity Association, 1985. 68 p.

1343. Pyne, Timothy, and Sammons, Thomas F. *Judicial Retirement Plans.* Chicago: American Judicature Society, 1984. 102 p.
There was also a 1980 edition of this.

1344. *Qualified Profit-Sharing Plans.* New York: Research Institute of America, 1985. 25 p.

1345. *Questions & Answers on the Pension and Profit Sharing Provisions of the New Tax Law, With an Explanation of the Retirement Plan Provisions of TEFRA.* Englewood Cliffs, NJ: Prentice-Hall, Inc., 1983. 92 p.

1346. Quinn, Joseph F. *The Early Retirement Decision; Evidence from the 1969 Retirement History Study.* Social Security Administration Staff Paper, 29. Washington, DC: U.S. Government Printing Office, 1978. 34 p.

1347. *Railroad Retirement System; Background Information.* Prepared for the use of the Committee on Interstate and Foreign Commerce. Washington, DC: U.S. Government Printing Office, 1978. 118 p.

1348. *The Railroad Retirement System; Economic Analysis of the Future Outlook for the Railroad Industry and Its Ability to Support the System, Staff Papers Supporting the Report to the President and the Congress.* Washington, DC: U.S. Commission on Railroad Retirement, 1972–1973. 3 vols.

1349. *The Railroad Retirement System; Its Coming Crisis, Report.* Washington, DC: U.S. Commission on Railroad Retirement, 1972. 570 p.

1350. Raish, David L. *Cash or Deferred Arrangements.* Tax Management Portfolios, 358. Washington, DC: Bureau of National Affairs, Inc., 1986. Various pagings.

1351. Rappaport, Anna M. *An Analysis of the Costs of Pension Accrual after Age 65.* Prepared for the Select Committee on Aging of the House of Representatives. Washington, DC: U.S. Government Printing Office, 1982. 33 p.

1352. *Reform of Social Security and Federal Pension Cost-of-Living Adjustments.* AEI Legislative Analyses, 49. Washington, DC: American Enterprise Institute for Public Policy Research, 1985. 27 p.

1353. *Reforming Retirement Policies.* A statement by the Research and Policy Committee of the Committee for Economic Development. New York: CED, 1981. 66 p.

1354. *Register of Retirement Benefit Plans Reported under the Welfare and Pension Plans Disclosure Act.* Washington, DC: U.S. Government Printing Office, 1972. 446 p.
There was an earlier edition in 1965.

1355. Reichard, Sherwood M. *Tax Sheltered Annuities; A Comparative Analysis.* Atlanta, GA: American Association of University Professors, Georgia Conference, 1979. 34 p.

1356. Reichler, Richard. *Employee Stock Ownership Plans; Problems and Potentials.* New York: Law Journal Press, 1978. 315 p.

1357. Reilly, Sarah C. *Public Pension Plans; The State Regulatory Framework.* Austin, TX: National Council on Teacher Retirement, 1985. 115 p.

1358. *Report by Academy Task Force on Pension Benefit Guaranty Corporation Multiemployer Study Required by PL 95–214.* Washington, DC: American Academy of Actuaries, 1978. 9 p.

1359. *Report on the Impact of ERISA on the Administration Costs of Small Retirement Plans.* New York?: Price Waterhouse & Co., 1977. Various pagings. This was done for the Department of Labor by Price Waterhouse.

1360. *Retirement before Age 65 Is a Growing Trend in the Private Sector.* Washington, DC: U.S. General Accounting Office, 1985. 17 p.

1361. *Retirement before Age 65; Trends, Costs, and National Issues.* Washington, DC: U.S. General Accounting Office, 1986. 73 p.

1362. *Retirement Benefits and Divorce.* Chicago: Commerce Clearing House, Inc., 1984. 218 p.

1363. *Retirement Equity Act of 1984; ALI-ABA Video Law Review Study Materials.* Philadelphia, PA: American Law Institute-American Bar Association. Committee on Continuing Professional Education, 1985. 282 p.

1364. *Retirement Equity Act of 1984; Law and Explanation, As Signed by the President on August 23, 1984.* Chicago: Commerce Clearing House, Inc., 1984. 88 p.

1365. *Retirement Equity & Deficit Reduction Acts of 1984.* Washington, DC: The Wyatt Co., 1984. 37 p.

1366. *Retirement Income Opportunities in an Aging America; Income Levels and Adequacy.* Washington, DC: Employee Benefit Research Institute, 1982. 121 p.

1367. *Retirement Income Policy; Considerations for Effective Decision Making, An Issues Report.* Washington, DC: Employee Benefit Research Institute, 1980. 76 p.

1368. *Retirement Income Programs; Directions for Future Research.* Washington, DC: Employee Benefit Research Institute, 1980. 41 p.

1369. *Retirement Income Systems; Coverage and Characteristics.* An EBRI Research Review, II. Washington, DC: Employee Benefit Research Institute, 1980. 118 p.

1370. *A Retirement Plan for Federal Workers Covered by Social Security; An Analysis of the Federal Employees Retirement System.* Washington, DC: Educational and Public Welfare Division. Civil Service Retirement Team, 1986. 55 p.

1371. *Retirement Plans for Small Business and Professionals Entering the Top-Heavy and Parity Age; ALI-ABA Video Law Review Study Materials.* Philadelphia, PA: American Law Institute-American Bar Association. Committee on Continuing Professional Education, 1984. 290 p.

1372. *Retirement Plans of Medical Groups in the United States.* Denver, CO: Center for Research in Ambulatory Health Care Administration, 1982. 39 p.

1373. *Retirement Plans of S Corporations under TEFRA.* Pension Planning Series. Englewood Cliffs, NJ: Prentice-Hall, Inc., 1983. 23 p.

1374. *Review of the Pension Benefit Guaranty Corporation's Progress towards Improving Accounting and Internal Control Weaknesses.* Washington, DC: U.S. General Accounting Office, 1983. 4 p.

1375. Rhodes, Theodore E. *Participation Requirements.* Pension and Profit-Sharing Plans. Series C, Folio 3. Philadelphia, PA: American Law Institute-American Bar Association. Committee on Continuing Professional Education, 1978. 13 p.

1376. *The RIA Complete Analysis of the '86 Tax Reform Act.* New York: Research Institute of America, Inc., 1986. 1,165 p.

1377. *The RIA Complete Analysis of the Tax Equity and Fiscal Responsibility Act of '82.* New York: Research Institute of America, Inc., 1982. 349 p.

1378. Rice, Leon L., Jr., and Schlaudt, Edward H. *Basic Pension and Profit-Sharing Plans.* Tax Handbook, 56. Philadelphia, PA: American Law Institute, 1957. 148 p.

1379. Richey, Louis R., and Colony, F. Austin. *Salary Continuation Plans.* A Market Builder Library Selection. Indianapolis, IN: Research & Review Service of America, 1980. 151 p.

1380. Rifkin, Jeremy, and Barber, Randy. *The North Will Rise Again; Pensions, Politics and Power in the 1980s.* Boston: Beacon Press, 1978. 279 p.

1381. Robbins, Rainard B. *Impact of Taxes on Industrial Pension Plans.* New York: Industrial Relations Counselors, Inc., 1949. 82 p.

1382. Robbins, Rainard B. *Retirement Plans for College Faculties.* New York: Teachers Insurance and Annuity Association of America, 1934. 68 p.

1383. Robinson, Jerry H., and Hargrove, John O. *Attorney's Guide to Pension and Profit-Sharing.* 2d ed. Berkeley, CA: California Continuing Education of the Bar, 1980. 524 p.

1384. Robinson, Robert A. *The Church Pension Fund; A Great Venture of Vision and Faith.* Newcomen Publication, 1129. New York: Newcomen Society in North America, 1980. 29 p.

1385. *The Role of an Actuary in a Pension Plan.* New York?: Harris Graham Consulting Actuaries, Inc., 197?-. 31 p.

1386. *The Role of TIAA-CREF in Higher Education.* New York: TIAA-CREF, 1986. 12 p.

1387. Rose, Henry. *Plan Termination Insurance.* Pension and Profit-Sharing Plans. Series F, Folio 3. Philadelphia, PA: American Law Institute-American Bar Association. Committee on Continuing Professional Education, 1978. 35 p.

1388. Rose, Robert D. *E.S.O.P.; Dilution of Ownership and Control.* Cincinnati, OH: The National Underwriter Co., 1976. 168 p.

1389. Rosen, Corey. *Employee Ownership; Issues, Resources and Legislation.* Washington, DC: Conference on Alternative State and Local Policies, 1981. 75 p.

1390. Rosen, Corey; Klein, Katherine J.; and Young, Karen M. *Employee Ownership in America; The Equity Solution.* Lexington, MA: Lexington Books, 1985. 270 p.

1391. Rosen, Kenneth T. *The Role of Pension Funds in Housing Finance.* Working Paper, 35. Cambridge, MA: Joint Center for Urban Studies of MIT and Harvard, 1975. 81 p.

1392. Rosenbloom, Jerry S., ed. *The Handbook of Employee Benefits; Design, Funding and Administration.* Homewood, IL: Dow Jones-Irwin, 1984. 1,096 p.

1393. Rosenbloom, Jerry S., and Hallman, G. Victor. *Employee Benefit Planning.* 2d ed. Englewood Cliffs, NJ: Prentice-Hall, Inc., 1986. 497 p.

1394. Ross, Stanford G. *Income Security Programs; Past, Present and Future.* Working Papers. Washington, DC: President's Commission on Pension Policy, 1980. 80 p.

1395. Rotgin, Philip N., and Jacobs, Arnold M. *Procedures for Qualification of Plans.* Pension and Profit-Sharing Plans. Series G, Folio 2. Philadelphia, PA: American Law Institute-American Bar Association, 1978. 42 p.

1396. Rothman, David C. *Contributions to Plans.* Pension and Profit-Sharing Plans. Series B, Folio 3. Philadelphia, PA: American Law Institute-American Bar Association. Committee on Continuing Professional Education, 1979. 26 p.

1397. Rothman, David C. *Establishing & Administering Pension & Profit Sharing Plans and Trust Funds.* Philadelphia, PA: American Law Institute-American Bar Association, 1967. 243 p.

1398. Rothman, David C. *Investment of Plan Assets.* Pension and Profit Sharing Plans. Series B, Folio 4. Philadelphia, PA: American Law Institute-American Bar Association. Committee on Continuing Professional Education, 1979. 19 p.

1399. Rothman, David C. *Plan Provisions Determining Eligibility to Participate.* Pension and Profit-Sharing Plans. Series B, Folio 1. Philadelphia, PA: American Law Institute-American Bar Association. Committee on Continuing Professional Education, 1978. 11 p.

1400. Rothschild, Walter S. *Fiduciary Responsibilities.* Pension and Profit-Sharing Plans. Series D, Folio 2. Philadelphia, PA: American Law Institute-American Bar Association. Committee on Continuing Professional Education, 1979. 78 p.

1401. Rubin, Harold. *Pensions and Employee Mobility in the Public Service.* New York: The Twentieth Century Fund, 1965. 105 p.

1402. *Rules and Financial Provisions of Industrial Pension Plans.* Princeton, NJ: Princeton University. Industrial Relations Section, 1928. 34 p.

1403. Rybka, John S. *Cash or Deferred Arrangements; Pros and Cons.* A Market Builder Library Selection. Indianapolis, IN: R&R Newkirk, 1982. 193 p.

1404. *S. 209, The ERISA Improvements Act of 1979; Summary and Analysis of Consideration.* Washington, DC: U.S. Government Printing Office, 1979. 186 p.

1405. Sahin, Izzet. *Job Mobility and Private Pensions.* Research Report, 86–2. Brookfield, WI: International Foundation of Employee Benefit Plans, 1986. 50 p.

1406. Sahin, Izzet, and Balcer, Yves. *Stochastic Models for Pensionable Service.* Discussion Papers. Madison, WI: University of Wisconsin. Institute for Research on Poverty, 1977. 34 p.

1407. Sakson, Jane. *State Pension Issues; An Overview.* Olympia, WA: State of Washington. Office of Financial Management Policy Analysis and Forecasting, 1984. 22 p.

1408. Salisbury, Dallas L., ed. *America in Transition; Implications for Employee Benefits.* Washington, DC: Employee Benefit Research Institute, 1982. 85 p.

1409. Salisbury, Dallas L., ed. *Economic Survival in Retirement; Which Pension Is for You?* An EBRI-ERF Policy Forum. Washington, DC: Employee Benefit Research Institute, 1982. 137 p.

1410. Salisbury, Dallas L., ed. *Retirement Income and the Economy; Increasing Income for the Aged?* Washington, DC: Employee Benefit Research Institute, 1981. 113 p.

1411. Salisbury, Dallas L., ed. *Retirement Income and the Economy; Policy Directions for the 80s.* An EBRI-ERF Policy Forum, May 6, 1981. Washington, DC: Employee Benefit Research Institute, 1981. 305 p.

1412. Salisbury, Dallas L., ed. *Should Pension Assets Be Managed for Social/Political Purposes?* An EBRI Policy Forum. Washington, DC: Employee Benefit Research Institute, 1980. 381 p.

1413. Salisbury, Dallas L., ed. *Why Tax Employee Benefits?* An EBRI-ERF Policy Forum. Washington, DC: Employee Benefit Research Institute, 1984. 105 p.

1414. *Sample Company Communications and Public Relations for ESOP Companies.* Washington, DC: The ESOP Association, n.d. Unpaged.

1415. Santora, Joseph C. *Employee Stock Ownership Plans; A Selected Bibliography.* Public Administration Series, P-1649. Monticello, IL: Vance Bibliographies, 1985. 17 p.

1416. Sarason, Harry M. *Advanced Pension Tables.* St. Louis, MO: Insurance and Pension Press, Inc., 1974. Unpaged.

1417. Sarason, Harry M. *Joint & Survivor Annuity Option Tables.* St. Louis, MO: Insurance & Pension Press, Inc., 1976. 3 vols.?
Each volume of tables comprises more than 120 pages and pertains to one particular actuarial interest rate assumption.

1418. Schieber, Sylvester J., and George, Patricia M. *Retirement Opportunities in an Aging America; Coverage and Benefit Entitlement.* Washington, DC: Employee Benefit Research Institute, 1981. 130 p.

1419. Schlesinger, Sanford J., and Hoffman, Paul Gordon. *Practical Pre-Retirement Planning.* Estate Planning and Administration Course Handbook Series, 164. New York: Practising Law Institute, 1986. 320 p.

1420. Schmitt, Ray. *Major Issues Facing the Private Pension System.* Washington, DC: Congressional Research Service, 1978. 43 p.

1421. Schmitt, Ray. *Pension Plans; Multiemployer Pension Plan Termination Insurance, Updated 01/08/86.* Washington, DC: Congressional Research Service, 1986. 17 p.

1422. Schmitt, Ray. *Pension Vesting, Integration, and Portability (VIP).* Washington, DC: Congressional Research Service, 1985. 13 p.

1423. Schreiber, David B. *The Legislative History of the Railroad Retirement and Railroad Unemployment Insurance Systems.* Washington, DC: U.S. Government Printing Office, 1978. 492 p.

1424. Schreiber, Irving, ed. *Integrating Pension and Profit Sharing Plans with Social Security.* Greenvale, NY: Panel Publishers, 1970. 42 p.

1425. Schuller, Tom. *Age, Capital & Democracy; The Management of Pension Funds.* Brookfield, VT: Gower Publishing Co., 1986.

1426. Schulz, James H. *The Economics of Aging.* 3d ed. New York: Van Nostrand Reinhold, 1985. 212 p.

1427. Schulz, James H. *Pension Aspects of the Economics of Aging; Present and Future Roles of Private Pensions. . . .* Washington, DC: U.S. Government Printing Office, 1970. 61 p.

1428. Schulz, James H., and Leavitt, Thomas D. *Pension Integration; Concepts, Issues and Proposals.* Washington, DC: Employee Benefit Research Institute, 1983. 83 p.

1429. Schulz, James H., et al. *Private Pension Benefits in the 1970's; A Study of Retirement and Survivor Benefit Levels in 1974 and 1979.* Bryn Mawr, PA: McCahan Foundation, 1982. 115 p.

1430. Schulz, James H., et al. *Providing Adequate Retirement Income; Pension Reform in the United States and Abroad.* Hanover, NH: University Press of New England, 1974. 330 p.

1431. Schwartz, Max J. *ERISA Litigation.* Litigation Course Handbook Series, 207. New York: Practising Law Institute, 1982. 264 p.

1432. Schwartz, Max J. *Employer Benefits under ERISA.* Tax Law and Practice Course Handbook Series, 190. New York: Practising Law Institute, 1983. 176 p.

1433. Schwimmer, Martin J., and Malca, Edward. *Pension and Institutional Portfolio Management.* New York: Praeger, 1976. 136 p.

1434. *The SEC Position on Employee Benefits after Daniel; Materials.* ALI-ABA Course of Study. Philadelphia, PA: American Law Institute-American Bar Association. Committee on Continuing Professional Education, 1980. 280 p.

1435. *Self-Employed Individuals Tax Retirement Act of 1961; Report to Accompany H.R. 10.* Washington, DC: Committee on Ways and Means, 1961. 94 p.

1436. *Self-Employed Individuals Tax Retirement Bill; Conference Version, Text of Senate-House with Prentice-Hall Explanation.* Englewood Cliffs, NJ, Prentice-Hall, Inc., 1962. 24 p.

1437. Seltz, Christine, and Gifford, Dale L. *Flexible Compensation; A Forward Look.* AMA Management Briefing. New York: American Management Associations, 1982. 44 p.

1438. Shepherd, A. G., ed. *Pension Fund Administration.* Portsmouth, NH: Longwood Publishing Group, 1984. 182 p.

1439. Sherman, Jeffrey G. *Pension Planning and Deferred Compensation.* Analysis and Skills Series. New York: Matthew Bender, 1985. 1,110 p.

1440. Shiller, Robert J., and Pound, John. *Survey Evidence on Diffusion of Interest among Institutional Investors.* NBER Working Paper, 1851. Cambridge, MA: National Bureau of Economic Research, 1986. 25 p.

1441. Shoobe, Joel L., and Deener, Jerome A., comps. *The Demise of the Professional Corporation? Seminar Materials.* Newark, NJ: New Jersey Institute for Continuing Legal Education, 1983. 67 p.

1442. Sibson, Robert E. *A Survey of Pension Planning.* Chicago: Commerce Clearing House, Inc., 1953. 184 p.

1443. Sickles, Robin C. and Taubman, Paul. *An Analysis of the Health and Retirement Status of the Elderly.* NBER Working Paper, 1459. Cambridge, MA: National Bureau of Economic Research, 1984. 29 p.

1444. Siegel, Mayer, and Buckman, Carol. *Executive's Guide to Pension and Retirement Benefits.* New York: Law & Business, 1982. 286 p.

1445. Simmons, Sherwin P. *Fiduciary Responsibility and Prohibited Transactions under the Employee Retirement Income Security Act.* Tax Law and Practice Course Handbook Series, 85. New York: Practising Law Institute, 1975. 336 p.

1446. Simone, Joseph R. *Introduction to Qualified Pension and Profit Sharing Plans.* Tax Law and Estate Planning Course Handbook Series, 172. New York: Practising Law Institute, 1982. 448 p.

1447. Simone, Joseph R. *Introduction to Qualified Pension and Profit Sharing Plans.* Tax Law and Practice Course Handbook Series, 186. New York: Practising Law Institute, 1983. 448 p.

1448. Simone, Joseph R., and Schwartz, Max J. *Employee Benefits Legislation, 1984.* Tax Law and Practice Course Handbook Series, 212. New York: Practising Law Institute, 1984. 280 p.

1449. Simone, Joseph R. *Introduction to Qualified Pension and Profit Sharing Plans, 1986.* Tax Law and Practice Course Handbook Series, 227. New York: Practising Law Institute, 1985. 376 p.

1450. Singer, Neil M. *Modifying Military Retirement.* A CBO Study. Washington, DC: U.S. Congressional Budget Office, 1984. 83 p.

1451. *Single-Employer Pension Plan Amendments Act of 1986; Law and Explanation; PL 99–272 as Signed by the President on April 7, 1986.* Chicago: Commerce Clearing House, Inc., 1986. 160 p.

1452. Slade, Frederic P. *Labor Force Entry and Exit of Older Men; A Longitudinal Study.* NBER Working Paper, 1029. Cambridge, MA: National Bureau of Economic Research, 1982. 18 p.

1453. Slimmon, Robert F. *Successful Pension Design for Small-to-Medium-Sized Businesses.* Reston, VA: Reston Publishing Co., Inc., 1985. 461 p.
    There was also a 1980 edition.

1454. Smith, Marvin M. *Accrual Accounting for Military Retirement; Alternative Approaches.* Staff Working Paper. Washington, DC: Congressional Budget Office, 1983. 25 p.

1455. Snider, H. Wayne, ed. *Employee Benefits Management.* New York: The Risk and Insurance Management Society, 1980. 228 p.

1456. Snyder, Bernhart R. *Fundamentals of Individual Retirement Plans.* Rockville Center, NY: Farnsworth Publishing Co., Inc., 1980. 121 p.

1457. Snyder, Bernhart R., ed. *Guide to Pension & Profit Sharing Plans under ERISA, 1975 Edition.* Rockville Center, NY: Farnsworth Publishing Co., 1975.

1458. Snyder, Bernhart R., and Hunter, Ronald J. *Fundamentals of Taxation of Qualified Plan Benefits.* Rockville Center, NY: Farnsworth Publishing Co., 1983. 114 p.

1459. Snyder, Donald C. *Private Pension Impacts on the Employment of Older Workers; An Annotated Bibliography.* Public Administration Series, P-1016. Monticello, IL: Vance Bibliographies, 1982. 77 p.

1460. *Social Security and Retirement; Private Goals, Public Policy.* Washington, DC: Congressional Quarterly, 1983. 246 p.

1461. Soldofsky, Robert M. *College and University Retirement Programs; A Review of Their Adequacy under Realistic Assumptions.* Iowa City, IA: University of Iowa. Bureau of Business and Economic Research, 1966. 55 p.

1462. Sollee, William L., and Shapiro, Larry E. *Pension Plans; Qualifications.* Tax Management Portfolios, 351. Washington, DC: Bureau of National Affairs, Inc., 1986. Various pagings.

1463. Sollee, William L., and Shapiro, Larry E. *Profit-Sharing Plans; Qualification.* Tax Management Portfolios, 352. Washington, DC: Bureau of National Affairs, Inc., 1986. Various pagings.

1464. Spalding, Albert D., Jr. *Deferred Compensation; Accounting, Taxation and Funding for Nonqualified Plans.* Englewood Cliffs, NJ: Prentice-Hall, Inc., 1985. 346 p.

1465. *Speakers' Outlines; Pension Plans after TEFRA, 1983.* Jefferson City, MO: Missouri Bar. Committee on Legal Education, 1983. 67 p.

1466. Sporn, Arthur D. *Retirement Bond Plans.* Pension and Profit-Sharing Plans. Series A, Folio 8. Philadelphia, PA: American Law Institute-American Bar Association. Committee on Continuing Professional Education, 1978. 11 p.

1467. Srb, Jozetta H. *Communicating with Employees about Pension & Welfare Benefits.* Key Issues Series, 8. Ithaca, NY: ILR Press, 1971. 44 p.

1468. Srb, Jozetta H. *Portable Pensions.* Key Issues Series, 4. Ithaca, NY: ILR Press, 1969.

1469. Stakes, Mary E. *Controlling Public Pensions.* Athens, GA: University of Georgia. Institute of Government, 1982. 40 p.

1470. *Statement of Financial Accounting Standards No. 35; Accounting and Reporting by Defined Benefit Pension Plans, Implementation Considerations for Plan Administrators, Actuaries and Auditors.* New York: Peat Marwick, Mitchell & Co., 1980. 47 p.

1471. Stein, Bruno. *Social Security and Pensions in Transition; Understanding the American Retirement System.* New York: Free Press, 1980. 308 p.

1472. Stein, Bruno. *Social Security and the Private Pension System.* New York: Industrial Relations Counselors, Inc., 1979. 46 p.

1473. Steinberg, Richard M., and Dankner, Harold. *Pensions; An ERISA Accounting and Management Guide.* 2d ed. New York: Wiley, 1983. 381 p.

1474. Steinforth, Alex W., ed. *Employee Benefits; A Guide for Hospitals.* Germantown, MD: Aspen Systems Corp., 1980. 107 p.
This is a reprint of *Topics in Health Care Financing,* vol. 6, no. 3.

1475. Stephens, Mark A. *Tax Service for Employee Retirement Plans.* Washington, DC: M. A. Stephens, 1978. 1,300 p.

1476. Stewart, Alva W. *American State Legislators; Pay and Perquisites, A Brief Checklist.* Public Administration Series, P-1559. Monticello, IL: Vance Bibliographies, 1984. 9 p.

1477. Stewart, Bryce M. *Financial Aspects of Industrial Pensions.* General Management Series, 87. New York: American Management Association, 1928. 24 p.

1478. Stewart, Bryce M., and Couper, Walter J. *Profit Sharing and Stock Ownership for Wage Earners and Executives.* Industrial Relations Monograph, 10. New York: Industrial Relations Counselors, 1945. 142 p.

1479. Stoeber, Edward A. *Pension Reform Act Explained; New Guidelines for Corporate, Keogh and Individual Retirement Plans.* Rev. ed. Cincinnati, OH: National Underwriters Co., 1976. 282 p.

1480. Stoeber, Edward A. *Tax and Fringe Benefit Planning for Professional Corporations.* Cincinnati, OH: National Underwriter Co., 1979. 212 p.

1481. Stone, Morris. *Benefit Plan Disputes; Arbitration Case Stories.* Brookfield, WI: International Foundation of Employee Benefit Plans, 1976. 92 p.
Jointly published with the American Arbitration Association.

1482. Storey, James R., and Hendricks, Gary. *Retirement Incomes Issues in an Aging Society.* Urban Institute Paper on Income Security and Pension Policy. Washington, DC: Urban Institute, 1979. 60 p.

1483. Strate, John. *Post-Retirement Benefit Increases in State Pension Plans; The Response to Inflation in the 1970's.* Waltham, MA: The Policy Center on Aging. Brandeis University, 1982. 79 p.

1484. Strong, Jay V. *Employee Benefit Plans in Operation.* University of Michigan. Reports of the Bureau of Industrial Relations, 4. Washington, DC: Bureau of National Affairs, Inc., 1951. 348 p.

1485. Stuchiner, Theresa B. *How to Integrate Your Retirement Plan with Social Security.* Englewood Cliffs, NJ: Prentice-Hall, Inc., 1972. 32 p.
An earlier edition was done in 1969.

1486. Studenski, Paul. *Teachers' Pension Systems in the United States.* New York: D. Appleton and Co., 1920. 24 p.

1487. *A Study of Cafeteria Plans and Flexible Spending Accounts.* Washington, DC: U.S. Department of Health and Human Services, 1985. Various pagings.

1488. *Study of the Administration of the Employee Retirement Income Security Act; Report to Congress.* Washington, DC: Office of Management and the Budget, 1980. 81 p.

1489. *Study of the Investment Performance of ERISA Plans.* Prepared for the Department of Labor by Berkowitz, Logue & Associates, Inc. Columbia, MD: Department of Labor, 1986. Various pagings.

1490. *Study of Total Compensation in the Federal, State and Private Sectors.* Prepared by Hay/Huggins Co. and Hay Management Consultants for the Committee on Post Office and Civil Service, House of Representatives. Washington, DC: U.S. Government Printing Office, 1984. 213 p.

1491. Sullivan, Timothy J. *Survey of Real Estate Investing by Pension Fund Investors.* New York: Money Market Directories, Inc., 1975. 78 p.

1492. *Summary of 1983 Federal Pension Plan Information.* Washington, DC: U.S. General Accounting Office, 1985. 36 p.

1493. Summers, Lawrence H. *Observations on the Indexation of Old Age Pensions.* NBER Working Paper, 1023. Cambridge, MA: National Bureau of Economic Research, 1982. 27 p.

1494. Summers, Lawrence H. *Tax Policy, the Rate of Return, and Savings.* NBER Working Paper, 995. Cambridge, MA: National Bureau of Economic Research, 1982. 46 p.

1495. *Survey of State Retirement Systems.* n.p.: National Association of State Retirement Administrators, 1974. Various pagings.

1496. Susko, A. Richard. *Plan Terminations; Asset or Liability?* Tax Law and Practice Course Handbook Series, 205. New York: Practising Law Institute, 1984. 680 p.

1497. Swanick, Margaret Lynne Struthers. *Women and Pensions; A Checklist of Publications.* Monticello, IL: Vance Bibliographies, 1979. 9 p.

1498. Tarver, Norman H. *Section 403(b) Manual.* Edited by Arvid L. Mortensen. Chicago: R&R Newkirk/Longman, 1985. Various pagings.

1499. Tauber, Yale D. *Executive Compensation, 1983.* Tax Law and Practice Course Handbook Series, 192. New York: Practising Law Institute, 1983. 496 p.

1500. Tauber, Yale D. *Executive Compensation, 1984.* Tax Law and Practice Course Handbook Series, 207. New York: Practising Law Institute, 1984. 704 p.

1501. Taubman, Paul. *Pensions and Mortality.* NBER Working Paper, 811. Cambridge, MA: National Bureau of Economic Research, 1981. 22 p.

1502. *Tax Equity and Fiscal Responsibility Act of 1982; Conference Report to Accompany H.R. 4961.* Chicago: Commerce Clearing House, Inc., 1982.

1503. *Tax Equity and Fiscal Responsibility Act of 1982; Law and Explanation.* Chicago: Commerce Clearing House, Inc., 1982. 536 p.

1504. *The Tax Reform Act of 1984.* Prepared by the law firm of Silverstein and Mullens. Edited by the staff of Tax Management, Inc. Washington, DC: Bureau of National Affairs, Inc., 1984. Various pagings.

1505. *Tax Reform Act of 1984 as Signed by the President on July 18, 1984; Law and Controlling Committee Reports.* Chicago: Commerce Clearing House, Inc., 1984. 1181 p.

1506. *The Tax Reform Act of 1986; Analysis of Employee Benefits and Compensation Provisions.* Washington, DC: The Wyatt Co., 1986. 40 p.

1507. *Tax Reform Act of 1986; Conference Bill, H.R. 3838 and Conference Report to Accompany H.R. 3838.* Washington, DC: U.S. Government Printing Office, 1986. 2 vols.
This was also republished in a Prentice-Hall edition.

1508. *Tax Reform Act of 1986; Law and Controlling Committee Reports.* Chicago: Commerce Clearing House, Inc., 1986. 1,728 p.

1509. *The Tax Reform Act of 1986; Legislative History.* Tax Management Portfolios, 986. Washington, DC: Bureau of National Affairs, Inc., 1986. 2 vols.

1510. *Tax Reform Bill of 1986 (H.R. 3838).* Standard Federal Tax Reports, Extra Edition, 41, September 21, 1986. Chicago: Commerce Clearing House, Inc., 1986. 2 vols.

1511. *Tax Reform Proposals; Pensions and Deferred Compensation.* For the use of the Committee on Ways and Means and the Committee on Finance. Washington, DC: U.S. Government Printing Office, 1985. 134 p.

1512. *Tax Reform Proposals; Tax Treatment of Employee Stock Ownership Plans.* For the use of the Committee on Ways and Means and the Committee on Finance. Washington, DC: U.S. Government Printing Office, 1985. 38 p.

1513. *Tax Revenues Lost and Beneficiaries Inadequately Protected When Private Pension Plans Terminate; Report to the Congress.* Washington, DC: U.S. General Accounting Office, 1981. 52 p.

1514. *Tax Saving Plans for the Self-Employed after Tax Reform.* Chicago: Commerce Clearing House, Inc., 1987. 72 p.
There were also 1980 and 1981 editions.

1515. *Tax Sheltered Annuities.* Washington, DC: Employee Benefit Research Institute, 1981. 5 p.

1516. *Tax-Sheltered Annuity Programs for Employees of Public Schools and Certain Tax-Exempt Organizations.* Publication 571. Washington, DC: Internal Revenue Service, 1983. 21 p.

1517. *Tax-Wise Ways to Handle Retirement Benefits in Marital Splitups.* Englewood Cliffs, NJ: Prentice-Hall, Inc., 1983. 32 p.

1518. Taylor, Suzanne Saunders. *Public Employee Retirement Systems; The Structure and Politics of Teacher Pensions.* Ithaca, NY: ILR Press, 1986. 187 p.

1519. Teague, Burton W. *Compensating Foreign Service Personnel.* Conference Board Report, 818. New York: Conference Board, 1982. 16 p.

1520. *Tenth Anniversary of the Employee Retirement Income Security Act of 1974; A Report of Conference Proceedings, Special Committee on Aging, September 11, 1984.* Washington, DC: U.S. Government Printing Office, 1985. 89 p.

1521. Tepper, Irwin. *Taxation and Corporate Pension Policy.* NBER Working Paper, 661. Cambridge, MA: National Bureau of Economic Research, 1981. 22 p.

1522. Terieckyj, Nestor E., and Levy, David M. *Cost of Retirement and U.S. Economic Growth Projections, 1980–2000.* National Economic Projections Series, 80–N-2. Washington, DC: National Planning Association, 1980. 62 p.

1523. *Termination of Plans with Excess Assets.* Washington, DC: U.S. General Accounting Office, 1986. 20 p.

1524. Testa, Michael H., and Bachelder, Joseph E., III. *ESOPs and TRASOPs; Employee Stock Ownership Plans.* Tax Law and Practice Course Handbook Series, 112. New York: Practising Law Institute, 1977. 480 p.

1525. Testa, Michael H., and Bachelder, Joseph E., III. *ESOPs and TRASOPs, 1979.* Tax Law and Practice Course Handbook Series, 140. New York: Practising Law Institute, 1979. 904 p.

1526. Testa, Michael H., and Bachelder, Joseph E., III. *ESOPs, TRASOPs and Other Employee Stock Ownership Plans.* Tax Law and Practice Course Handbook Series, 126. New York: Practising Law Institute, 1978. 928 p.

1527. *The Thrift Plan.* Washington, DC: Employee Benefit Research Institute, 1979. 4 p.

1528. Tilove, Robert. *Pension Funds and Economic Freedom.* New York: The Fund for the Republic, 1959. 91 p.

1529. Tilove, Robert. *Public Employee Pension Funds.* A Twentieth Century Fund Report. New York: Columbia University Press, 1976. 370 p.

1530. Todd, Jerry D. *A Deterministic Model for Evaluating the Optimal Use of Tax Sheltered Annuities.* Working paper. Austin, TX: University of Texas. Bureau of Business Research, 1977?. 14 p.

1531. Tolo, Kenneth W., ed. *Pension Plan Termination Insurance; Does the Foreign Experience Have Relevance for the United States?* An EBRI Policy Forum, June 25, 1979. Washington, DC: Employee Benefit Research Institute, 1979. 160 p.

1532. Torrey, Barbara Boyle. *Demographic Shifts and Projections; The Implications for Pension Systems.* Working Papers. Washington, DC: President's Commission on Pension Policy, 1980?. 39 p.

1533. Torrey, Barbara Boyle, et al. *An International Comparison of Pension Systems.* Working Papers. Washington, DC: President's Commission on Pension Policy, 1980. 52 p.

1534. *Trends in Company Pension Plans.* New York: National Industrial Conference Board, 1944. 52 p.

1535. *Trends in Employee Health and Pension Plans. . . .* Personnel Series, 118. New York: American Management Association, 1948. 30 p.

1536. Treynor, Jack L.; Regan, Patrick J.; and Prust, William W., Jr. *The Financial Reality of Pension Funding under ERISA.* Homewood, IL: Dow Jones-Irwin, 1976. 149 p.

1537. Tropper, Peter, and Kaufman, Anne. *Pension Power for Economic Development.* Washington, DC: Northeast-Midwest Institute, 1980. 35 p.

1538. Trowbridge, C. L., and Farr, C. E. *The Theory and Practice of Pension Funding.* Homewood, IL: Richard D. Irwin, Inc., 1976. 154 p.

1539. Trudeau, G. B. *But the Pension Fund Was Just Sitting There.* A Doonesbury Book. New York: Holt, Rinehart and Winston, 1979. 128 p.
There is probably only one pension joke. This is a book of cartoons, but the title is indicative of the attitude of many toward pension funds.

1540. Tucker, J. Richard. *State and Local Pension Funds, 1972; Digest of Authorized Investments and Actual Investments.* New York: Securities Industry Association, 1972. 98 p.

1541. Ture, Norman B., and Fields, Barbara A. *The Future of Private Pension Plans.* Washington, DC: American Enterprise Institute for Public Policy Research, 1976. 128 p.

1542. *12 Major Tax-Saving Opportunities for Closely Held Corporations.* Greenvale, NY: Panel Publishers, Inc., 1986. 106 p.

1543. Udell, Gilman G., comp. *Civil Service Preference Retirement and Salary Classification Laws.* Washington, DC: U.S. Government Printing Office, 1962. 279 p.

1544. Udell, Gilman G., comp. *Railroad Retirement and Unemployment Insurance Act as Amended.* Washington, DC: U.S. Government Printing Office, 1978. 313 p.

1545. Ullman, James Michael, and Bercoon, Norman. *The Dow Jones-Irwin Guide to Using IRAs.* Homewood, IL: Dow Jones-Irwin, 1986. 320 p.

1546. Unthank, L. L. *What You Should Know about Individual Retirement Accounts; Detailed Answers to the 350 Most Frequently Asked Questions about IRAs.* Homewood, IL: Dow Jones-Irwin, 1978. 351 p.

1547. *Valuing ESOP Shares.* Washington, DC: The ESOP Association, 1984. 76 p.

1548. Van Tassel, David, and Stearns, Peter N. *Old Age in a Bureaucratic Society; The Elderly, the Experts, and the State in American History.* Contributions to the Study of Aging, 4. Westport, CT: Greenwood Press, 1986. 259 p.

1549. Vance, Mary A. *Employee Ownership; A Bibliography.* Public Administration Series, P-1161. Monticello, IL: Vance Bibliographies, 1983. 8 p.

1550. Venti, Steven F., and Wise, David A. *The Determinants of IRA Contributions and the Effect of Limit Changes.* NBER Working Paper, 1731. Cambridge, MA: National Bureau of Economic Research, 1985. 51 p.

1551. Venti, Steven F., and Wise, David A. *IRAs and Saving.* NBER Working Paper, 1879. Cambridge, MA: National Bureau of Economic Research, 1986. 67 p.

1552. *Veterans' Administration Analysis and Evaluation of the Non-Service-Connected Pension Program; A Report.* Washington, DC: U.S. Government Printing Office, 1978. 708 p.

1553. Vicker, Ray. *The Dow Jones-Irwin Guide to Retirement Planning.* Homewood, IL: Dow Jones-Irwin, 1985. 332 p.

1554. Victor, Richard B., and Pease, Sara R. *The Financial Condition of Teacher Retirement Systems.* Prepared for the National Institute of Education. Rand Report. Santa Monica, CA: Rand Corp., 1980. 50 p.

1555. Vieira, Edwin. *Social Investing; Its Character, Causes, Consequences, and Legality under the Employee Retirement Income Security Act of 1974.* Washington, DC: U.S. Department of Labor. Labor-Management Services Administration, 1983. 104 p.

1556. Vine, John M. *Elective Savings Plans under the Tax Reform Act of 1986.* Washington, DC: The ERISA Industry Committee, 1986. 23 p.

1557. Vogel, Mark A. *Pension Plan Revisions.* New York: Law & Business, Inc., 1984. 403 p.

1558. Voorheis, Frank L. *Bank Administered Pooled Equity Funds for Employee Benefit Plans.* MSU Business Studies. East Lansing, MI: Michigan State University. Bureau of Business and Economic Research, 1967. 96 p.

1559. Vroman, Wayne. *Employment Termination Benefits in the U.S. Economy.* Washington, DC: Employee Benefit Research Institute, 1983. 247 p.

1560. Wachter, Susan M. "Inflation's Impact on Pensions." Unpublished manuscript. Philadelphia, PA: 1985. 2 vols. Various pagings.

1561. Wade, Alice. *Actuarial Tables Based on the U.S. Life Tables, 1979–81.* Actuarial Study, 96. Baltimore, MD: U.S. Social Security Administration, Office of the Actuary, 1986. 134 p.

1562. Waldman, Saul. *Retirement Systems for Employees of State and Local Governments . . . 1966; Findings of a Survey of Systems Whose Members Were Not Covered under the OASDHI Program.* Research Report, 23. Washington, DC: Social Security Administration, 1968. 115 p.

1563. Walker, James W., and Lazer, Harriet L. *The End of Mandatory Retirement; Implications for Management.* New York: John Wiley & Sons, 1978. 223 p.

1564. Wallfesh, Henry M. *The Effects of Extending the Mandatory Retirement Age.* New York: AMACOM, 1978. 41 p.

1565. Walsh, Francis J. *New Rules for Pension Accounting.* Research Bulletin, 135. New York: Conference Board, 1983. 15 p.

1566. Walsh, Sandra A. *Bibliography on Public and Private Pension Plans.* Public Administration Series, P-136. Monticello, IL: Vance Bibliographies, 1978. 12 p.

1567. Walton, W. Robert. *The Retirement Decision; How the New Social Security and Retirement Age Laws Affect You.* Kansas City, MO: Sheed Andrews and McMeel, 1978. 116 p.

1568. Waters, William R. *Employer Pension Plan Membership and Household Wealth.* S. S. Huebner Foundation Monograph Series, 10. Homewood, IL: Richard D. Irwin, Inc., 1981. 110 p.

1569. Watts, Timothy J. *Executive Economics.* Chicago: Probus Publishing, 1985.

1570. Weeks, David A., ed. *Rethinking Employee Benefit Assumptions.* Conference Board Report, 739. New York: Conference Board, 1978. 97 p.

1571. Weiss, Marc A. *Pension Funds Investments; The Issue of Control.* Washington, DC: Conference on Alternative State and Local Policies, 1978. 50 p.

1572. Weiss, Randall D., and Schiller, Bradley R. *The Value of Defined Benefit Pension Plans; A Test of the Equalizing Differences Hypothesis.* College Park, MD: University of Maryland. Department of Economics, 1976. 38 p.
Submitted to U.S. Department of Labor (DOL Contract No. J-9–M-5–0038).

1573. Weiss, Willard A. *A Critical Analysis of Trustee and Insurance Company Administered Employee Retirement Plans.* Reprinted from the Proceedings of the Conference of Actuaries in Public Practice, vols. 5, 1955–56. Cleveland, OH: Eugene M. Klein and Associates, 1956?. 231 p.

1574. Wendling, Wayne; Crabb-Velez, Connie Ann; and Carlsen, Melody A. *The Regulatory Impact on Pensions.* Brookfield, WI: International Foundation of Employee Benefit Plans, 1986. 91 p.

1575. Weyher, Harry F., and Knott, Hiram. *ESOP; The Employee Stock Ownership Plan.* 2d ed. Chicago: Commerce Clearing House, Inc., 1985. 291 p.
    The earlier edition was published in 1982.

1576. *What You Should Know about the Pension Law. [A Guide to ERISA as Amended by REA].* Washington, DC: U.S. Government Printing Office, 1985. 57 p.

1577. *What You Should Know about Your Retirement Income Now.* New York: Research Institute of America, 1985. 44 p.

1578. White, Frank J., Jr. *Construction Employer Liability and Rights under Title IV of ERISA.* Woodbridge, CT: WM Press, 1982. 75 p.

1579. Wilkin, John C. *United States Population Projection by Marital Status for CASDI Cost Estimates, 1980.* Baltimore, MD: Actuarial Study, 84. U.S. Social Security Administration, Office of the Actuary, 1980. 40 p.

1580. Williams, Arthur. *Managing Your Investment Manager; The Complete Guide to Selection, Measurement and Control.* 2d ed. Homewood, IL: Dow Jones-Irwin, 1986. 393 p.

1581. *The Williams-Javits Pension Reform Proposal.* Legislative Analysis Series. Washington, DC: American Enterprise Institute for Public Policy Research, 1973. 57 p.

1582. Wilson, Thomas. *Pensions Inflation & Growth.* New York: Irvington Publications, 1974. 422 p.

1583. Winklevoss, Howard E. *Pension Mathematics with Numerical Illustrations.* Homewood, IL: Published for the Pension Research Council by Richard D. Irwin, Inc., 1977. 243 p.

1584. Winklevoss, Howard E., and McGill, Dan. *Public Pension Plans; Standards of Design, Funding and Reporting.* Homewood, IL: Dow Jones-Irwin, 1979. 364 p.

1585. Winslow, Clarence Morton. *Profit Sharing and Pension Plans; Practical Planning and Administration.* Chicago: Commerce Clearing House, Inc., 1946. 272 p.

1586. Winthrop, Ralph. *Setting up and Administering Pension, Profit Sharing & Employee Benefit Programs and Professional Corporations; Forms and Workbook.* Greenvale, NY: Panel Publishers, 1977. 2 vols.

1587. Wise, David A. *Pensions and the Labor Market.* NBER Summary Report. Cambridge, MA: National Bureau of Economic Research, 1985. 24 p.

1588. Wise, David A., ed. *Pensions, Labor, and Individual Choice.* National Bureau of Economic Research Project Report. Chicago: University of Chicago Press, 1985. 453 p.

1589. Wise, David A., and Kotlikoff, Laurence J. *Labor Compensation and the Structure of Private Pension Plans; Evidence for Contractual Versus Spot Labor Markets.* NBER Working Paper, 1290. Cambridge, MA: National Bureau of Economic Research, 1984. 33 p.

1590. Wistert, Francis M. *Fringe Benefits.* Reinhold Management Science Series. New York: Reinhold Publishing Corp., 1959. 155 p.

1591. Wolf, Gerald P. *Non-Qualified Deferred Compensation Plans, 1985.* Tax Law and Practice Course Handbook Series, 228. New York: Practising Law Institute, 1985. 720 p.

1592. *Women and Retirement Income Programs; Current Issues of Equity and Adequacy, A Report.* Prepared by the Congressional Research Service. Washington, DC: U.S. Government Printing Office, 1979. 119 p.

1593. Woodruff, Thomas C. *Dollars and Sense; The Case for State and Local Pension Reform.* Washington, DC: American Federation of State, County and Municipal Employees, 1984. 37 p.

1594. Woyke, John F. *Qualified Plans; Integration.* Tax Management Portfolios, 356. Washington, DC: Bureau of National Affairs, Inc., 1986. Various pagings.

1595. Wright, Becky A., ed. *Handbook for Benefit Plan Professionals, 1983.* Brookfield, WI: International Foundation of Employee Benefit Plans, 1983. 142 p.

1596. Wyatt, Arthur R.; Dieter, Richard; and Stewart, John E. *Accounting for Deferred Compensation.* Tax Management Portfolios, 393. Washington, DC: Bureau of National Affairs, Inc., 1978. Various pagings.

1597. Wyatt, Birchard E. *Private Group Retirement Plans.* Washington, DC: Graphic Arts Press, Inc., 1936. 145 p.

1598. Wyatt, Birchard E., et al. *Employee Retirement Plans.* Washington, DC: Graphic Arts Press, Inc., 1945. 110 p.

1599. Young, Fay, and Young, Leo. *Everything You Should Know about Pension Plans.* 2d ed. Cockeysville, MD: Liberty Publishing Co., 1978.

1600. *Your Guide to the 1962 Federal Disclosure Law.* 3d ed. Englewood Cliffs, NJ: Prentice-Hall, Inc., 1965. 24 p.

1601. *Your Retirement; A Complete Planning Guide.* New York: A&W Publishers, Inc., 1981. 128 p.

1602. Zax, Jeffrey S. *Pure Price Effects of Nonwage Compensation.* NBER Working Paper, 1630. Cambridge, MA: National Bureau of Economic Research, 1985. 50 p.

1603. Zorn, Paul. *Small Business Barriers; Public Pension Investment Restrictions and Small Business Capital, A Report.* Washington, DC: Government Finance Officers Association, Government Finance Research Center. 1985. 138 p.

Theses

1604. Addy, Noel D., Jr. "Interest Rate Expectations for Pension Plans; Incentives for Divergent Actuarial Assumptions between DOL and FASB Disclosures." Ph.D. dissertation, University of Florida, 1985. 134 p.

1605. Alderson, Michael J. "Unfunded Pension Liabilities and Empirical Investigation." Ph.D. dissertation, University of Illinois, 1984. 239 p.

1606. Andrews, Victor L., Jr. "Investment Practices of Corporate Pension Funds." Ph.D. dissertation, Massachusetts Institute of Technology, 1958.

1607. Arnold, Frank S. "State and Local Employee Pension Funding; Theory, Evidence, and Implications." Ph.D. dissertation, Harvard University, 1983. 222 p.

1608. Atkins, Gerald L. "Distributions from Employer-Sponsored Pension Plans at Termination; Implications for Retirement Income and Tax Policy." Ph.D. dissertation, Brandeis University, 1985. 319 p.

1609. Baker, Leroy E. "Accounting for Pension Costs; An Historical Survey." Ph.D. dissertation, Harvard University, 1962.

1610. Bartell, Harry R., Jr. "Unions and Pension Funds." Ph.D. dissertation, Columbia University, 1963.

1611. Bayer, Frieda A. F. "An Analysis of the Relationship between the Discretionary Actuarial Factors Used by a Firm and Certain Firm-Specific Variables." Ph.D. dissertation, University of Texas at Arlington, 1984. 118 p.

1612. Bazzoli, Gloria J. "The Early Retirement Decision; The Influence of Health, Pensions, and Social Security." Ph.D. dissertation, Cornell University, 1983. 252 p.

1613. Beier, Emerson H. "A Study of Pension Plan Management and Its Public Policy Implications." Ph.D. dissertation, University of Wisconsin, 1969. 209 p.

1614. Ben-Artzy, Andy. "An Analysis of Institutional Investment Performance; The Case of Pension Funds." Ph.D. dissertation, New York University, 1979. 317 p.

1615. Bergen, Aaron H. "An Analysis of Retirement Plans in Selected Independent Colleges." Ph.D. dissertation, University of Denver, 1955. 105 p.

1616. Broman, Keith L. "Some Effects of Noncontributory Pension Plans on the Financial Policy of Corporations." Ph.D. dissertation, University of Nebraska, 1955. 310 p.

1617. Brooks, William A. "Accounting for the Enterprise Pension Benefit; An Examination Based upon a Statistical Study of Quit Rates for 207 Pension and Nonpension Metropolitan Kansas City Manufacturing Firms for the Period, 1965–1968." Ph.D. dissertation, University of Kansas, 1970. 331 p.

1618. Browning, Colin A. "Why Pension Funds Should Buy Common Stocks." Thesis, National Graduate Trust School, 1969. 81 p.

1619. Brucker, Maurice H. "A Computer-Based Retirement Planning System for Farmers with Low Income." Ph.D. dissertation, University of Illinois, 1973. 237 p.

1620. Burkhauser, Richard V. "The Early Pension Decision and Its Effect on Exit from the Labor Market." Ph.D. dissertation, University of Chicago, 1976.

1621. Carberry, Pauline R. "Taxation of Pension Plans for Self-Employed Individuals with Recommended Reforms." Ph.D. dissertation, The Ohio State University, 1970. 175 p.

1622. Carlson, Arthur E. "Some Management Problems in the Administration of Deferred-Payment Profit Sharing Plans." Ph.D. dissertation, Northwestern University, 1954. 442 p.

1623. Caswell, Jerry W. "Economic Efficiency in Pension Plan Administration; A Study of the Construction Industry." Ph.D. dissertation, University of Pennsylvania, 1974. 229 p.

1624. Cavanagh, Walter F. "The Economic Effects of Defined Benefit Pension Funding Policy on the Value of the Firm." Ph.D. dissertation, SUNY at Buffalo, 1985. 144 p.

1625. Clark, Arben O. "Employee Perception of and Attitude toward the Pension Plans of Employing Organizations." DBA dissertation, Indiana University, 1963. 171 p.

1626. Cohen, Cynthia F. "Estimation and Analysis of Differentials in Expected Retirement Benefits Provided by the Private Pension System for Men and Women." Ph.D. dissertation, Georgia State University, 1980. 180 p.

1627. Collins, Adrian A. "Pension Regulation; A Study of Need and Feasibility." DBA dissertation, George Washington University, 1967. 300 p.

1628. Collins, Julie H. "An Analysis of the Effect of Integration on the Private Pension Tax Subsidy." Ph.D. dissertation, University of Florida, 1983. 218 p.

1629. Corpus, Janet M. "Private Old-Age Pensions; A Study of Corporate Needs and Social Welfare." Ph.D. dissertation, Massachusetts Institute of Technology, 1980.

1630. Cozort, Larry A. "The Effect of Accrued Pension Benefit Preservation on Worker Mobility in Multiemployer Plans." Ph.D. dissertation, Virginia Polytechnic Institute and State University, 1985. 129 p.

1631. Cramer, Joe J., Jr. "Accounting and Reporting Requirements of the Private Pension Trust." DBA dissertation, Indiana University, 1963. 182 p.

1632. Crosby, William M. "An Examination of the Effects Which a Change in the Interest Rate Has on Pension Costs and Liabilities in Companies with Defined Benefit Pension Plans." Ph.D. dissertation, University of Georgia, 1985. 159 p.

1633. Cymrot, Donald J. "An Economic Analysis of Private Pensions. . . ." Ph.D. dissertation, Brown University, 1978. 176 p.

1634. Dahlin, Michel R. "From Poorhouse to Pension; The Changing View of Old Age in America, 1890–1929." Ph.D. dissertation, Stanford University, 1983. 249 p.

1635. Daley, Lane A. "The Valuation of Reported Pension Measures for Firms Sponsoring Defined Benefit Plans." Ph.D. dissertation, University of Washington, 1982. 297 p.

1636. DaMotta, Luiz F. J. "Multiperiod Contingent Claim Models with Stochastic Exercise Prices; An Application to Pension Fund Liability Insurance and Valuation of Firms." Ph.D. dissertation, University of Southern California, 1979.

1637. DeBard, Robert. "Economics of Hedging Corporate Pension Fund Reinvestment Rate Uncertainty." Ph.D. dissertation, Claremont Graduate School, 1981. 134 p.

1638. Delaney, Michael M. "Integration of Private Pension Plans with Social Security." Ph.D. dissertation, University of Pennsylvania, 1976. 203 p.

1639. Dietz, Peter O. "Evaluating the Investment Performance of Noninsured Pension Funds." Ph.D. dissertation, Columbia University, 1965. 212 p.

1640. Douthitt, Robin A. "Pension Information and the Retirement Decision of Married Women." Ph.D. dissertation, Cornell University, 1982. 120 p.

1641. DuPree, Dempsey M. "An Evaluation of Tax-Qualified Retirement Plans for Self-Employed Individuals." Ph.D. dissertation, Michigan State University, 1967. 159 p.

1642. Edmonds, Lucia K. "Financing State and Local Public Employee Retirement Plans." Ph.D. dissertation, Massachusetts Institute of Technology, 1979.

1643. Ellis, Charles D. "Investment Policies of Large Corporate Pension Funds." Ph.D. dissertation, New York University, 1979. 171 p.

1644. Emmet, Boris. "Profit Sharing in the United States." Ph.D. dissertation, Johns Hopkins University, 1917. 188 p.

1645. Entwisle, Barbara D. "Education, Pension Programs, and Fertility; A Cross-National Investigation with Special Reference to the Potential Held by Education and Pension Programs as Fertility Reduction Policies." Ph.D. dissertation, Brown University, 1980. 318 p.

1646. Erb, Charlotte M. "Savings and Investment Decisions in the Retirement Plans of Working Women." Ph.D. dissertation, University of Wisconsin, 1969. 204 p.

1647. Estrella, Arturo. "Portfolio Effects of Asset Idiosyncrasies; The Cases of Money and Pensions." Ph.D. dissertation, Harvard University, 1983. 169 p.

1648. Faram, Harvey D. "Pension Costs and Population Maturity." DBA dissertation, University of Colorado, 1981. 237 p.

1649. Ferguson, Dennis H. "The Economic Impact of the Employee Retirement Income Security Act on Firms with Active and Terminated Pension Plans." Ph.D. dissertation, Cornell University, 1981. 165 p.

1650. Fertig, Paul E. "The Accounting Aspects of Industrial Pension Plans." Ph.D. dissertation, The Ohio State University, 1952. 291 p.

1651. Flanagan, Edward J. "Incompletely Vested Pension Plans and Labor Mobility." Ph.D. dissertation, Michigan State University, 1969. 102 p.

1652. Flippo, Edwin B. "An Analysis of Methods Used to Maintain and Sustain Employee Profit Sharing Plans in Selected Companies." Ph.D. dissertation, The Ohio State University, 1953. 289 p.

1653. Ford, Gary R. "Statewide Assessment Survey of Michigan Public School Employees Retirement System Members to Determine Pension Benefit Awareness." Ph.D. dissertation, University of Michigan, 1975. 143 p.

1654. Foster, Ronald S. "Noninsured Corporate Pension Funds as a Source of Funds for Savings and Loan Associations," Ph.D. dissertation, The Ohio State University, 1961. 289 p.

1655. Galloway, James C. "An Analysis of the Employee Stock Ownership Plan Financing Technique with Examples of Its Use Prior to 1977." DBA dissertation, University of Virginia, 1980. 382 p.

1656. Galper, Jeffry H. "Private Pension Plans; Determinants of Benefit Receipt and Amount." Ph.D. dissertation, Bryn Mawr College, 1972. 302 p.

1657. Garfin, Louis. "On Pension Fund Reserves." Ph.D. dissertation, University of Iowa, 1942.

1658. Gass, Sylvester F. "Ecclesiastical Pensions." Ph.D. dissertation, Catholic University of America, 1942.

1659. Ghicas, Dimitrios C. "An Analysis of the Change of Actuarial Cost Methods for Pension Accounting and Funding." Ph.D. dissertation, University of Florida, 1985. 127 p.

1660. Gile, Frank L. "Some Economic Implications of the Pension Reform Act of 1974 for Fixed Benefit Pension Plans." Ph.D. dissertation, University of Illinois, 1979. 300 p.

1661. Glasson, William Henry. "History of Military Pension Legislation in the United States." Ph.D. dissertation, Columbia University, 1900. 135 p.

1662. Godfrey, Lon H. "An Inquiry into the Significance and Disclosure of Year-to-Year Variations in Pension Expense Reported by Selected Corporations." Ph.D. dissertation, University of Alabama, 1975. 258 p.

1663. Graaskamp, James A. "Pension Termination Due to Business Failure, Liquidation, or Migration." Ph.D. dissertation, University of Wisconsin, 1965. 518 p.

1664. Gradison, Willis D., Jr. "Management Problems in Pension Investing." Ph.D. dissertation, Harvard University, 1954.

1665. Graham, Sharon S. "The Hedged Operating Risk Mode; A Pension Asset Investment Strategy." DBA dissertation, University of Virginia, 1984. 212 p.

1666. Green, Mitzi C. "An Empirical Study of Employers' Administrative Costs and Benefits of Providing a Defined Benefit Pension Plan in Mississippi." DBA dissertation, Mississippi State University, 1983. 170 p.

1667. Gustavson, Sandra G. "Pension Plans and the Writing of Fully-Covered, Exchange Traded Call Options." Ph.D. dissertation, University of Illinois, 1979. 160 p.

1668. Hagigi, Moshe. "Investment Objectives and Policies of Large Corporate Pension Funds; Implications for Investment and Accounting Regulations." Ph.D. dissertation, New York University, 1981. 95 p.

1669. Hailstones, Thomas J. "Historical and Economic Aspects of Pension Plans in the Automobile Industry." Ph.D. dissertation, Saint Louis University, 1951.

1670. Hamdallah, Ahmed El-Sayed. "An Investigation of Motivation for Voluntarily Terminating Overfunded Pension Plans." Ph.D. dissertation, City University of New York, 1985. 123 p.

1671. Hammond, James D. "The Effect of Mergers on Private Pensions." Ph.D. dissertation, University of Pennsylvania, 1961. 203 p.

1672. Harbrecht, Paul P. "Pension Funds and Economic Power." Ph.D. dissertation, Columbia University, 1960.

1673. Harvey, Ernest C. "Public and Private Pension Plans and Group Preferences for Economic Security in Old Age." Ph.D. dissertation, Columbia University, 1961. 292 p.

1674. Haselkorn, Michael. "APB Opinion No. 8 and Fluctuation in Pension Expense; A Case Study in the Effectiveness of Accounting Regulation." Ph.D. dissertation, University of Chicago, 1981.

1675. Helburn, Isadore B., III. "An Analysis of the Industrial Relations Climate in Unionized Profit-Sharing Firms." Ph.D. dissertation, University of Wisconsin, 1966. 330 p.

1676. Higgins, Neal O. "The Early Pension Plans of the Baltimore and Ohio and the Pennsylvania Railroads, 1880–1937." Ph.D. dissertation, University of Nebraska, 1974. 117 p.

1677. Hill, Joanne M. "Pension Fund Management; A Framework for Investment and Funding Decisions." Ph.D. dissertation, Syracuse University, 1978. 255 p.

1678. Holland, Rodger Gene. "The Information Content of Three Pension Cost Measures; Theoretical and Empirical Analysis." Ph.D. dissertation, The Ohio State University, 1981. 114 p.

1679. Hoogstraat, Emerson E. "Investment Policy for Deferred Distribution Profit Sharing Trust Funds." DBA dissertation, University of Washington, 1963. 213 p.

1680. Ibrahim, Ibrahim B. "An Econometric Model for Life Insurance Companies' and Pension Funds' Investment Behavior." Ph.D. dissertation, New York University, 1969. 148 p.

1681. Ilse, Louise W. "The History of Group Insurance and Retirement Plans in the United States." Ph.D. dissertation, Columbia University, 1951. 498 p.

1682. Inzunza, Gilbert. "A Multiple Employer Pension Plan for Middle Management Salaried Aerospace Employees." Ph.D. dissertation, United States International University, 1983. 84 p.

1683. Ireland, Ralph R. "The Aging Industrial Worker; Retirement Plans and Preparations. . . ." Ph.D. dissertation, University of Chicago, 1951. 354 p.

1684. Jarboe, Norma J. "Pension Funds as a Source of Investment in Residential Real Estate in the 1980's." Thesis, Stonier Graduate School of Banking, 1981. 90 p.

1685. Jenkins, David O. "Accounting for Industrial Pension Plans." DBA dissertation, University of Southern California, 1963. 306 p.

1686. Joanette, Francois P. "Managing Corporate Pension Funds; A Study of the Determinants of Pension Funding and Assets Allocation Decisions." Ph.D. dissertation, University of Pennsylvania, 1985. 327 p.

1687. Johnson, Alton C. "A Suggested Analytical Procedure for Pension Design and Appraisal." Ph.D. dissertation, University of Wisconsin, 1957. 196 p.

1688. Jones, Gene K. "A Study of Profit-Sharing Plans of Selected Banks in Texas." Ph.D. dissertation, University of Texas, 1964. 203 p.

1689. Keeley, Robert H. "Pension Plan Decisions and Corporate Financial Policy." Ph.D. dissertation, Stanford University, 1969. 371 p.

1690. Klein, Katherine J. "The Effects of Employee Stock Ownership on Employees' Job Satisfaction, Organization Commitment and Well-Being." Ph.D. dissertation, University of Texas, 1984. 313 p.

1691. Krueger, James M. "Information Needed for the Management of Locally Administered Municipal Pension Funds with Indiana Municipal Pension Funds as a Specific Case." DBA dissertation, Indiana University, 1976. 219 p.

1692. Landsman, Wayne R. "An Investigation of Pension Fund Property Rights." Ph.D. dissertation, Stanford University, 1984. 188 p.

1693. Lazar, Laura Kristen. "Effects of Pension Information on Credit Quality Judgments of Municipal Bond Analysts." Ph.D. dissertation, Indiana University, 1986. 127 p.

1694. Leeds, Michael A. "The Underfunding of Municipal Pensions and its Effect on Property Values, Wages and Strike Activity in the Local Public Sector." Ph.D. dissertation, Princeton University, 1983. 152 p.

1695. Lenarcic, Michael Alan. "Forecasting Pension Plan Cash Flows in an Inflationary Environment." Ph.D. dissertation, Harvard University, 1977.

1696. Levi, Donald R. "An Economic Analysis of Farmer Participation in Keogh Retirement Plans." Ph.D. dissertation, Washington State University, 1974. 223 p.

1697. Louie, Charles F. "Accounting for Pension Costs; The Measurement of Pension Costs in the National Accounts." Ph.D. dissertation, University of California, 1963. 135 p.

1698. Love, William H. "Simulated Pension Scenarios with Stochastic Demographic and Investment Experience Utilizing Alternative Actuarial Cost Methods and Accounting Principles." Ph.D. dissertation, University of Arkansas, 1986. 355 p.

1699. Lucas, Vane B., Jr. "Influence of Collective Bargaining on Pension Plan Design." Ph.D. dissertation, University of Pennsylvania, 1964. 358 p.

1700. Luzadis, Rebecca A. "Defined Benefit, Defined Contribution, or No Pension?" Ph.D. dissertation, Cornell University, 1986. 188 p.

1701. Maher, John J. "Pension Obligations and the Bond Credit Market; An Empirical Analysis of Accounting Numbers." Ph.D. dissertation, Pennsylvania State University, 1985. 168 p.

1702. Malley, Susan L. "Unfunded Pension Liabilities; Risk of Costly Default and the Cost of Equity Capital." Ph.D. dissertation, New York University, 1979. 154 p.

1703. Margotta, Donald G. "The Effect of Institutional Ownership of Shares on Financial Decisions of the Firm." Ph.D. dissertation, University of North Carolina, 1984. 174 p.

1704. Markwalder, Alice M. S. "An Evaluation of the Effectiveness of ERISA; Assessed from the Termination of Defined Benefit Pension Plans in Georgia, 1974–1979." Ph.D. dissertation, University of Georgia, 1982. 315 p.

1705. Marshall, James N., II. "The Pension Fund Asset Mix Decision in a World of Economic Uncertainty; A Simulation Approach." Ph.D. dissertation, Lehigh University, 1982. 121 p.

1706. Marshall, Stanmore B. "Fixed-Income Securities in the Pension Fund; The Effect on Market Valuation." DBA dissertation, University of Virginia, 1986. 201 p.

1707. McDonald, Maurice E. "Reciprocity among Private Multiemployer Pension Plans." Ph.D. dissertation, University of Pennsylvania, 1972. 424 p.

1708. McKenna, Fred W. "Pension Costs under Stochastic Inflation Rate, Salary Rate, and Investment Rate Assumptions." Ph.D. dissertation, University of South Carolina, 1980. 230 p.

1709. McMillan, Henry M. "Essays in the Economics of Pensions." Ph.D. dissertation, University of Wisconsin, 1982. 182 p.

1710. McMurry, D. "The Political Significance of the Pension Question, 1885–1897." Ph.D. dissertation, University of Wisconsin, 1921. 8 p.

1711. McVey, Phillip. "Pension Plans for Outside Salesmen." Ph.D. dissertation, The Ohio State University, 1954. 237 p.

1712. Melone, Joseph J. "Collectively-Bargained Multi-Employer Pension Plans." Ph.D. dissertation, University of Pennsylvania, 1961. 296 p.

1713. Merz, Thomas E. "Analysis of the Underfunding of Municipal Pensions." Ph.D. dissertation, University of Pittsburgh, 1980. 117 p.

1714. Mielke, David Ervin. "Theoretical Framework for Pension Costs." Ph.D. dissertation, University of Wisconsin, 1981. 202 p.

1715. Miljus, Robert C. "A Comparative Analysis of Work History Data Reported by Wisconsin Workers in Order to Determine the Relative Influence of Private Pensions on Labor Mobility." Ph.D. dissertation, University of Wisconsin, 1963. 395 p.

1716. Mills, Donald R. "A Conceptual Model of Retirement Plans for Professional Personnel in Selected Universities." Ed.D. dissertation, University of Missouri, 1971. 216 p.

1717. Mittelman, Jonas E. "The Vesting of Private Pensions." Ph.D. dissertation, University of Pennsylvania, 1959. 219 p.

1718. Modlin, George M. "Industrial Old Age Pensions." Ph.D. dissertation, Princeton University, 1932.

1719. Monroe, Paul. "Profit Sharing; A Study in Social Economics." Ph.D. dissertation, University of Chicago, 1897. 1,923 p.

1720. Morris, William J. "Accounting for Common Stocks for Church Pension Funds, an Empirical Evaluation." Ph.D. dissertation, Michigan State University, 1971. 210 p.

1721. Nektarios, Miltiades. "The Economic Theory of Dynamic Pensions and Their Impact on Capital Formation and Economic Growth." Ph.D. dissertation, Temple University, 1980. 254 p.

1722. Niehaus, Gregory R. "The Economic Effects of ERISA." Ph.D. dissertation, Washington University, 1985. 127 p.

1723. Novomestky, Frederick. "A Multiple Criteria Decision Making Approach to the Pension Funding and Management Problem." Ph.D. dissertation, Polytechnic Institute of New York, 1982. 394 p.

1724. O'Brien, John C. "An Analysis of the Standards of Administration of Union Welfare and Pension Funds." Ph.D. dissertation, University of Notre Dame, 1961. 495 p.

1725. O'Leary, Harold E. "An Analysis of the Composition, Operating Characteristics and Performance of Trustee-Managed Municipal Pension Funds in Florida." DBA dissertation, Florida State University, 1980. 214 p.

1726. Olson, Shirley F. "A Model for the Financing of Current and Future Pension Systems for Municipal Governments with Special Application to Jackson, Mississippi." DBA dissertation, Mississippi State University, 1978. 162 p.

1727. Parker, Mary V. "Population Dynamics and Benefit Allocation Patterns for Defined Benefit Pension Plans Subject to FASB Statement 35 Requirements." DBA dissertation, University of Colorado, 1982. 174 p.

1728. Parlar, Mahmut. "Extensions of Some Discrete Time Optimal Control Models with Applications to Pension Planning." Ph.D. dissertation, University of Waterloo, 1979.

1729. Pascucci, John Joseph. "The Investment Policies of Collectively Bargained Pension Funds." Ph.D. dissertation, Stanford University, 1964. 294 p.

1730. Pavelka, Deborah D. "Pension Liabilities and Bankers' Loan Decisions." Ph.D. dissertation, University of Missouri, 1985. 220 p.

1731. Pope, Ralph A. "An Examination of the Economic Efficiency of State and Municipal Pension Plans." DBA dissertation, Mississippi State University, 1984. 131 p.

1732. Power, Mark L. "An Analysis of Post-ERISA Growth in the Number of Private Pension Plans." Ph.D. dissertation, University of Iowa, 1981. 210 p.

1733. Pullara, Santo J. "Retirement Plans; A Study of Small Firms and Large Firms." Ph.D. dissertation, Syracuse University, 1962. 214 p.

1734. Reiter, Sara A. "The Effect of Defined Benefit Pension Plan Disclosures on Bond Risk Premiums and Bond Ratings." Ph.D. dissertation, University of Missouri, 1985. 181 p.

1735. Reuter, John H. "Retirement Plans and Medium Sized Trust Departments." Thesis, National Graduate Trust School, 1967. 144 p.

1736. Scanlan, Burt K. "Some Aspects of Industrial Pension Plan Development." Ph.D. dissertation, University of Nebraska, 1964. 376 p.

1737. Schofield, Rosalie F. "The Private Pension Coverage of Part-Time Workers." Ph.D. dissertation, Brandeis University, 1985. 282 p.

1738. Schulz, James H. "The Future Economic Circumstances of the Aged; A Simulation Projection of Aged Pension Income and Asset Distributions, 1980." Ph.D. dissertation, Yale University, 1966. 204 p.

1739. Schwartz, Charles M. "Asset Purchase and Revision Policies for Pension Portfolios. . . ." Ph.D. dissertation, New York University, 1973. 79 p.

1740. Scott, Harold W. "The Investment of Trusteed Pension Funds." Ph.D. dissertation, New York University, 1959.

1741. Seow, Gim-Seong. "The Valuation of Corporate Pension Obligations; A Contingent Claims Model and Some Empirical Tests." Ph.D. dissertation, University of Oregon, 1985. 121 p.

1742. Seyed-Kazami, Mohammad Hossein. "A Comparison of Relative Rates of Return on Private and Public Pension Funds." Ph.D. dissertation, Clark University, 1983. 107 p.

1743. Shapiro, Arnold F. "A General Model of Expected Pension Costs." Ph.D. dissertation, University of Pennsylvania, 1975. 317 p.

1744. Sharif, Kamarrudin Bin. "Pension Funding and Investments; A Multiple Criteria Decision Making Approach." Ph.D. dissertation, The Ohio State University, 1985. 147 p.

1745. Sil, Amar Nath. "Valuation of a Corporate Pension Put Option and Its Effect on Pension Liability." Ph.D. dissertation, Columbia University, 1984. 86 p.

1746. Slocum, Clarence A. "The Practice and Operation of Industrial Pensions." Ph.D. dissertation, The Ohio State University, 1953. 401 p.

1747. Smith, Lowell C. "An Evaluation of Public Policy Proposal for the Regulation of Private Pension Plan Eligibility Requirements and Vesting Provisions." Ph.D. dissertation, University of Alabama, 1969. 380 p.

1748. Snyder, Donald C. "Changes in Pension Provisions and Firm Attachment; A Longitudinal Analysis." Ph.D. dissertation, University of Maryland, 1981. 309 p.

1749. Spector, William D. "The Adequacy of the Private Pension System for Women; A Look at Survivor Benefits and Vesting Provisions." Ph.D. dissertation, Brandeis University, 1981. 197 p.

1750. Stewart, Douglas S. "Retirement Plan Alternatives for Medical Professionals; Self-Employed vs. Incorporated." Thesis, National Graduate Trust School, 1980. 138 p.

1751. Stone, Mary S. "An Examination of the Effect of Disclosures Concerning Unfunded Pension Benefits on Market Risk Measures." Ph.D. dissertation, University of Illinois. 1981. 251 p.

1752. Studenski, Paul. "Teachers' Pension Systems in the United States; A Critical and Descriptive Study." Ph.D. dissertation, Columbia University, 1921. 460 p.

1753. Sullens, Robert T. "Evaluation of Current Pension Reporting Practices." DBA dissertation, Kent State University, 1974. 242 p.

1754. Swil, Samuel R. "Actuarial Assumptions for the Determination of Pension Scheme Funding Rates in an Inflationary Economy." MBA thesis, University of the Witwatersrand, 1983.

1755. Swindle, Charles B. "Accounting Ratios as Measures of Benefits to Companies Initiating Pension Plans." Ph.D. dissertation, Louisiana State University, 1979. 106 p.

1756. Sze, Man-Bing. "Pension Funding Policy and Corporate Finance." Ph.D. dissertation, The Rand Graduate Institute, 1985. 121 p.

1757. Tepper, Irwin. "Optimal Financial Strategies for Trusteed Pension Plans." Ph.D. dissertation, University of Pennsylvania, 1972. 269 p.

1758. Thomas, Jacob K. "Taxes and Corporate Pension Policy; Some Empirical Tests." Ph.D. dissertation, University of Michigan, 1984. 90 p.

1759. Thompson, Brian C. "A Dynamic Programming Approach to the Pension Fund Asset Structure Problem." Ph.D. dissertation, Southern Methodist University, 1974. 188 p.

1760. Thompson, Gerald E. "The Role and Effect of Private Pensions in the American Economy." Ph.D. dissertation, University of Iowa, 1953. 260 p.

1761. Tobin, Charles J. "A Theory of Socioeconomic Organization; The Economics of Profit Sharing." Ph.D. dissertation, Georgetown University, 1957.

1762. Tosh, David E. "An Empirical Evaluation of Alternative Accounting Measures of Defined Benefit Pension Plan Liabilities." Ph.D. dissertation, The Pennsylvania State University, 1985. 209 p.

1763. Tsay, Bor-Yi. "The Relationship between Pension Disclosure and Bond Risk Premium." Ph.D. dissertation, University of Houston, 1986. 113 p.

1764. Turner, Jennie Willing McMullin. "Thinking and Planning, Health and Happiness, Profit-Sharing That Failed; From Scientific Management to Unionism, Joint Control." Ph.D. dissertation, University of Wisconsin, 1927.

1765. Utz, John L., Jr. "A Comparative Study of the Investments of Union Pension Funds, Corporate Pension Funds and Balanced Mutual Funds." MBA Thesis, Duquesne University, 1970. 199 p.

1766. Vaughan, Therese M. "The Trade-Off between Pensions and Wages in an Implicit Contracts Labor Market." Ph.D. dissertation, University of Pennsylvania, 1985. 156 p.

1767. Von der Linde, Gert. "Growth, Functions and Financial Administration of Private Pension Plans." Ph.D. dissertation, University of California, 1963. 429 p.

1768. Vu, Liem Quy. "The Effect of Pension Leverage on the Systematic Risk of Common Stocks." Ph.D. dissertation, University of Arkansas, 1983. 192 p.

1769. Wagner, Shelby E. "Early Retirement Plans for Certificated Public School Employees in California." Ed.D. dissertation, UCLA, 1976. 165 p.

1770. Wardlow, Penelope S. "Towards Building a Conceptual Framework of Financial Reporting for State and Local Government Defined-Benefit Pension Plans." Ph.D. dissertation. University of Georgia, 1985. 398 p.

1771. Warren, Charles W. "Synthesis of a Skeleton for College Retirement Plans in North Carolina." Ed.D. dissertation, University of Northern Colorado, 1976. 192 p.

1772. Waters, William R. "The Effect of Employer Pension Plan Membership on the Level of Household Wealth." Ph.D. dissertation, University of Chicago, 1976.

1773. Whiting, Jack E. "Compensating Wage Differentials and Pension Coverage; The Implicit Market for Pensions." Ph.D. dissertation, Cornell University, 1979. 279 p.

1774. Williams, Robert B. "Inside the Labor-Managed Firm; An Economic Analysis." Ph.D. dissertation, University of North Carolina, 1984. 495 p.

1775. Willinger, Geoffrey L. "A Contingent Claims Model for Pensions Costs." DBA dissertation, The Florida State University, 1982. 140 p.

1776. Wilson, Joseph W. "The Impact of the Employee Retirement Income Security Act of 1974 on Small Private Pension and Profit Sharing Plans in Arkansas." Ph.D. dissertation, University of Arkansas, 1980. 259 p.

1777. Wimberly, Jack C. "Private Industrial Pension Plans in the United States; A Comparative Analysis." Ph.D. dissertation, The Louisiana State University, 1967. 178 p.

1778. Winklevoss, Howard E. "A Quantitative Analysis of the Factors Affecting Pension Costs." DBA dissertation, University of Oregon, 1970. 422 p.

1779. Wood, Richard H. "The Principles and Practices of Profit Sharing Illustrated from the Profit Sharing Plans of the Eastman Kodak Company, the Procter and Gamble Company, Sears Roebuck and Company." Ph.D. dissertation, Princeton University, 1943. 230 p.

1780. Woolrych, Edmund H. "Corporate Pension Funds and Their Effects on Other Saving Institutions." Ph.D. dissertation, Syracuse University, 1958. 234 p.

1781. Wrightsman, Dwayne E. "An Analysis of the Extent of Corporate Ownership and Control by Private Pension Funds." Ph.D. dissertation, Michigan State University, 1964. 210 p.

1782. Wyatt, Birchard E. "Private Group Retirement Plans." Ph.D. dissertation, Columbia University, 1937. 146 p.

1783. Zock, Richard, "Equities and Private Pension Plans." DBA dissertation, University of Colorado, 1971. 236 p.

Miscellaneous Sources

DATABASES

Several bibliographic databases are useful to the researcher in the retirement plan area. All have limitations. The weakness of abstracted bibliographic databases is that the abstracters have to be very knowledgeable and the most knowledgeable and successful business people are the least likely to be abstracters.

Furthermore, the retirement plan area is characterized by obscure and vague or ambiguous terminology. Even an abstracter well schooled in general business language will encounter articles that will befuddle or confuse.

As a consequence, the researcher, whether using a controlled thesaurus of subjects or a buzzword approach, can never be certain of getting at all of the literature in a database on a certain topic. One can prove this very easily. The two best bibliographic databases on our topic at this writing are ABI/INFORM and MANAGEMENT CONTENTS. Because they have a great deal of overlap, one can easily find journal articles on retirement literature that *should* be indexed in both. If one were to search for literature on asset mix or pension investment policy or privatization of the Pension Benefit Guaranty Corporation or cutbacks or phased retirement, one would often find that the result of the search in one of the databases contains cites that are missing from the result of the search in the other. If one checks the list of journals indexed, one will usually find that there should have been hits where there were misses. Of course, searching by author or title will get much more nearly identical results, but most searches are conducted by subject.

No doubt a mediocre abstract is better than no abstract at all. My little experience with BUSINESS PERIODICALS INDEX on WILSONLINE has certainly convinced me of that. Furthermore, one should not blame the abstracters for misses. The editorial policies as to the depth of indexing or the wording of abstracts no doubt cause some of them. The point is that one can never be absolutely certain of thoroughness when utilizing only database approaches.

Of course, one can never be certain of thoroughness with a paper approach either. The more traditional tools are far more time consuming and afford only a thesaurus approach. The ability to reach into a well-written abstract for searching purposes can only be afforded by computerized bibliographic databases. It behooves researchers to know their limitations.

1784. ABI/INFORM. Data Courier, Inc. Louisville, KY, 1971–.
At this writing, this is the best general purpose online bibliographic database for retirement plan literature. It indexes around 700 business journals and has long abstracts which allows for more hits. The use of cc=6400 will frequently help to eliminate false positives, but one should use it with caution.

1785. BEST'S ONLINE DATABASE. A.M. Best Company, Inc. Oldwick, NJ, n.d.
This contains much of the information published in the *Best's Reports*.

1786. BUSINESS PERIODICALS INDEX. H.W. Wilson Co., New York, New York, 1982–.
An excellent paper bibliography, this is available online via Wilsonline. But the only reason I would search it is if articles were requested from a particular periodical not indexed by ABI/INFORM. There are no abstracts, and buzzword searching leads to poor results.

1787. CIS. Congressional Information Service, Inc. Bethesda, MD, 1970–.
Available also in paper, this source had a profound effect on the shape of this book. Reminded of its existence by Alice Wickizer of the Government Publications Department at Indiana University, I searched it with the term "pension?" On March 12, 1987, there were 5,566 documents mentioning pension or pensions and about 4,000 of them were congressional committee hearings. I had to be reminded of the existence of this database because I had never used it. No doubt there are researchers delving into the legislative history of retirement plans who use it frequently. At any rate, I dropped most congressional literature from this book because it is readily discoverable here. See also the discussion at FEDERAL INDEX, entry 1791.

1788. CUMULATIVE BOOK INDEX. H.W. Wilson Co. New York, New York, 1982–.
Online this only goes back to 1982. It is bibliographic. information on books only.

1789. DISSERTATION ABSTRACTS. University Microfilms International, Ann Arbor, MI, 1962–.
This database has a paper counterpart, but it is much easier to search online. There have been several hundred theses on retirement plan subjects. This was the source of the vast majority of my thesis chapter. Most of the theses, by the way, are available from University Microfilms in Ann Arbor, Michigan.

1790. EMPLOYEE BENEFIT INFORMATION SYSTEM (EBIS). International Foundation of Employee Benefit Plans, Brookfield, WI, 1988–.
As I write this, EBIS is not yet available. It is scheduled to be included in the DIALOG family of databases in early 1988. EBIS will consist of references and abstracts from more than 400 journals as well as numerous books and pamphlets relating to the benefits field. Because it is being produced by the International Foundation of Employee Benefit Plans, it is sure to be useful.

1791. FEDERAL INDEX (once called PTS Federal Index). Predicasts, Inc., Cleveland, OH, 1976–.
This looks to cover virtually the same congressional literature as CIS. It also covers the various outputs of the executive and the judiciary although these branches are nowhere near so prolific. A search on April 18, 1987, disclosed 3,284 documents having mention of pensions or retirement. This is also available in paper. See also the discussion of Congressional Information Service, entry 1787.

1792. FEDERAL REGISTER ABSTRACTS. Capitol Services, Inc., Washington, DC, 1977–.
This is an excellent replacement for dredging through *Federal Register* indexes themselves. It is retrospective to 1977, and it is updated weekly.

1793. GPO MONTHLY CATALOG and GPO PUBLICATIONS REFERENCE FILE. U.S. Government Printing Office, Washington, DC, 1976–.
These are actually separate databases. The first is simply an index to *some* U.S. government publications. From July 1976 through April 1987, there are 1,533 mentions of pension(s) or retirement. Those seeking government literature prior to July 1976 must have recourse to the paper equivalent. The second is an index to publications for sale by the Superintendent of Documents. In April 1987 there were only eighty-five hits for pension(s) or retirement.

1794. HRIN (The Human Resource Information Network). ETS, Inc., Indianapolis, IN, 1974–.
One module of HRIN contains full text access to various Bureau of National Affairs publications of interest to retirement plan professionals.

1795. INSURANCE ABSTRACTS. University Microfilms International, Ann Arbor, MI, 1979–1984.
This database ceased being updated as of the end of 1984, meaning that it becomes less useful with each passing day. It indexed only seventy journals that might touch upon retirement plan literature, but in the short space of six years, it amassed 10,165 items with mention of pension(s) or retirement. Each journal must have been indexed exhaustively.

1796. IRS TAXINFO. U.S. Internal Revenue Service, Washington, DC, n.d.
This contains full text of most of the IRS publications described elsewhere in this book and also contained in the Commerce Clearing House *IRS Publications*. I can scarcely conceive of anyone using this except in emergencies or if the new editions of the publications are loaded significantly before paper become available.

1797. LC MARC and REMARC. U.S. Library of Congress, Washington, DC, 1968–.
These databases contain bibliographic entries for books and pamphlets gathered from various sources but mostly from the holdings of the Library of Congress. The databases are massive and prone to error, but they do contain a lot of retirement plan literature.

1798. LEGAL RESOURCE INDEX. Information Access Co., Belmont, CA, 1980–.
This index to legal periodical literature covers about 700 journals and is getting more useful as time goes by. It is retrospective only to 1980, however.

1799. LEXIS. Mead Data Central, Dayton, OH, dates vary.
This is not really a database; instead it is a family of databases. Of interest to retirement plan practitioners are full-text access to IRS manuals and handbooks, revenue rulings and procedures, private letter rulings, general counsel memoranda, insurance codes for the fifty states, court reporters, Pension Benefit Guaranty Corporation publications, and (since January 1982) *BNA Pension Reporter*. See also treatment at WESTLAW, entry 1802.

1800. MANAGEMENT CONTENTS. Information Access Co., Belmont, CA, 1974–.
This database indexes about a hundred business publications very thoroughly. It is very slightly less expensive per printed or typed hit than ABI/INFORM. There are few searches for retirement plan literature where I would prefer MANAGEMENT CONTENTS over ABI/INFORM, however. The index is skewed to management theory.

1801. PHINET. Prentice-Hall, Inc., Englewood Cliffs, NJ, 1985–.
This database contains full text of materials relevant to federal tax. Of particular interest to retirement plan practitioners are the private letter rulings, revenue rulings and procedures, general counsel memoranda, and access to the *PH Pension and Profit Sharing Service.*

1802. WESTLAW. West Publishing Co., St. Paul, MN, dates vary.
This database family has such a high overlap with LEXIS that reading the LEXIS, entry 1799, treatment is probably sufficient as a description of WESTLAW.

OTHER PERIODICAL INDICES

1803. *Business Index.* Information Access Co., Belmont, CA, 1979–.
This is a microfilm guide to periodical literature in business. It is a good deal more timely and easy to use than traditional paper indices, and it indexes more than 500 publications. It is, however, a bit sloppy in that there are errors now and then in alphabetization. The subject scheme is too articulated, and some of the indexers are not where they should be in understanding the literature. The microfiche format makes it an unlikely find in many libraries.

1804. *Business Periodicals Index.* H.W. Wilson Co., New York, New York, 1958–.
This high quality book and pamphlet format index goes back to 1958. It split off in that year from *Industrial Arts Index.* Any periodical literature on retirement plans which was indexed before 1971 came out in *BPI* or its predecessor. For a decade after that, it was still more comprehensive in its coverage than the online alternatives. Even now when its primary drawback is that it is not timely, there is a lot to recommend the paper version. Of course, it is a nuisance to go from volume to volume, but one still picks up things one does not catch online. Finally, although the cost varies with the holdings of the purchasing library, it may be accounted inexpensive. The time spent in bibliographic searching is often discounted.

1805. *Business Publications Index and Abstracts.* Information Access Co., Belmont, CA.
This is the paper equivalent of MANAGEMENT CONTENTS, which is discussed in entry 1800.

OTHER-THAN-PRINT-MEDIA

Audiocassettes have long since appeared in the retirement plan arena. The various actuarial bodies are publishing some of the proceedings at their meetings in this way. In my library there are tapes from both the Conference of Actuaries in Public Practice and the Society of Actuaries. The Practising Law Institute is publishing its seminars on audiotape with accompanying course handbooks. Both Bureau of National Affairs and Commerce Clearing House have published in the area on audiotape. *Nutshell*, described in the periodicals chapter, has been coming out on audiotape since early 1985 or before. It is fairly obvious from the title or subtitle "Video Law Review" that the American Law Institute-American Bar Association must be doing some of its programs on videocassette. Finally, there is a bulletin board for the industry in the entity of Employee Benefit Information Network (EBIN). EBIN has information on legislation, studies being published, and seminars being held, and a message board is also featured. It is accessible with virtually any make of personal computer.

Core Library Collection

The perfect retirement plan library probably does not exist. Even the library at the International Foundation of Employee Benefit Plans, which has a relatively long and organized existence, probably does not include a current edition of everything in the following list. It is not so much the considerable expense that precludes this state. Several of the surveys listed are proprietary and obtaining them is close to impossible unless one is a participant.

Another factor is that perfection depends on the clientele. A perfect survey library would be of small use to most of the lawyers in the industry. Prevalence of various practices is only of marginal interest to them. They are more concerned with operating within the legal and regulatory framework and with changes in the framework. Of course, the clientele of a library depends on its situation, but to a typical library, the legal profession is likely to be the heaviest user contingent. All lawyers go through a course that requires that they learn how to do research. Moreover, as Tom Paxton reminds us, "in ten years we're gonna have one million lawyers" (phonorecord. *One Million Lawyers and Other Disasters*. Flying Fish, 1985).

SURVEYS

Benefit managers are voracious consumers of survey information. The nature of the retirement package offered by competitors is important to them, but that information is generally only available in proprietary surveys and Department of Labor files.

Those interested in some aspect of government policy are also consumers of survey information. They tend, however, not to be interested in benefits afforded by a particular firm or segment of industry. They are more interested in the aggregate picture.

The following list contains both kinds of surveys. Several of them are not readily obtainable, but a superlative survey cannot be ignored for that reason. Although I include more surveys by my own employer than by most publishers, I do not feel that I have been unfair. They are just good surveys.

1806. *Employee Benefits.* Washington, DC: U.S. Chamber of Commerce. Survey, Research Section, 1949?–. (Annual)

This important survey is primarily concerned with benefits as a whole, but several of its tables break out pension plan payments and profit sharing and thrift plan payments. One can thus learn percentage of payroll, cents per hour, and dollars per year per employee figures which are interesting to many. A shortcoming of the survey is that it treats only employees who are not exempt from the provisions of the Fair Labor Standards Act. Except in banking, professional employees are not covered. Another shortcoming is that the data is over a year old when first published. This is nevertheless the best known and most used benefits survey.

1807. *Employee Benefits in Medium and Large Firms.* Washington, DC: U.S. Department of Labor, Bureau of Labor Statistics, n.d. (Annual)

Three-eighths of the 1985 survey, published in July 1986, has to do with retirement plans. This is an excellent survey if your approach is from the macro level. Government policymakers no doubt find it extremely useful. But, if you are in charge of benefits for a 400-employee, $30 million-revenue, consumer goods manufacturer in Oklahoma, you should not expect it to tell you what companies in your situation are affording their employees.

1808. *ESOP Survey.* Washington, DC: The ESOP Association, n.d. (Annual)

A survey of firms having employee stock ownership plans and belonging to the publishing association.

1809. *Executive Report on Large Corporate Pension Plans.* New York: Johnson & Higgins, 1978–. (Annual)

This is a study of corporate pension expense and funding. The introduction treats current issues in the area. The figures for expense as a percentage of corporate profit and the funding ratios to be found here are useful.

1810. *The Hay/Huggins Benefits Comparison.* Philadelphia?, PA: Hay/Huggins Co., Inc., n.d. (Annual)

Formerly entitled the *Noncash Compensation Comparison*, this is reputedly an excellent survey that includes a good deal of information on numerous plan provisions. Although about a thousand organizations are surveyed, no company names are mentioned, and the industry breakdown is rudimentary. The survey is tightly controlled. I believe that a copy may be obtained only by participants.

1811. *Hewitt Associates SpecBook.* Lincolnshire, IL: Hewitt Associates, 1979?–. (Annual)

Reputed recently to have grown to three volumes from two, this survey has extensive coverage of retirement plans. The specifications of the plans are not summarized as in most surveys. Instead, for 700 to 800 named companies, information such as benefit formula, integration provisions, eligibility requirements, and type of plan are listed. This survey is strictly controlled and, I believe, available to participants only. Summaries are sold to all comers under the title *Salaried Employee Benefits*. These are described in entries 120 and 121.

1812. *Large Corporate Pensions; Report to Participants.* Greenwich, CT: Greenwich Associates, 1973–. (Annual)

This has coverage of things not surveyed elsewhere. Mainly, it has to do with the investment practices of pension funds, but there is treatment of gross contributions and distributions; actuarial assumptions; participants' age, service, and vesting; postretirement increases; and use of 401(k)s. The 1973 edition has a statistical history of pensions.

1813. *Profit Sharing Survey.* Conducted by Hewitt Associates in cooperation with the Profit Sharing Council of America. Chicago: Profit Sharing Council of America, 1958–. (Annual)
>This item surveys contributions as a percentage of pay, investment choices, asset mix, rates of return, and a number of other provisions of profit sharing plans.

1814. *Salaried Employee Benefits Provided by Major U.S. Employers.* Lincolnshire, IL: Hewitt Associates, n.d. (Annual)
>About a quarter of each survey has to do with stipulations of retirement and capital accumulation plans.

1815. *Salaried Employee Benefits Provided by Major U.S. Employers; A Comparison Study.* Lincolnshire, IL: Hewitt Associates, 1980?–. (Annual)
>This survey shows changes in benefits over time, year by year, since 1979.

1816. *Survey of Actuarial Assumptions and Funding; Pension Plans with 1,000 or More Active Participants.* Washington, DC: The Wyatt Co., 1969?–. (Annual)
>The title varied slightly in earlier editions. The 1985 edition says it is the seventeenth in a series. This publication covers, for 948 plans, interest rate and salary growth assumptions, the Social Security and retirement age assumptions, security ratios, and value of assets and disclosure interest rates.

1817. *Survey of Retirement and Savings/Capital Accumulation Benefit Plans Covering Salaried Employees of U.S. Employers.* Washington, DC: The Wyatt Co., 1987–. (Biennial)
>At this writing, the first edition of this has yet to see the light of day. Judging from the survey instrument, it is to be an all-encompassing survey of prevalence of plan provisions in minute detail. How much of the detail will be published and whether the survey will be available to nonparticipants are yet moot points.

1818. *Top 50; A Survey of Retirement, Thrift and Profit-Sharing Plans Covering Salaried Employees of 50 Large U.S. Industrial Companies.* Washington, DC: The Wyatt Co., 1968–. (Annual)
>This is the only survey I know of which attempts to project the retirement benefits that will be received by employees covered by certain plans. Admittedly employees of the firms surveyed here are hardly typical of the labor force as a whole. There are hundreds of thousands of them, however. Furthermore, the plan provisions are given, and hundreds of other companies are thus able to assess roughly the adequacy of their own retirement plans.

PROMOTIONAL LITERATURE

As I stated in the introduction to the chapter on this topic, I regard most of these items as fungible. They are divided by category pretty much into those which are newsy and those which essay exhaustive treatments of particular topics. You might try to get on the mailing list for a couple of each kind.

PERIODICALS

Here, I have chosen to break out loose leafs and annuals into separate rubrics. Those that follow are the most important among journals and magazines.

1819. *Benefits News Analysis.* New Haven, CT: Benefits News Analysis, Inc., 1979–. (10/yr.)

Most of the articles have to do with how a particular company is handling a particular benefit or problem. Because interest in how others do the job is nothing short of avid, this is a very useful periodical.

1820. *Benefits Quarterly.* Brookfield, WI: International Society of Certified Employee Benefits Specialists, 1985–. (Quarterly)

This is a scholarly, referred journal. In addition to articles, there are book reviews, abstracts of articles appearing in other publications, and a legal/legislative update. The latter is analytic rather than newsy.

1821. *BNA Pension Reporter.* Washington, DC: Bureau of National Affairs, Inc., 1974–. (Weekly)

This extremely important publication covers legislation, the courts, and regulations by the various federal agencies. It is indexed frequently, but the indexing is not cumulative beyond the quarterly, and the index is always at least two weeks behind the issues. This shortcoming can be overcome by accessing BNA via HRIN (see entry 1794). Included are lists of upcoming educational seminars.

1822. *Business Insurance.* Chicago: Crain Communications, Inc., 1967–. (Weekly)

This publication is extremely important to the retirement plan practitioner. Although it targets all benefits as well as risk management and the insurance industry, there is considerable coverage of retirement plan news. Special issues include a directory of employee benefit plan computer systems that appears around May each year and a late December issue listing employee benefit consultants. A July or August issue announces employee benefit communications awards. Through sponsoring such awards, this magazine may have done more to make benefits comprehensible to employees than all government regulations yet printed.

1823. *Daily Tax Report.* Washington, DC: Bureau of National Affairs, Inc., 1954–. (Daily)

A typical issue has about 25 percent of its pages relevent to retirement plan topics. Because of its daily currency, this title is of great usefulness to those who must be on top of government legislation, regulation, and court decisions as they happen. The majority of practitioners should be able to do without it, however. The indexing is frequent and good but always less up to date than one wishes.

1824. *EBRI Issue Brief.* Washington, DC: Employee Benefit Research Institute, n.d. (Irregular)

Each *Issue Brief* is a thorough treatment of a particular topic, and many of the topics are retirement plan related.

1825. *Employee Benefit Plan Review.* Chicago: Charles D. Spencer & Associates, Inc., 1946–. (Monthly)

This is aimed at the benefits manager instead of at the actuary or attorney, but it is useful to the latter as well. The articles are brief and newsy. Each issue contains an internal section entitled "Multinational Benefits Review," which is a good way to keep up with foreign trends. There is also a good listing of upcoming educational seminars.

1826. *Employee Benefits Journal.* Brookfield, WI: International Foundation of Employee Benefit Plans, 1975–. (Quarterly)

This publication specializes in substantive but readable articles that cover the entire gamut of employee benefits.

1827. *Federal Register.* Washington, DC: Office of the Federal Register, National Archives and Records Administration, n.d. (Daily)

Regulations promulgated by the Department of Labor, the Internal Revenue Service, the Pension Benefit Guaranty Corp., and other agencies first see the light of day in this publication. An employee benefits attorney will need access to this in order to do his or her job.

1828. *Journal of Compensation and Benefits.* Boston: Warren, Gorham & Lamont, Inc., 1985–. (Bimonthly)

Much of the material published here is relevant to retirement plans. This publication is very important to practitioners.

1829. *Journal of Pension Planning & Compliance.* Greenvale, NY: Panel Publishers, Inc., 1974–. (Quarterly)

This journal is indispensable to the retirement plan practitioner.

1830. *Journal of Taxation.* Boston: Warren, Gorham & Lamont, Inc., 1954–. (Monthly)

Practitioners interested in the legal and regulatory environment have pronounced this to be an indispensable publication. It is generally not easy reading.

1831. *Nutshell: A Monthly Digest of Employee Benefits Publications.* Aspen, CO: The Country Press, Inc., n.d. (Monthly)

Nutshell can be extremely useful in keeping its subscriber informed. It is especially useful to those who have no access to a good benefits library. Because there are few such libraries, its potential audience is wide. It consists of abstracts of articles appearing in a broad array of publications, most of them listed in this book. The weakness of the publication is that it is inevitably slow. A May issue, consisting of abstracts written on items mostly dated in May was received in my library on 1 July. Thus the average item in the issue hits the street about six weeks before *Nutshell* can represent it to its reader. That said, one must admit that *Nutshell* is useful even in a good benefits library. It can be used to make certain that important acquisitions were made, and its article supply service is modestly priced.

1832. *Pension World.* Atlanta, GA: Communication Channels, Inc., 1964–. (Monthly)

In addition to publishing excellent and authoritative articles, this journal makes awards to outstanding achievers in the retirement area and publishes an annual compliance calendar. Other special features include an annual software directory, listings of master and directed trust services, real estate portfolio managers and third party administrators, and an annual survey of state retirement systems.

1833. *Pensions & Investment Age.* Chicago: Crain Communications, Inc., 1973–. (Fortnightly)

Formerly *Pensions and Investments*, this publication serves up general news in addition to a concentration on the investment of pension assets. Its quarterly *PIPER* (*Pensions Investment Performance Evaluation Report*) is a relatively cheap way of following the performance of investment managers. It runs a monthly listing of proprietary capital market indices that are otherwise hard to get at. The Russell 3000, the Ryan Index, and the Shearson Lehman Government/Corporate bond index graced one recent issue. In addition, there are lists of underwriters, large pension funds, GIC rates, largest issuers of securities, financial associations and organizations, largest money mangers, service providers in cash management, investment consultants, and "best" brokers, some of which are the only directories of their kind. Many of the articles require some background in finance, but there is a refreshing propensity toward informal English.

1834. *Wall Street Journal.* New York: Dow Jones & Co., 1889–. (Daily)

LOOSE LEAF

1835. *EBPR Research Reports.* Chicago: Charles D. Spencer & Associates, Inc. 1954–. (Weekly)
Less than half of this seven-volume loose-leaf service is concerned with the retirement area, but that is enough to render it indispensable. It is published in tandem with *Employee Benefit Plan Review* which is reviewed in entry 272. It is accompanied by *Weekly News Digest*, a newsletter that is intended to be routed and then filed with the service. The emphasis is on surveying the world of benefits and explaining it to someone at the level of a personnel practitioner. Prevalence of various practices, samples of particular plans, and synopses of exemplary studies are the main content. Considerable pieces of regulation lifted from the *Federal Register* and other background documents are placed in context. The weakness of this service is in its arrangement. The use of decimals in the page numbers is no hindrance to the seasoned user. It constitutes a formidable barrier to the new or occasional user. The index could be much better. More thought should be given to the range of vocabulary with which users approach the index.

1836. *Employee Benefits Cases.* Washington, DC: Bureau of National Affairs, Inc., 1981–. (Weekly)
This loose-leaf service includes bound volumes that provide text and indexed coverage of opinions of federal and state courts and selected decisions of the National Labor Relations Board and arbitrators on employee benefits issues from September 1974 to the point at which the loose leaf takes over. All of this is available in various sources in a good law library, but to have it in one-half shelf is a great advantage to an employee benefits attorney.

1837. *Pension and Profit Sharing.* Englewood Cliffs, NJ: Prentice-Hall, Inc., 1978–. (Weekly)
This is a six-volume loose-leaf service which is very much the same sort of thing as the *Pension Plan Guide* from Commerce Clearing House. Users tend to have a favorite between the two, and representatives will summon up tomes of reasons for theirs being the better service. There probably are differences between these services, but I would avoid making a choice if possible. Buy them both, if you can. Librarians should solicit user opinion if they cannot afford both. If a decision between them is necessary, I suggest flipping a coin. There are better ways to spend your energy. (cf. the CCH treatment in *Pension Plan Guide*, entry 1839.)

1838. *Pension Coordinator.* New York: Research Institute of America, Inc., 1987?–. 11 vols.
This loose-leaf service is scheduled for publication in 1987. It will include a two-volume forms service from Corbel & Co. Research Institute of America has a reputation for making tax law comprehensible to nonlawyers. This service will no doubt be roughly comparable to the Commerce Clearing House *Pension Plan Guide*, entry 1839, and the Prentice-Hall *Pension and Profit Sharing*, entry 1837.

1839. *Pension Plan Guide.* Chicago: Commerce Clearing House, Inc., 1953–. (Weekly)
This is a seven-volume loose-leaf service that concentrates purely on the legal and taxation aspects of retirement plans. It is accompanied by a weekly newsletter intended for routing. The endeavor is to bring all federal laws, regulations, court decisions, and near law, such as private letter rulings, that bear on retirement plans into a useable body. The endeavor is quite successful. This or the Prentice-Hall equivalent, entry 1837, is indispensable in a library that needs a good collection in this area.

ANNUALS AND IRREGULARS

1840. *Employee Benefit Plans under ERISA; Federal Regulations.* Englewood Cliffs, NJ: Prentice-Hall, Inc., 197?-. (Annual)

1841. *Pension and Employee Benefits; Code, ERISA, Regulations.* Chicago: Commerce Clearing House, Inc., n.d.
> Editions of this irregular serial have appeared "on" 4/15/78, 5/8/81, 8/19/83, and 4/5/85. A 1987 edition is said to be forthcoming.

1842. *Pension Facts.* Washington, DC: American Council of Life Insurance, 1974. (Annual?)
> The frequency of appearance of this publication is probably determined on the basis of what resources are available to produce it. It is handy for statistics, and it has a bibliography in some issues.

1843. *Pension Reform Handbook; Employee Retirement Income Security Act of 1974 and Later Amendments.* By Martin E. Holbrook. Englewood Cliffs, NJ: Prentice-Hall, Inc., 1982?-. (Annual)

MONOGRAPHS

These are not necessarily the most profound books available, but they are the ones I have found most useful. They include two basic textbooks, several books used for "something simple" questions, a book on trends in the industry, and one on economic policy. Several books have content bearing on the questions of what to do with all that money. That is what makes retirement plans interesting to a lot of people.

1844. Allen, Everett T., Jr.; Melone, Joseph J.; and Rosenbloom, Jerry S. *Pension Planning; Pensions, Profit Sharing and Other Deferred Compensation Plans.* 5th ed. The Irwin Series in Insurance and Economic Security. Homewood, IL: Richard D. Irwin, Inc., 1984. 448 p.

1845. Ambachtsheer, Keith P. *Pension Funds and the Bottom Line; Managing the Corporate Pension Fund as a Financial Business.* Homewood, IL: Dow Jones-Irwin, 1986. 167 p.

1846. Andrews, Emily S. *The Changing Profile of Pensions in America.* An EBRIERF Policy Study. Washington, DC: Employee Benefit Research Institute, 1985. 234 p.

1847. Canan, Michael J., and Baker, David R. *Qualified Retirement Plans.* West's Handbook Series. St. Paul, MN: West Publishing Co., 1977.

1848. *Employee Benefit Plans; A Glossary of Terms.* 6th ed. Brookfield, WI: International Foundation of Employee Benefit Plans, 1987. 157 p.
> A very useful, but not encyclopedic, book which can help in coping with the jargon that infests the industry. It gets more useful with every edition.

1849. *Fundamentals of Employee Benefit Programs.* 2d ed. Washington, DC: Employee Benefit Research Institute, 1985. 235 p.
> This is composed of the various pamphlets on each benefit that have been published by EBRI.

1850. *Investment Policy Guidebook for Corporate Pension Plan Trustees.* Brookfield, WI: International Foundation of Employee Benefit Plans, 1984. 185 p.

1851. Ippolito, Richard A. *Pensions, Economics and Public Policy.* Homewood, IL: Published for the Pension Research Council by Dow Jones-Irwin, 1986. 267 p.

1852. Maginn, John L., and Tuttle, Donald L. *Managing Investment Portfolios; A Dynamic Process.* Sponsored by the Institute of Chartered Financial Analysts. Boston: Warren, Gorham & Lamont, 1983. 712 p.

1853. McGill, Dan M., and Grubbs, Donald S., Jr. *Fundamentals of Private Pensions.* Homewood, IL: Published for the Pension Research Council by Richard D. Irwin, Inc., 1984. 754 p.
> This is the most often used basic text in the retirement plan area. Its resemblance to the first edition of 1955 is minute.

1854. McGinn, Daniel F. *Actuarial Fundamentals for Multiemployer Plans.* Brookfield, WI: International Foundation of Employee Benefit Plans, 1982. 122 p.
> I have what appears to be a 1975 edition entitled *Actuarial Primer for Trustees.*

Organizations

This chapter lists organizations that can be sources of information on retirement plans. Usually the organizations impose some form of fee or require that the information seeker have membership status before information can be accessed. Although an effort was made to ascertain that the addresses and phone numbers provided are correct, it is expected that this accuracy will deteriorate rapidly. Some of these organizations operate out of shoe boxes that are given by the past president to the current one. Others find moves frequently necessary because of burgeoning staff sizes. As this writing ages, the reader may want to consult *Encyclopedia of Associations* either in print or online. A source for some of the more obscure groups is a listing published in *Pensions & Investment Age*. The March 31, 1986, issue carried it under the title "Financial Associations and Organizations" commencing on page 19. I believe that PIA intends to update its list occasionally, and *Encyclopedia of Associations* is frequently updated. These sources together can update the majority but not the entirety of this section. Where reference is made to a Segal Associates statement of percentages of membership, the citation is to a 1984 survey, *A Confidential Survey of Benefit Managers*, by Segal Associates (see entry 20).

Administrative Management Society. Maryland Rd., Willow Grove, PA 19090 (215) 659-4300.
The membership has a heavy bent toward personnel management. There is therefore information published and otherwise available that is at least tangent to retirement plans.

American Academy of Actuaries. 1720 I St., N.W., Ste. 700, Washington, DC 20006 (202) 223-8916.
This is the umbrella organization for the other actuarial bodies in the U.S. Actuaries utilize their mathematical talents for a variety of tasks. Some have determined the optimum patterns for depth charge operations. One has designed a tennis racquet handle. There may be as many as a thousand of them who confine themselves to pension work.

American Association of Retired Persons. 1909 K St., N.W., Washington, DC 20049 (202) 872-4700.
Retirement plans are not exactly central to the activities of this enormous and influential group, but one of its goals is "to improve every aspect of living for older people." The association therefore cannot and does not ignore sources of retired persons' income.

American Compensation Association. P.O. Box 1176, Scottsdale, AZ 85252 (602) 951-9191.

Although this association is primarily composed of persons interested in cash compensation, there is some interest in retirement plans, and Segal says that 10.2 percent of benefit managers belong.

American Council of Life Insurance. 1850 K St., N.W., Washington, DC 20006 (202) 862-4000.

This is an association of which the members are insurance companies. In addition to publishing *Pension Facts*, ACLI has an excellent library and a number of researchers whom I have found helpful. Members come first, however. They pay the bills.

American Institute of Certified Public Accountants. 1211 Avenue of the Americas, New York, NY 10036 (212) 575-6200.

Since the first employer adopted a pension plan, some poor accountant has been struggling with the question of how (or whether) to report it on an income statement and a balance sheet. AICPA is a source of guidance.

American Law Institute-American Bar Association (ALI-ABA). 4025 Chestnut St., Philadelphia, PA 19104 (215) 243-1600.

This is a joint program of the two associations named above. It exists to further the professional education of lawyers. It publishes in print, audio, and video formats and puts on courses of study around the country. Retirement plans get a fair share of treatment.

American Management Association. 135 W. 50th St., New York, NY 10020 (212) 586-8100.

Members have access to the library. There are occasional courses, seminars, and publications on retirement plans, and nonmembers can get access to these.

American Pension Conference. (212) 957-1780.

This is an organization the headquarters of which moves with every election. I believe that it is regional and primarily East Coast in operation. I have many printed speeches from its meetings in the 60s and 70s, so I know it to have some substance.

American Society for Personnel Administration. 606 N. Washington St., Alexandria, VA 22314 (703) 548-3440.

According to Segal, 13.8 percent of benefit managers belong to this society.

American Society of Pension Actuaries. 1413 K St., N.W., Ste 500, Washington, DC 20005 (202) 737-4360.

This organization exists to educate its members and to lobby.

Association of Private Pension and Welfare Plans. 1331 Pennsylvania Ave., N.W., Washington, DC 20004 (202) 737-6666.

This is primarily a lobbying organization, but it is a significant publisher in legislative and regulatory matters.

Bureau of National Affairs. 1231 25th St., N.W., Washington, DC 20037.

BNA has a research department that will do tailored research for a fee. Because they are also a major publisher in the area, they are all the more capable of a good quality of research.

Chamber of Commerce of the United States. 1615 H St., N.W., Washington, DC 20062 (202) 659-6000.

The chamber is mostly involved with lobbying and publishing.

Chicago Pension Forum. (312) 498-8249.

This is a local or regional group concerned with fund management.

Church Pensions Conference. c/o Hay Huggins, 229 S. 18th St., Philadelphia, PA 19103 (215) 875-2469.
Administrators of some denominational pension funds.

The College of Insurance. One Insurance Plaza, 101 Murray St., New York, NY 10007 (212) 962-4111.
This is an accredited degree-granting institution that boasts an excellent library of general insurance materials. The amount of retirement plan information of which this organization disposes is probably considerable.

Committee on Finance. SD-219 Dirksen Senate Office Bldg., Washington, DC 20510 (202) 224-4515.
Through this committee of the U.S. Senate must pass most legislation on retirement plans. There is a subcommittee on savings, pensions, and investment policy. Hearings and other topical publications appear frequently. Staffers are knowledgeable and harried.

Committee on Ways and Means. 1102 Longworth House Office Bldg., Washington, DC 20515 (202) 225-3625.
This is the committee of the House of Representatives through which must pass most measures dealing with retirement plans. There are staff members who are conversant with current legislation, and there is frequent publication of topical material.

The Conference Board. 845 Third Ave., New York, NY 10022 (212) 759-0900.
This is a prestigious research organization that produces important and authoritative surveys in the retirement area on an irregular basis. Membership is expensive, but the publications are available to nonassociates at reasonable rates.

Congressional Research Service. Library of Congress, 101 Independence Ave., S.E., Washington, DC 20540 (202) 287-5775.
Although there is considerable publication on our topic and even some expertise in it available from CRS, it is often not available directly to the public. The best way to get at a CRS publication is through your local congressman. CRS serves Congress.

Council of Institutional Investors. 818 Connecticut Ave., N.W., Washington, DC 20006 (202) 452-0754.
Dedicated to the idea that pension funds should use the power that comes from their ownership of society to better society.

Council on Employee Benefits. c/o Goodyear Relief Assn., 1144 E. Market St., Akron, OH 44316 (216) 796-4008.
This is an employer's group which exchanges information informally. Segal says that 12.2 percent of benefit managers belong.

Council on Multiemployer Pension Security. 220 I St., N.E., Ste. 280, Washington, DC 20002 (202) 223-0409.
This is a lobbying group of employers subject to a particular law, the Multiemployer Pension Plan Amendments Act of 1980.

Dallas-Fort Worth Metroplex Pension Sponsor Group. (817) 355-1525.
A local group founded for dialogue.

Department of Labor. 200 Constitution Ave., N.W., Washington, DC 20210 (202) 523-7316.
DOL has an extensive library for historical research, an office of public disclosure where the general public can obtain forms 5500 and SPDs and a whole Assistant Secretariat for Pension and Welfare Benefit Programs full of people who know something about retirement plans. DOL also has a

major problem. They are understaffed for the enormity of the tasks that they are called upon to perform. Furthermore, if you approach any government organization with an abstruse question, you must be furnished with a fund of patience. As you are referred from person to person, each succeeding person will sound a little more like he or she knows what you are talking about. Eventually you will probably find that one person in the bureaucracy who knows. Do yourself a favor and make a note of the name and number.

Employee Benefit Research Institute. 2121 K St., N.W., Ste. 860, Washington, DC 20037 (202) 659-0670.
This is a lobbying and research organization which also publishes extensively. It has done some very useful books and pamphlets.

Employers Council on Flexible Compensation. 1660 L St., N.W., Ste. 715, Washington, DC 20036 (202) 659-4300.
This is a lobbying and educative group for employers who have established a cafeteria plan.

ERISA Industry Committee. 1726 M St., N.W., Ste. 1101, Washington, DC 20036 (202) 833-2800.
Known as ERIC, this body has members drawn from the *Fortune* 100 only. It is a source of information but only for very large manufacturers.

ESOP Association. 1725 DeSales St., N.W., Ste. 400, Washington, DC 20036 (202) 293-2971.
Information on employee stock ownership plans.

Financial Executives Institute. 10 Madison Ave., P.O. Box 1938, Morristown, NJ 07960 (201) 898-4600.
This body has a committee on the investment of retirement plan assets that has only recently begun to function. The allied Financial Executives Research Foundation has commissioned a number of studies of interest to pension fund investors.

General Accounting Office. 441 G St., N.W., Washington, DC 20548 (202) 275-6241.
GAO is frequently asked to investigate retirement subjects. The resulting documents are often useful, but they are sometimes baffling. A number of the useful and the baffling are described in this book.

Houston Council on Retirement Plans. (713) 654-6502.
A local discussion group.

Internal Revenue Service. 1111 Constitution Ave., N.W., Washington, DC 20224 (202) 566-3990.
IRS promulgates more paper that concerns retirement plans than any other federal agency. Much of it appears in the *Federal Register* or *Internal Revenue Bulletin*.

International Foundation of Employee Benefit Plans. P.O. Box 69, 18700 Bluemound Rd., Brookfield, WI 53008 (414) 786-6700.
This is the closest the employee benefits industry comes to an umbrella industry association. According to Segal, 20.5 percent of benefit managers belong. There is extensive research and publication from this body. There is also some lobbying, and the library is the best on the topic anywhere.

International Society of Certified Employee Benefit Specialists. 18700 Bluemound Rd., Brookfield, WI 53005 (414) 786-8771.
This body promotes education and professional development of practitioners. It publishes as well, and it is affiliated with the International Foundation of Employee Benefit Plans.

Joint Board for the Enrollment of Actuaries. Internal Revenue Service, Director of Practice, PM:HR:DP, New Post Office Bldg., Room 1416, 1111 Constitution Ave., N.W., Washington, DC 20224 (202) 535-6787.
This is a creature of the Department of Labor and the Internal Revenue Service which enrolls actuaries. It does this by requiring passage of two examinations to determine the fitness of an actuary to practice. Not only actuaries are enrolled, but also attorneys and accountants.

Judy Diamond Associates, Inc. 450 Fifth St., N.W., 9th Floor South, Washington, DC 20001 (202) 639-8820.
For a fee, this organization will retrieve forms 5500 and summary plan descriptions from government depositories.

Midwest Pension Conference. Jack Stone, Ex-Cell-O Corp., 2855 Coolidge Hwy., Troy, MI 48084 (313) 637-1020.
This is a regional discussion group.

National Association of Manufacturers. 1776 F St., N.W., Washington, DC 20006 (202) 637-3000.
This is an influential lobbying organization that is very much interested in retirement plan legislation. Its members bear a considerable portion of the nation's expenditures on pensions.

National Association of Pension Consultants and Administrators. P.O. Box 53017, 359 E. Paces Ferry Rd., Atlanta, GA 30355 (404) 231-0100.
Lobbying organization for small plans.

National Association of State Retirement Administrators. Bert D. Hunsaker, Utah State Retirement Office, 540 E. Second, S., Salt Lake City, UT 84111 (801) 355-3884.

National Center for Employee Ownership. 927 S. Walter Reed, No. 1, Arlington, VA 22204 (703) 979-2375.
This is a research group in the ESOP area.

National Commission on Public Employee Pension Systems. 1221 Connecticut Ave., N.W., Washington, DC 20036 (202) 293-3960.
Provides information on waste and excess in public plans.

National Conference on Public Employee Retirement Systems. 275 E. Broad St., Columbus, OH 43215 (614) 227-4090.
Promotes and safeguards the rights and benefits of public employees with respect to their retirement plans.

National Council of Real Estate Investment Fiduciaries. 1090 Vermont Ave., N.W., Washington, DC 20005 (202) 289-7713.
Members are companies that have substantial amounts of their retirement plan funds invested in real estate.

National Employee Benefits Institute. 2550 M St., N.W., Ste. 785, Washington, DC 20037 (800) 558-7258.
Fortune 1000 companies interested in government legislation and regulation.

National Institute of Pension Administrators. P.O. Box 15466, 1700 E. Dyer Rd., Ste. 165, Santa Ana, CA 92705 (714) 832-0159.
Runs an educational and accreditation program.

National Investment Sponsor Federation. (412) 263-3200.

This is a nascent umbrella organization for local and regional discussion groups.

Pension Benefit Guaranty Corp. 2020 K St., N.W., Washington, DC 20006 (202) 254-4817.

Established by ERISA, this government corporation insures most private plans in the U.S. As a provider of information, it has some flaws. It publishes a monthly list of termination interest rates and factors which is essential in plan termination. This comes out at midmonth, but it reaches the addressee very late in the month. It is true that PBGC staffs a telephone, (202) 778-8840, to impart the figures orally, but actuaries and attorneys prefer paper for obvious reasons. PBGC also publishes PBGC opinion letters, and woe betide you if you want a recent one. The letters are published on a quarterly basis through the National Technical Information Service, and in January 1987, we were informed that the second and third quarters of 1986 had just gone to press. The PBGC library is neither staffed nor budgeted for much in the way of public service.

Pension Group East. (914) 939-0200.

This is a regional discussion group.

Pension Real Estate Association. 1101 17th St., N.W., Ste. 700, Washington, DC 20036 (202) 296-4141.

This organization monitors government activities and educates in the area of real estate investment for pension funds.

Pension Research Council. 3641 Locust Walk, Philadelphia, PA 19104 (215) 898-7762.

Sponsors nonpartisan research in the private pension area. There is a connection to the Wharton School. This is an influential publisher, and I believe that Wharton and the PRC are academia's cynosure for the retirement plan industry.

Pension Rights Center. 1701 K St., N.W., Ste. 300, Washington, DC 20006 (202) 296-3778.

This is a lobbying group in the public interest. It promotes the rights of individuals with regard to pensions. There is a referral service for those with retirement plan problems.

Pension 21.

This is a national discussion group that has no officers and is not open to new members.

Pension West. (213) 647-1716.

A local discussion group.

President's Commission on Pension Policy.

This organization went out of existence in 1981. Because it published some important material, there are occasional requests for its whereabouts. It is now in the bosom of Abraham.

Profit Sharing Council of America. 20 N. Wacker Dr., Chicago, IL 60606 (312) 372-3411.

Provides information and lobbies in respect to profit sharing.

Profit Sharing Research Foundation. 1718 Sherman Ave., Evanston, IL 60201 (312) 869-8787.

This organization is affiliated with the Profit Sharing Council of America described above. The distinction between the functions of the council and the foundation is somewhat fuzzy. Between them, they cover profit sharing thoroughly.

Railroad Retirement Board. 844 Rush St., Chicago, IL 60611 (312) 751-4500.
This is an agency of the U.S. government that administers the railroad retirement system. Like social security, this is a creature of the New Deal. Unlike social security, the majority of the citizenry has probably forgotten its existence.

St. Louis Pension Group. (314) 982-2983.
This is a local discussion group.

Small Business Administration. 1441 L St., N.W., Washington, DC 20416 (202) 653-7561.
Very occasionally one sees from this source some action or publication on benefits in the small business sector.

Social Security Administration. 6401 Security Blvd., Baltimore, MD 21235 (301) 594-3120.

Society of Actuaries. 500 Park Blvd., Itasca, IL 60143 (312) 773-3010.
This organization is the largest sponsor of the examinations that lead to the designations FSA and ASA. It also does considerable publishing in the pension area.

Society of Professional Benefit Administrators. 2033 M St., N.W., Ste. 605, Washington, DC 20036 (202) 223-6413.
An association of firms that administer plans for employers.

Southern Ohio Pension Group.
This is a local discussion group.

Southern Pension Conference.
This is a regional discussion group.

Teachers Insurance and Annuity Association/College Retirement Equity Fund. 730 Third Ave., New York, NY 10017 (212) 490-9000.
There is a research department that has published a considerable amount of material on academic retirement. Because most academics are participants, this is a retirement plan information source for an important segment of society.

Townsend Plan National Lobby. 5500 Quincy St., Hyattsville, MD 20784 (301) 864-1988.
Lobbyist for a radical change in the social security system which would result in nationalization of the pension system.

Twin Cities Pension Group. (612) 773-7377.
A local discussion group.

Washington Pension Forum. (202) 857-9705.
A local discussion group.

Western Michigan Pension Group. (616) 928-2000.
This is a local discussion group.

Western Pension Conference.
A regional discussion group.

Author Index

Numbers in italic refer to page numbers. All other numbers refer to citation numbers.

Title Index

Numbers refer to citation numbers, not page numbers.

Subject Index

Numbers refer to citation numbers, not page numbers.